This is a volume in the Arno Press collection

THE DEVELOPMENT OF CONTEMPORARY ACCOUNTING THOUGHT

See last pages of this volume for a complete list of titles.

THREE CENTURIES OF ACCOUNTING IN MASSACHUSETTS

William Holmes, Linda H. Kistler
and Louis S. Corsini

ARNO PRESS
A New York Times Company
New York • 1978

Editorial Supervision: LUCILLE MAIORCA

First publication 1978 by Arno Press Inc.

THE DEVELOPMENT OF CONTEMPORARY ACCOUNTING THOUGHT
ISBN for complete set: 0-405-10891-5
See last pages of this volume for titles.

Manufactured in the United States of America

Library of Congress Cataloging in Publication Data

Holmes, William, 1919-
Three centuries of accounting in Massachusetts.

(The Development of contemporary accounting thought)
Some of the readings have been previously published in the Massachusetts CPA review, during 1975.
1. Accounting--Massachusetts--History. 2. Massachusetts Society of Certified Public Accountants--History. I. Kistler, Linda H. II. Corsini, Louis S. III. Title. IV. Series.
HF5616.U5H63 657'.09744 77-87295
ISBN 0-405-10922-9

THREE CENTURIES OF ACCOUNTING IN MASSACHUSETTS

by

William Holmes
Linda H. Kistler
and
Louis S. Corsini

THREE CENTURIES OF ACCOUNTING IN MASSACHUSETTS

by

William Holmes, Linda H. Kistler, and Louis S. Corsini

TABLE OF CONTENTS

Part I - Early Massachusetts Accounting

Part II - History of the Massachusetts Society of CPAs

INTRODUCTION

Preliminary discussions on a project to prepare a permanent record of the history of accountancy in Massachusetts began several years ago. Anthony Krzystofik, editor of the Massachusetts CPA Review, believed that a comprehensive history of the Massachusetts Society of CPAs would be appropriate to commemorate the occasion of the Society's Seventy-Fifth Anniversary in 1975. His enthusiasm was transmitted to the Society's officers and executive committee, which supported the project from inception on 1974 to completion in 1976. Once under way, the project grew of its own volition into a much wider study and required the commitment of several individuals in order to complete the project on a timely basis. Linda H. Kistler, William Holmes, and Louis S. Corsini, all members of the Society Publications Committee and Associate Editors of the CPA Review, agreed to write the history and prepare materials for publication during 1974, 1975 and 1976.

A primary objective has been to combine high quality research with a readable format; to satisfy the appetite of the professional accountant or historian, and at the same time to tickle the palate of the non-professional. Accounting history is more than the history of accounting. There is always present in addition the wider perspective of history *through* accounting. Old accounts offer fascinating vignettes of the social and economic life of bygone years; and the authors have included a few of these episodes in this volume.

The book is divided into two parts. Part I presents a series of studies on accounting in Massachusetts from the days of the Pilgrims until the 1890s. Part II is a comprehensive history of the Massachusetts Society of CPAs from its founding in 1900 to 1970.

PART I

The first five chapters are of national interest to accounting historians and educators desiring to trace the evolution of accounting theory and practice in this country. Chapter One offers a different view of the Pilgrims, neophytes in business matters and at the mercy of a "wheeler-dealer" bookkeeper to the point that their financial debts threatened the very survival of the Plymouth Colony during the period from 1620 to 1645.

The second chapter, on the other hand, shows the early mangers of the Massachusetts Bay Colony as a responsible and able group of businessmen and discusses a surprising amount of auditing of both public and commercial accounts in the hundred years following 1630.

Chapter Three explores the evolution of municipal accounting in the Plymouth Colony from 1657 to 1686. Contrary to established opinion, this study reveals a high level of sophistication in public records maintained by the Pilgrims more than three hundred years ago.

Chapter Four sets forth the accounts of a joint venture in 1666 which is probably typical of many similar ventures of that period. Samuel Eliot Morison has noted the paucity of accounts from this period, and those set forth in this chapter have probably not been offered in print before. This work required Bill Holmes to laboriously translate the document from the manuscript on file in the Judicial Files of the Massachusetts Archives.

The witches of Salem are the subject of Chapter Five. The accounts are elementary in form and add little to our knowledge of accounting. The appeal in this instance is purely in the context of a fascinating glimpse of that communal madness called witch-hunting in 1692, written from the viewpoint of the keeper of the Boston jail.

The authors believe the chapters on 17th century accounting are particularly valuable. These studies provide unusual glimpses of Massachusetts' rich contribution to the economic development of the United States. They also offer source materials for future research of early financial data which can be used to trace the evolution of accounting theory and practice during the three hundred years since our country's founding. The presence of these historical documents which are not available elsewhere in the country offers a unique opportunity and a corollary responsibility to present this information to a national audience.

Historians of accounting in the United States have concentrated on the period following the late 1700s, with a primary emphasis on the development of public accountancy from the 1880s onward. The publication of studies in accounting during the 1600s is therefore an important contribution by Massachusetts accountants to professional colleagues in the rest of the country.

Chapters Six, Seven and Eight are a three-part examination of accounting and accountants in Massachusetts during the eighteenth and nineteenth centuries. Boston accountants and the business schools which prepared students for careers in counting houses and commercial businesses during the 1800s are emphasized. The growth of public accounting in Western Massachusetts is discussed in Chapter Nine, and a review of early public accounting firms and pioneer practitioners is the subject of Chapter Ten.

PART II

Part II consists of five chapters which offer a comprehensive history of the Massachusetts Society of Certified Public Accountants and its predecessor organization from the 1890s to 1970. The authors acknowledge a debt of gratitude to Miss Ethel Kingman, who wrote a monograph on the history of the Society which was published in 1952. Miss Kingman was the first female Fellow of the Society, having been admitted in 1925; and her review of the Society's early years provided much valuable information in developing this comprehensive history of public accounting in Massachusetts.

Early public accountancy in Massachusetts is reviewed in Chapter Eleven. The movement to form a professional accounting organization began in the 1890s and culminated in the establishment of the Incorporated Public Accountants of Massachusetts in 1900. Early CPA legislation, professional development, and ethical conduct were topics of considerable interest during this period.

The years from 1910 to 1930 are the subject of Chapter Twelve. Passage of the income tax amendment created new opportunities for accountants to serve the public. The nation's industrial growth during the 1920s, followed the 1929 collapse, are the setting for a developing professional society of accountants. Several Massachusetts accountants became national leaders during this period; and the Society won state-wide respect as a professional organization during this period.

Chapter Thirteen is devoted to the depression years, 1930 to 1940. This era is an improtant one in the history of accountancy because of the passage of reform laws by the Congress and the first utterances of accounting and auditing procedure by the American Institute of CPAs. During this decade, the practice of public accounting in the United States began to emerge as a recognized profession.

Chapter Fourteen covers the twenty years from 1940 to 1960. The Society was relatively limited in its activities from 1940 to 1945 because of the pressing demands of World War II. The return to normalcy following the war took a few years, but it was not long before the Society was engaged in legal battles with lawyers as to who has the right to proffer tax advice. Then CPAs began to think about placing restrictions on non-certified accountants practicing public accounting in Massachusetts.

Chapter Fifteen, dealing with the period from 1960 to 1970, opens with the differences between public accountants and certified public accountants still unresolved - it would take another three years to settle the matter. The decade of the sixties is characterized by a proliferation of working committees, some good public relations, and the beginning of professional development programs on a formal basis.

Some of the readings in this volume have been previously published in the Massachusetts CPA Review during 1975. The authors appreciate the Society's willingness to permit these chapters to be included in this permanent volume which would be incomplete without them.

THE AUTHORS

Principal authors of this history of Massachusetts accountancy are William Holmes, Linda H. Kistler, and Louis S. Corsini.

Bill Holmes is a manager in the Boston Office of Peat, Marwick, Mitchell and Co. Born and educated in Scotland, he emigrated to the United States in 1951. He is a Massachusetts CPA, a British Certified Accountant, and a Fellow of the Society. A prolific writer, his articles on professional accounting matters and on accounting history have appeared in numerous publications including the Journal of Accountancy. He was a Charter Member of the Academy of Accounting Historians, and has recently been appointed to the editorial board of this organization. He also serves as an Associate Editor of the Massachusetts CPA Review and is a member of the Society's Publications Committee.

Linda H. Kistler, CPA, is Professor of Accounting at the University of Lowell. She is a Massachusetts CPA and Fellow of the Society. Professor Kistler earned Bachelor of Science and Master of Science degrees in Business Administration from Colorado State University. Her research on both financial and management accounting topics as well as accounting history have been published in numerous national and regional accounting journals, including the Accounting Review and the Journal of Accountancy. She is a member of the Academy of Accounting Historians and participates in its committee activities; and she is an Associate Editor of the Massachusetts CPA Review and a member of the Society's Publications Committee.

Louis S. Corsini is Associate Professor of Accounting at Boston College, and holds a PhD. in accounting from Louisiana State University. A Massachusetts CPA and a Fellow of the Society, Dr. Corsini has published in professional journals. Professor Corsini is Editor of the CPA Review, and he writes a bi-monthly column on auditing theory and practice for the journal. He also serves on the Society's Publications Committee.

Individuals who have contributed single chapters to this volume of readings are: Williard Stone, CPA, Professor of Accounting at the University of Florida; Anthony T. Krzystofik, CPA, Professor of Accounting at the University of Massachusetts, Amherst; and Ernest Berg, CPA, past president of the Society and partner in Hitchcock & Co., in Springfield until his retirement in 1972.

ACKNOWLEDGEMENTS

The authors wish to express their appreciation to the many individuals who assisted in the preparation of this history of accountancy in Massachusetts. Presidents Paul Finnegan, Jordan Golding, and Edward H. Pendergast, Jr. supported the project during its development period. The Executive Committees of the Massachusetts Society of CPAs in 1975, 1976 and 1977 approved the project and agreed to provide financial support for the publication of this volume as a permanent record of accountancy in Massachusetts. Ethel Kingman's contribution has been noted above and is reiterated here. Ruth Welton, Agnes Bixby, and Marianne Brush all deserve special mention for providing research notes and editorial comments on those periods of time when they were very close to Society operations. Anthony Krzystofik and Thomas Dunn of the Publications Committee were especially helpful in coordinating final details of publication.

CHAPTER ONE

ACCOUNTING WOES, PILGRIM STYLE

Williard Stone

Lack of a qualified accountant added greatly to the hardships of the Pilgrim Fathers over many of their early years. Beginning with the first major expenditure in 1620 and ending with the final settlement by the Pilgrims with their London backers in 1641, the records of the Pilgrim Colony business transactions were chaotic. The Fathers took several books on farming and fishing but a book on bookkeeping by the Italian method would have brought greater comfort and profit. Much of the surplus from the farming, fishing, and trading went to settle unwarranted claims, according to Governor William Bradford.[1]

The Agreement

As early as November 1617 the Pilgrims began negotiations to secure a charter and financial backing for a colony in the New World. It was not until 1620 that they found the necessary capital and they never did receive a valid charter. Thomas Weston, merchant of London, and a group of friends formed "The Adventurers" and supplied financial support and the Pilgrims, designated "The Planters" were to settle in the New World and repay the Adventurers from the surpluses of farming, timbering and fishing. The formal agreement provided that:

1. Each person 16 and upward going to to the colony be given a £10 share.

2. Each person 16 and upward going and taking £10 in money or provisions be given two shares.

3. Planters to fish and build houses.

4. At end of 7 years, profits to be divided between adventurers based upon shares. Every man to be free of debt or detriment.

Robert Cushman and Deacon John Carver signed this agreement as agents for the Pilgrims. Obvious deficiencies existed in the agreement such as the failure to specify the amount of the contribution of the Adventurers and the lack of assignment of responsibility for maintaining records. Specifically, the Pilgrims were upset by the omission of two provisions agreed upon in preliminary discussions and accused Robert Cushman of exceeding his authority in signing the agreement without provisions for:

1. Planters to have two days each week for private employment and

2. Planters to have title to "ye houses, & land improved espetialy gardens & home lotts" at the end of 7 years.

Book-keeping Without Books

Their accounting woes began promptly for Cushman gave no satisfactory accounting for money had by him of the Adventurers. Even the exact amount was not known beyond that it was "I know not how many 100£". No record was available of the use to which this was put. It can be assumed that the Adventurers carefully recorded the advances but the Planters had no clear idea of financial transactions. Cushman also authorized repairs to the Speedwell totaling £ 700 at Southampton. The Speedwell joined the Mayflower at Southampton and on August 5 set out for the New World but sprang a leak and put into Dartmouth for repairs. Another start was aborted by a leak and the ships turned back to Plymouth where the Speedwell was turned back to the Adventurers. On September 6 the Mayflower set forth with 102 passengers to land at Plymouth rock on December 16, 1620.

Cushman was joined in Southampton by Christopher Martin, of Billivike in Essex, who became the Pilgrims' first treasurer. Together with agents for the Adventurers they settled upon the advances made and "brought them into better forme & write them in a booke". The amount is not shown but later when the first shipload of products was sent to London it was stated that the value of the cargo, Ł500, was nearly half the amount due to the Adventurers. Cushman came under great criticism for his handling of business affairs in general and the lost provisions of the agreement in particular. On August 17, 1620, he withdrew from the group, but not before he complained about Martin, the new treasurer. "Mr Martin saith he neither can nor will give any accounts; he crieth out of unthankfullness for his paines & care, that we are susspitious of him, and flings away, & will end nothing."

In a letter dated July 6, 1621, received by William Bradford on November 10, Weston complained of many things and requested: "and likewise give us accounte as perticulerly as you can how our moneys were laid out". There is no record that he received a satisfactory reply. In November the ship Fortune was "speedily dispatcht away, being laden with good clapboard.-., and 2 Hoggsheads of beaver and otter skins. The fraight was estimated to be worth near Ł500". The Fortune arrived safely but had been "robbed by ye Frenchmen" and did not repay any of the Pilgrims debt. This began a series of misadventures, although some shipments reached London safely, others did not. The Little James loaded with cod and beaver valued at Ł277 was captured by pirates of Morocco with a loss of cargo, ship and crew who were sold into slavery. By 1625 the debt of the Pilgrims to the Adventurers amounted to Ł1,400 ($70,000) according to William Bradford.

The accounts of the Pilgrims (and their business affairs) from a poor beginning continued in a chaotic condition. Martin, the first treausrer, died in the winter of 1621 and his accounts were found to be in great disorder. He was succeeded by Deacon William Paddy who served as Treasurer until 1644 when Captain Myles Standish took the post. Paddy appears to have had little acquaintance with bookkeeping for he left the matter entirely in the hands of the business manager and the London merchants. Myles Standish was an efficient treasurer and collected taxes, made disbursements and maintained adequate accounts for his five year term of office. He was replaced in 1649 by John Alden who held the office until 1659.

The Business Manager

In 1624 Issac Allerton appeared on the scene, first as a factor representing the Adventurers but he was highly recommended by the London Underwriters and soon became business manger (and bookkeeper) of the Pilgrims. Fishing did not prove to be profitable because the Pilgrims knew little about it and a venture in manufacturing salt to preserve fish failed after two years of bungling. The Pilgrims found timbering and trading with the Indians for skins to result in their best cash crops. Shiploads were sent to London and things seemed to be going well except that no one in the Colony knew where they stood with respect to the debt to the London merchants. Another problem was their lack of a charter. In 1626 Allerton was sent to London to procure a charter and to borrow such sums as he needed for the purpose at "reasonable rates of interest."

Allerton found many willing to help secure the charter but all had open palms. He borrowed £500 at the "reasonable rate" of 50% per annum. This was quickly spent on gifts and travel. Even at that time it cost a great deal to live well in London. The quest for the charter was to continue until 1630 when a charter was secured and success seemed within their grasp until it was discovered that the charter lacked the great seal and was invalid. Allerton was never able to secure the seal although he did succeed in placing the Pilgrims even deeper in debt in the quest. Allerton was subsequently found to have invested Ŀ400 in a London Pub during that period.

Allerton must have been a persuasive man for he led the Puritans through many ventures in which he acted as both principal and agent (involving conflict of interest) always to his advantage and to the disadvantage of the Pilgrims. He bought Ŀ113 of salt which he could have sold at a profit of Ŀ30 for the Pilgroms but elected instead to place the salt into a joint venture with Mr. Winslow, who had come to the New World to attempt an accounting. Whether the venture was successful is not known but the Pilgrims received no profit from it.

Although unsuccessful in procuring a charter for the Pilgrim Colony Allerton did get a patent for himself for a tract along the Penobscot River where he started a trading post in competition with the Pilgrims whose most profitable venture thus far had been the fur trading in this area. Allerton subsequently made several trips to England to purchase supplies jointly for the Pilgrim colony and for his store. When the goods arrived it was usually found that all the most useful and profitable merchandise was consigned to Allerton's store and the Pilgrims were forced to buy their winter clothing from him.

The Friendship was purchased by Allerton as agent for the Colony but when it arrived in the New World with a full cargo of merchandise it was discovered that only two bundles of rugs and two hogsheads of mead (most of which the crew "had drunke up under ye name of leackage") were for the Pilgrims and the balance for Allerton's store. At a later date Allerton purchased another ship, the White Angel. He assured the Pilgrims that this was for a private fishing venture of his but the cost was discovered in the London merchant's accounts of the Planters. On the White Angel's first voyage with a full cargo of merchandise, it went aground and cost Ł100 to refloat. The Pilgrim Fathers were assured that it was their merchandise but refused both the merchandise and the charge. They should have accepted the merchandise because the Ł100 appeared on their account anyhow.

The amazing patience of the Pilgrim Fathers gave way under the weight of the charges for the Friendship and the White Angel and Allerton was dismissed as their agent. Even then they displayed remarkable forebearance for Bradford wrote "With pitie and compassion (touching Mr. Allerton) I may say with ye apostle to Timothy, 1. Timothy 6.9 'They that will be rich fall into many temptations and snares, etc., and pearce themselves throw with many sorrows, etc.; for the love of money is ye root of all evil."

The Day of Reckoning

The affairs of the Pilgrims were in a horrible state. Bradford states that their total debt to the Adventurers at the end of "ye year 1628 did not amounte to much above Ł400." The accounts kept by the Adventurers in London placed the debt at Ł4,700 two years later. Many attempts were made by both parties to get some semblance of order in the Planters' accounts. Because no one in the Colony had any training or aptitude for record keeping, the London Underwriters in 1630 sent Mr. Hatherley as an auditor to go over the accounts "knowing he will be a comforte to Mr. Allerton, a joye to you,... and a great stay to ye business."

Hatherley appears to have been a greater comfort to Mr. Allerton than a joy to the Pilgrom Fathers for he approved the accounts and stayed in the Colony to become a partner with Mr. Allerton in his later private ventures.

In 1630 the London Underwriters wrote suggesting (as they had a year earlier) that they send over a "new-acountante". The Pilgrim Fathers replied indignantly "that their charge was great allready, and they neede not increase it, as this would; but if they were well delte with, and had their goods well sent over, they could keep their accounts hear them selves." Despite this reply, the London Merchants had Josiah Winslow, a younger brother of Edward Winslow, trained in bookkeeping and sent over. Because of his connection with one of their respected members, he was well received but labored two years with small success. At any rate the Pilgrims' records were lost at sea along with a shipment of beaver skins in December 1632.

In 1636 the London Adventurers laid claim to Ł4,770 "still due for ye purchase yet unpayed." The Pilgrim Fathers pointed out that this included the large losses due to the Friendship and the White Angel which they would not accept and "... some things were obscure, and some things twise charged...or thrise charged." The matter apparently exhausted the patience of the Pilgrim Fathers. They stated "ye new accountante (Josiah Winslow) which they in England would needs presse upon them, did wholy faile them, and could never give them any accounte; but trusting to his memorie, * lose papers, let things rune into such confusion, that neither he, nor any with him, could bring things to rights." They concluded that "...they could not estimate that all ye supplies since sent them, & bills paid for them, could come to above Ł2,000; so as they conceived their debts had been payed, with advantage or intrest." The dispute carried on until October

15, 1641 when an agreement was reached by the parties that the Pilgrims would make a payment of Ł1,800 in final settlement of all claims.

Their unfortunate experience with accounting appears to have finally borne some fruit. Not only did the new treasurer, Myles Standish, keep adequate records but in 1671 when the first school in the Colony was established, John Morton was hired to teach the young how to "read and write & cast up accounts."

FOOTNOTES

[1] William Bradford, Hisotry of Plymouth Plantation, Boston Wright & Potter Printing Co., State Printers, 1898, p. 346. All information in this article was gathered from this transcript of the original manuscript.

CHAPTER TWO

AUDITING IN COLONIAL MASSACHUSETTS

William Holmes

Most accountants are aware, in a general sort of way, that the word "auditor" is derived from "audire", the Latin verb "to hear"; and that at some time in the distant past auditing consisted of listening with both ears akimbo while the bookkeeper "read" his accounts. Most accountants would also date "modern" auditing as commencing about 1850, when railroads developed their internal audit departments and the Chartered Accountant appeared on the business scene in Scotland. But what of the period between the distant past and 1850 - say, for instance, the hundred years between 1630 and 1730 in Colonial America?

On March 4, 1629, the London Managers of the New England Company, as a means towards settling conflicting territorial claims in Massachusetts, obtained a new Royal Charter from King James I in the name of The Massachusetts Bay Company. The Charter provided for a managing board consisting of a Governor, Deputy Governor, Treasurer and eighteen "Assistants", collectively called the Court of Assistants, which was to meet "every moneth or oftener at their pleasure". In addition a General Court to be attended by the "Generalities" of stockholders was to be held four times a year.

The predecessor New England Company had already settled some "Planters" in Massachusetts, but plans were afoot to expand the operation quickly, and more money was urgently needed to pay the costs of recruiting Planters, buying tools and provisions and hiring ships and crews. From the first, a high proportion of the Adventurers (stockholders) were men of business, many involved with other Joint Stock Companies, who showed a commendable concern for the Company's affairs, as is shown by the following extracts from the Company's Records:

On March 9, 1629:

> "This day John Washborne is intertayned for Secretary for one whole yeere, to enter the Courts, to keepe the Companys accounts, to make warrants for all moneys to bee browght in or payd out, & to geeue nottice at euery meeting of such as are backward in payment of there subscriptions, as also for all ꝑuission to bee made reddy, to call vppon such as haue ye chardge thereof, w^{r} by the shippes nowe bound ffor Newe England may bee dispatched by the 25 of this month at ffurdest;

At a General Court on May 13, 1629 a new Court of Assistants was appointed and a few weeks later, on June 11, 1629.

> "The Court was appointed to take consideracon of raising of moneys for paym^{t} of divers debts & bills; and thereupon an estimate was made of what was owing, sev̄alls bills, & W^{ch} are of necessitie to bee presently paid."

However, this Court was sparsely attended and it was felt proper to submit these money matters to a larger audience. A special effort was made to get members to attend another General Court on June 17, 1629 and 26 members heeded the summons. They got down to some serious financial planning to raise some extra money and the minutes of the meeting made note of the following:

> "Audito^{r}s appointed for auditing the accompts, viz, Mr Symon

> Whetcombe, Mr Nathaniell Wright, Mr Noell, Mr Perry, Mr Crane, Mr Clarke, Mr Eaton, and M^{r}Andrewes; these 8, or any 4 of them to meete at a convenyent tyme & place to audite the accompts./"

A little over a month later, at another General Court, the matter came up again and was acted on as follows:

> "The business treated on at the last meeting was now read; and thervpon the accomptes of Mr Gouno^{r}, Mr Deputie, and Mr Trer, being now ꝑ sented to this Court, the Audito^{rs}, formly appointed for auditing the Comp accompts, were now desired to meete & ꝑuse & audite thee accompts; wch they haue agreed to doe to morrow in th'afternoone./"

Commenting on these proceedings, Frances Rose-Troup in her authoritative The Massachusetts Bay Colony and its Predecessors says

> "These were not professional auditors such as would be employed now, but eight Adventurers empowered to act on this occasion only."

Her remarks warrant some consideration. There probably were no "professional auditors" around in these days, but neither was the appointment a meaningless formality, similar say to appointing Mrs Smith, the church organist to be auditor for the local garden club. The occupations of the eight Auditors names are a follows:

Symon Whetcombe	Woollen merchant
Nathaniell Wright	Merchant
Mr Noell (Increase Nowell)	A future Secretary of the Colony
Mr Perry	Merchant tailor
Mr Crane	Grocer

Mr Clarke	Not known
Mr Eaton	Merchant adventurer
Mr Andrewes	Probably a haberdasher and an Alderman

This group of merchants, versed in financial affairs, and used to scrutinizing financial records, was probably the next best thing to professional auditors in existence at the time. It is probable also that the purpose of the audit was not so much to check the correctness of the books as to help the Treasurer and Secretary arrive at the best estimate of the Company's financial condition. A similar situation arose a few months later, which is mentioned below, where this was clearly the primary consideration.

On July 28, 1929 it was proposed, principally on behalf of a new group of stockholders that in order to advance the plantation, and to encourage persons of means and social standing to emigrate, the governments of the plantation should be transferred "to those that shall inhabit there not continue in subordination to the Company in England as it now is". The proposal occasioned considerable opposition and debate, mainly between the old merchant group and the newcomers, but, with modifications, was adopted at a meeting on August 29, 1629. The die was cast and the centre of gravity of the Corporation was to be moved to Massachusetts as soon as possible.

Bernard Bailyn in his The New England Merchants in the Seventeenth Century made the following comment about this action

> "By this vote the company effected its own elimination. Though they were sincerely interested in the establishment of a Puritan colony, the original investors, with a few exceptions,

were not themselves prepared to emigrate. The trading company they had organized in hope of profits was dead, and they proceeded to inter its remains."

On October 16, 1629 the Court of Assistants made note

> "But for that there is great debt owing by the ioynt stock, it was moved that some course might bee taken for cleering thereof, before the goūnm^{t} bee transferred; and to this purpose it was first thought fitt that the accompts should bee audited, to see what the debt is; but the business not admitting any such delay, it was desired that M^{r} Goūno^{r} & M^{r} Trēr would meete to morrow & make an estimate of the debts, & ꝑpare the same against a meeting to bee on Monday next, to determine this question."

Two further entries in the London records are of particular interest. The first pertains to a meeting on November 20, 1629 of the Court of Assistants when

> "Mr. Smith, the accomptant, attended them wth their accompts, and after ꝑusal thereof, it appearing that divers were behynde wth their whole subscripc̄ons, of ꝑt thereof, it was thought fitt, that for the ꝑsent supply of monys, ticketts should bee sent unto them to desire them to send in the sōmes by them underwritten; to wch purpose a list of their names & sōmes was now drawne out."

Mr. Smith shows up again at a General Court on November 25, 1629 at which

> "The accomptant having made an estimate of the acc^{o}, the joynt stock appears to bee in arreare 3000 & upward"

Mr. Smith is a mystery figure of whom not much is known. His appearances, as recorded, are limited to the two mentioned above and his services to the Company are not further defined.

The scene was now set for the move to Massachusetts, and by the end of

February 1630 a fleet of fourteen sail was ready to transport 1500 men, women, and children to New England under their new Governor, John Winthrop. The old merchant group of stockholders was noticeably missing, and to quote Bailyn again

> "Thereafter the leadership of the company was securely in the hands of men whose main occupation was not trade."

It should also be pointed out that in future the "business" of the Company became more and more the organization and administration of a civil government, with the power to assess local taxes to provide for its financial requirements. The Planters soon dispersed through the small towns that quickly established themselves - Charlestown, Boston, Salem, Newton, etc. - and fiscal relationships between these towns and the Company became matters of concern. The story of how Winthrop tried to circumvent the General Court and maintain his arbitrary rule as Governor from 1630 to 1634 is well known. In 1634 after a secret ballot "by papers" he was not re-elected and Dudley took over as Governor. I believe it is more than a coincidence that shortly after Winthrop's defeat on March 3, 1636, the Court voted as follows apparently appointing auditors for the first time on Massachusetts soil.

> Mr Tresurer & Mr Nowell being deputed to take the accompts of Mr Roger Ludlowe, for moneyes that hee hath receaved & disbursed for the publ, hath nowe exhibited the said accompt into Court vnder their hands, & it appeares that the country owed him the some of iij^l vij^s vij^d & for losses in beav^r soe much as makes the s^d sōme vpp x^l, wch the Court appoynts the Tresurer forthwth to pay him.
>
> Mr Hutchinson & Mr Willm Spencer are deputed to take the accompts of Mr Simkins, & to returne the same into the nexte Court.

The town Deputies, representing the Planters, were now the watchdogs of the Money matters of the Company, and from this time on the Treasurer's accompts were regularly "taken" by a committee appointed by the Court. They went further and on September 8, 1636 appointed a Committee to clean up what appears to be "old business".

> "Increase Nowell, Mr Willi : Spencer, & Mr Natha : Duncan are chosen comittes to examine the accounts of all such ꝑsons as the country owes money vnto, as also to make inquiry after such debts as are oweing to the country, & to make report to the next Courte what they have done therein. To this order is aded the examination of the accounts of the m^{r}shall & Mr Brenton./

Between 1636 and 1645 such references to "taking" the accounts of the Treasurer and appointing Committees to examine accompts for other particular matters occur frequently. For instance in May 1640

> Mr Natha : Duncan & Capt Rob^{r}t Sedgwick were appointed to joyne wth the newe Treasurer to take the accounts of the ould Treasurers./ The former three are appointed to examine Sr Rich^{r}d Saltonstalls demands of 160 & od pounds layd out 8 years ago./

Between 1630 - 1640 almost 20,000 souls were transported from old England to New England. The absorption of this flood of emigrants into the existing and newly established towns must have strained considerably fiscal control at both the town and Company levels. The problem apparently became acute in 1645 and the Company sought to improve the situation by creating the post of "Auditor Gen^{r}all for ye Country" and outlining his duties under thirteen headings. The more important paragraphs are worth setting forth in full -

1. It is therefore ord^{r}ed by ye Co^{r}t y^{t} ye said auditor gen^{r}all shalbe carefull to place no debt upon ye country wch doth not rightly belong to y^{m} to pay, or wch doth more ꝑperly belong to any colony, towne, or ꝑticul^{r} ꝑson to discharge; & if y^{r} should be any doubts arising herein, or in any such like paym^{t}, y^{t} he suspend ye paym^{t} y^{r} of till y^{s} Co^{r}t hath determined ye same.

2. That he shall examine all notes, bylls, & accounts upon wch ye country is to make paym^{t} or satisfaction to any ꝑson, & to agree wth y^{m} about ye rates & prizes set downe, if they seeme to him unreasonable, or if they have not before *bene agreed wth, & y^{t} for ye future he shall passe no bills to ye Treasurer to pay, except they bring ꝑticular notes und^{r} ye hands of such y^{t} have received or taken up any thing wch ye country is to be charged wth, as for ferrages, messages, dyet, & such like things; & ye Treasurer shall not allow any bill, etc, before it hath bene signed by ye auditor, who is to be as an equall judge between ye creditor & ye country, y^{t} wrong may not willingly be done either way.

3. That he keepe ꝑfect books of account of all such things y^{t} shall passe through his hands, apertaining to ye country, or signed by him, to be paid by ye country,as also of all debts & dues belonging to ye country, eith^{r} by fines, rates, gifts, legacies, rents, customes, impositions, or any oth^{r} wayes; & y^{t} hee may ye better do it, ye Secretary fro^{m} time to time shall, after every session of ye Gen^{e}all Co^{r}t, & at ye end of every Quarter Co^{r}t, or any other, give notes of all fines, or oth^{r} ꝑfits y^{t} shall arise or appertaine to ye country, by entering of actions, or any oth^{r} way, y^{t} he may enter y^{m} into his booke, & take order for their recovery at ye times agreed upon; & to y^{t} end pow^{r} is hereby given him to sumon & call before him all farm^{rs} or oth^{r} officers y^{t} are to receive any customes, impositions, or rents belonging to ye country, & to take their accounts, & to ord^{r}

their paying of y^{m} in to ye Treasurer according to ye times agreed upon; also to call before him anyꝑson y^{t} is indebted to ye country, at such time & place as hee shall appoint, to give account of such debts.

5. That he take notice of every rate y^{t} is granted fro^{m} time to time, & how it is ꝑportioned to ev^{r}y towne, & make ye Treasurer debter for so much, y^{t} so ye country may have a iust account of ye same; & he hath power at any time to examine & view ye Treasurers accounts, *that so his owne bookes & accounts may be ye more ꝑfect & ready; & if any difference or difficulty should arise between ye audit^{r} & Treausrer about any thing y^{t} may seeme to aꝑptaine to ye office of ye Treasurer, or y^{t} ye Treasurer should thinke it aꝑptines to ye auditor to looke after, y^{t} in such cases they joyne togeth^{r} to do what they can, y^{t} ye business of ye country be not neglected, untill ye Gen^{r}all Co^{r}t shall ord^{r} it between them.

11. That at all oth^{r} Co^{r}ts held wthin y^{s} iurisdiction, eith^{r} ye secretary or clarke of y^{t} Co^{r}t, or some oth^{r} w^{m} y^{t} Co^{r}t, shall appoint, shall take a ꝑticul^{r} account of ye charge of y^{t} Co^{r}t, & leave a note und^{r} his hand wth him y^{t} hath ꝑvided for^{n}y^{t} Co^{r}t, wch he is to bring to ye auditor to enter into his booke before he appoint ye Treasurer to discharge it.

In effect this created a commendable division of duties between the Treasurer and the Auditor General with two sets of books, either of which could be used to check the other. Notice that paragraph 5 also set up a central system of Appropriation accounting as a check against the Town Treasurers. The document in its entirety sets up an extremely interesting and sophisticated exercise in fiscal control and one wonders who was the author. England, of course, had an Auditor General's department dating back to 1314, and it is possible some of the ideas were borrowed from this source.

We see the system at work in the records for May 10, 1648 when it is ordered by the board

> "that the audito^{r} gen^{r}all & Capt Ting shall take the Treasurers account once ev^{r}y yeare, & ꝑsent the same to this Co^{r}te the first session of the Courte of Elections yearely, & that they shall take the account of the ꝑsent Treasurer for the time past before the next session of this ꝑsent Co^{r}te, that so it may appeare, from time to time, what is in the treasury, or what we are indebted. It is also ordered, that the commission^{rs} for the rates in every sheire shall, wthin one month after their sheire meeting, send into the audito^{r} gen^{r}all a true transcript of the rates of the sev^{r}all townes.

And on May 2, 1649 the Court further ordered

> "Mr Nowell, Capt Keayne, & Capt Ting are appointed a com ittee to take the Treasurers account & audito^{r} gen^{r}alls between this & the next session of this Courte, make^{g} returne thereof to this Co^{r}te."

And so the accounts of the auditor General himself were to be independently audited.

It is interesting to see the standing in the community of some of these persons appointed as auditors from 1636 to 1649.

Nathaniel Duncan, who was appointed Auditor General, was one of the original group who emigrated in 1630. He is listed in The Pioneers of Massachusetts (Charles Henry Pope - 1900) as a selectmen, auditor and deputy. Pope, however, makes reference to an old text written in New England which states that Duncan was "Learned in Latin and French a very good accountant".

Robert Keayne was a London merchant tailor who came to New England in

1635 and who Pope says "Carried on a Large business and left great estate".

Capt. Ting was probably Edward Tyng, a London merchant who emigrated to Boston some time prior to 1636.

Increase Nowell arrived in 1630, settled in Charlestown, and was at one time or another an Assistant, Deputy, Secretary of the Colony, and town officer.

I believe we see here a repeat of the situation in London. The men appointed to the audit committees were responsible,well educated people, and often with a business background.

The comments so far obviously relate to auditing public finances. What about auditing the business sector of the Massachusetts economy? Few of the London merchants comprising the "old brigade" of the shareholders emigrated. However, by the early 1640's a new breed of local merchants began to evolve out of the melting pot of emigrants flowing into New England. One of the largest of the commercial ventures was the attempt to establish a local iron works. In the early 1640's the Court granted a franchise to a group of "Undertakers & Adventurers" who formed a separate Joint Stock Company to dig the local bog ore, and to set up facilities to refine it and make iron products. The first venture was in Braintree, but this was moved within a short period to Saugus. The local management of the venture was turned over to John Gyfford as agent.

In 1654 it appeared as though there had been some suspicious goings-on at the foundry properties and auditors were sent in to examine the situation. The records for 1654 include the following under date of November 22, 1656:

> "Itt was also put to the quaestion, whither the Courte, in the case of the vndertakers of the iron works, by theire dep^{ts}, plaintiffs, & Mr Jno Gifford, defendant, would so accept of the

first auditt as to beginne where they left, reserving the plaintives just liberty in point of plea for damage in theire second action for the defendants not following his orders and instruccons. Itt was resolved on the affirmative by the whole Court."

Two days later on November 24, 1654 the matter came up again.

"After the whole Court had heard what the plaintiffs & defendants could say, & ꝑvsed seuerall of the evidences & audito^{rs} retourne, they proceeded as foll : Whereas thereis an accon of thirteene thowsand pounds vppon accoumpt depending in this Court betwixt Mr Josiah Winslow & Capt Robt Keayne, deputjes and attourneys for the vndertakers of the iron workes, plaintiffs, against Mr Jno Gifford, late agent, defendant, the Court findes that, vppon the sajd Giffords presenting his bookes of accompt in a County Court by theire order, where the action was first comenced, the sajd Court refer^{d} the auditting of the saijd accompts to certaine select meete persons, who, having spent much tjme about the same, made a retourne so farr as they had ꝑceeded, but left the consideracon of many particculars in Mr Giffords charge, wch they wanted evidenc to passe, to the valew of three thowsand five hundred severty-two pounds sixteene shillings and eleven pence, to the consideracon and determination of the Court: but this some consisting of too many ꝑticculars for the Court to examine, was againe referred, together with the effects of the iron workes, to other audito^{rs}, who, after much tjme expended about the same, made theire retourne, and left the defendant debot^{r} vppon the whole the some heereafter exprest, against wch the plaintiffs made many just and considerable objections, which occasioned this Court to enter into a more strict consideracon & examination of the whole accompt, wherein they finde many false charges, vast expences & guifts, some tonns of iron disposed of more then he gives the iron works creditt for, the proffitt of the ffarme, &, which he made vse of for himself, not brought to acco^{t}, together with diuerse other improbable disbursements putt vppon accoumpt. The Court also found that the last audito^{rs} had respect only to the accoumpts as they stood in the bookes, without reference to the defendant orders or coṁission, and so issued the same in an arbitrary way, and much of it wthout proofe, which this Court could not allow off; but after much tjme spent about this case, finding the whole accoumpts intricate, & very many of the particculars coteyned in fower papers left by the first auditers to the determinacon of the Court, to the valew of three thowsand five hundred seventy two pounds sixteene shillings & eleven pence, very doubtful and suspitious, the plaintiffs also objecting against the whole as being donne wthout order, and the defendant peremptorily refusing to shew his order or com ission for the same, the Court judged it meete to order, that the defendant should be allowed two thousand and five hundred and odd pounds exprest in the foote of the audit, leaving the defendant to his liberty, by due proofe, according to his orders and instructions, to proove what he may or cann more, the defendant paying the workemens wages, and giving securitje for the same."

The case was in and out of the Court for several years, but the interesting aspect is the attempts by successive teams of auditors to make sense out or what appears to have been an exceedingly messy set of books. This also appears to have been an attempt to audit the entire undertaking.

A more normal happening before the court was the question of disputes between merchants on specific matters. These were of common enough occurrence that in 1654 the Court prescribed the method of proving a debt and requiring that along with the Waste Book and Journal a merchant must also make available his Ledger.

> "Wherein as well, ye buyer, as creditor, and his particular payments are written, as on ye other side, what he is debtor for."

In these instances also, the Court turned to the use of a Committee of court-appointed auditors to examine the accounts and make recommendations.

A good example of this shows up in Volume 39 (page 204) of the Massachusetts Archives. Apparently in this case a former set of auditors had narrowed the issues between the parties and left three items still to be settled. The Court appointed a second set of auditors who reported as follows:

> "We the subscribed being appointed to this Court to Audit Accompts between John Hoare, Attorney to Daniel Hoare, and Mr Richard Cook in these severall actions as hereafter follow do make, in obedience there unto, this our Report.
>
> As to the 1st October, being an action of review of 1000^l. Having perused all papers produced by both sydes, in reference to the said action, and the said John Hoare owning th former Audit out only in three ꝑticulars which we sufficiently satisfied about we allow of and conceed with the former Audit as to all particulars. And as to ye interest we find not now evidence. And the evidence formerly produced to be obscure & doubtful, therefore leave it to this honourable Court to Judge thereof.
>
> As to the second action for non ꝑformance of an Agreement Covenant or Bond from the said Richard Cook to Daniel Hoare as in there mentioned, we find no such agreem^t Covenant, of Bond of Said Cook's. And further if it could be produced, we find that the said Richard Cook hath performed, as is

> demonstrated of the former Audit.
>
> As to the 3rd Action being an action of Probiter concerning an account of the Barke Hopewell, we find (as the former Audit) that there were three Accompt given by Daniel Hoare of the said Barke which upon examination we find to differ one from another and all to be contradictory to the oaths of Samuel Arnalt & Richard Cook and therefore conceive them justly to be Excepted against, as not being without error."
>
> February 24, 1663
>
> | | |
> |---|---|
> | Wm Davis | Thomas Charles |
> | John Richards | Anthony Stoddard |

The audit of public finances commented on so far has been related to the accounts of the Province of Massachusetts. However, in 1689 the town of Boston climbed on the bandwagon at the town meeting.

March 10, 1689/90

> At a publique meeting of the inhabitants of Boston "Voted that Mr. Peter Sergeant, Mr. Benj Alford, and Mr. Samson Sheafe be desired to Audit the Townes Acct with ye Selectmen for the two years past."

The auditors apparently went at the task with due deliberation and raised enough questions that only an interim report could be made a year later, for at the meeting of March 9, 1690/91 they were "desired to perfect what remaines to be done of the Acct^s of those 2 yeares, as also to audit the accomp^t of the Selectmen in the year 1690".

They finally got the first two years out of the way at the meeting on March 14, 1691/92 when their report was unanimously adopted. In 1695 the meeting voted "that the Treasurer's accompt be audited once in every year". Peter Sergeant was again one of the three auditors chosen and by that time had about five years experience in the business.

It should be noted that Peter Sergeant was one of the most successful merchants in Boston at the time and his appointment is in keeping with the practice at the Provincial level of selecting persons well versed in business affairs to the position of Auditor.

A new dimension is added for the first time to the audit reports in 1709 and I believe the first report of this type bears printing in full. It is Chapter 33 in the Acts & Resolves for 1709-10.

CHAPTER 33

ORDER ACCEPTING THE COMMITTEES REPORT ON THE COMMISSARY GENERALS ACCOMPTS

Boston June 15: 1709.

PURSUANT to the Order of the House appointing us a Committee, to Examine, & Audit, the Accompts of Andrew Belcher Esqr Com̄issary Generall:

We Attended the Said Service, & Examined his Accompts from March 30th 1706, to Janu^{ry} 23th 170^{6}/7 (his accompts before that time having been Pass'd by this Court) and find them right Cast, and well Avouch'd. And upon the 23th of Janu^{ry} 170^{6}/7, there was due from the Province to the S^{d} Com̄issary Generall to Ballance his Accompt the Sum of One Thousand Eight Hundred, fifty Six Pounds, Six Shillings & eleven pence, halfe peny, as was Reported, by the Com̄ittee, appointed by the Honble Board to Examin the Same. The House Rqviring our Attendance has Prevented our further Proceeding, at this time.

JOS: WOLCOT
JAMES BARNES

THO: FITCH
JOHN BROWNE
Cōmittee

Ordered That the above-Report, be Accepted. (Passed June 15)

"right cast, and well Avouch'd!" These words, with minor variants, are included in almost all reports of audits of public accounts during the next hundred years. They were also used on occasion in audits of commerical matters.

Another interesting report appears as Chapter 37 of the Acts & Resolves for the year 1720-21.

CHAPTER 37

ORDER FOR COMMITTING THE ACC^{TS} OF THE Ł100,000 LOAN

In the House of Representat^{ves}

Ordered that Mr William Clark, Mr Treasurer Allen & Mr John White Clerk of this House, be a Committee in the Recess of this Court, To Inspect the Accompts of the Commissioners of the Hundred Thousand Pound Loan of the Province Bills that are brought in & prepare them for the Court to pass upon at their next Session, And that such of the Commissioners as have not return'd their Accompts framed according to a Model sent to them, by Mr William Clark & c, formerly a Committee appointed by this Court, be strictly required without Delay to confirm their Accompts to the said Model, & return them to the Committee hereby appointed.

"Accompts framed according to a Model sent to them" and "Commissioners be strictly required ... to conform their Accompts to the said Model." This probably represents the earliest attempt to design a uniform system of accounts in New England and possibly in America.

The growing sophistication of Audit Committees which led them to look at the substance of accounts instead of merely vouching amounts to bills and making sure the arithmetic was right is shown in Chapter 55 of the Acts and Resolves for the 1720-21.

CHAPTER 55

ORDER ACCEPTING THE REPORT OF THE COMMITTEE IN REGARD TO ACC^{TS} OF THE CHARGE OF Y^{E} ADDITIONAL BUILDING AT HARVARD COLLEGE, AND MAKING A PRESENT TO THE COMMITTEE FOR THEIR SERVICES.

> THE ACCOMPTS of Jonathan Remington, Charles Chambers Esqr & Mr Andrew Boardman a Committee appointed by the Court to Oversee the Additional Building at Harward College, Of the Charge of Building & Finishing said House, the Ballance of which due to the Province, being One hundred, sixteen pounds, & one Penny, Together with, The Report of Mr William Clark in behalf of the Com^{te} appointed by the House of Representat^{ves} to view the said Building, Whic Report is as follows,
>
> In Obedience to the Order of this Honb^{l} House, The Committee went to Cambridge & View'd the Additional Brick Building at Harvard College, lately erected there at the Province Charge, And Report that they find it a well build & finished House, & well adapted to the Reception of Students. The Committee have also examined & Audited the Accompts of the Committee that had the Care of Building the same, And Report, That they find them well vouch'd & rightly cast, And the several Charges in the many Trades mens Bills no more than what is usual & Customary.

Physical observation of new fixed assets and a critical review of the reasonableness of charges represent an advanced level of audit techniques in use two hundred and fifty years ago!

I like the report in Chapter 46 of the Acts & Resolves for 1721.

CHAPTER 46

RESOLVE ON COMMITTES REPORT ON CAP^{T} ZECHARIAH TUTHILLS ACCOMPT OF VICTUALLING THE GARRISON AT CASTLE WILLIAM.

> AN ACCOMPT presented, by Mr Zechariah Tuthill of Victualling the Garrison at his Majesties Castle William, From Jany 13th 1720, to June 29th 1721, both days Included.
>
> The Committee having Exam^{d} the Accompts,of Victuall^{g} the officers, Soldiers & c^{a} of his Majesties Castle William, & find it right Cast, & Vouched from the Former Accompt, but would observe that there is Charged in Said accompt, Subsistence for three men Negroes & Servants to his Honour the Lt Govr, which have not done any Duty at the Castle, Viz^{t} Thomas, Quaco, John Cooper, & Peter Slaughter, the Former his Waiting man, the othr Two his Servants Employed on his Farm at Newbury & never at the Castle on Duty, whose Victualling, being Thirtten pounds Four Shillings. The Committee are Humbly of opinion, ought not to be paid by the Province, So have taken the Same out of the Amount of the Victualling being Ł274. 0.7 So that there Remains Due for the discharge of the Said Victualling Accompt, Two hundred Sixty one pounds Sixteen Shill^{gs} & Seven pence, As by the Accompts on the Other Side.
>
> By Order of the Committe,
>
> W^{M} CLARKE

It was apparently a ticklish business to challenge the "Lt Govr" - note the "Humbly of opinion" - but the Committee did it anyway. The Court, incidentally, agreed with them in the matter and disallowed the amount objected to. This is not an isolated instance. The Acts & Resolves are full of examples of "qualified opinions", good evidence that the Auditors did an honest job and were not inclined merely to "rubber-stamp" the accompts. After all, in most instances it was their own tax money they were saving.

What the can we say about auditing in Colonial America? The first thing is to take note of the surprising amount of auditing going on, particularly in the public sector at all levels of government. The appointment of the Auditor General in 1645 in the middle of what was still basically a wilderness was, to say the least, surprising. The "job description" that went with the post, everything considered, is astounding!

The "auditors" appointed throughout the period for the most part meet the definition ascribed to those to be appointed in the iron works examination as "certain select meete persons". By education, background and business experience they were of a high calibre and eminently suited to the task. The number of instances where they took exception to the accounts bear witness to their zeal and objective honesty.

At the commercial level, other than the isolated instance of suspected fraud in the iron works, there appears to be little evidence of auditing the affairs of a whole busiess. The family business or small partnership typical of the times was accountable only to itself and there was accordingly no motivation for audit. The commercial sector turned to the auditor mostly to settle its intermittent squabbles in the Courts and was apparently satisfied with the results, although the instances of "second" audits indicates some right of appeal from the findings of "first" audits. In these instances also the Courts took care to appoint "certain select meete persons".

Everything considered, the auditing effort must have contributed much to the probity of civil government and people's trust in it, and to the orderly development and application of the lex mercatoria - surely a worthwhile undertaking.

It would be interesting to compare experience in Massachusetts during this period with New York and Pennsylvania, particularly to study the impact of the early Dutch control in New York. It would not be amiss either to compare experience in the public sector with conditions in Britain during the same period.

A final note! In 1871 the auditors for the town of Boscawen in New Hampshire submitted the following report on the town accounts -

> "The undersigned, appointed to audit the accounts of the Selectmen of Boscawen, for the 1870-71, report that they have examined said accounts, and find the receipts from March 1, 1870, to March 1, 1871, to have been $20,010.28, and the disbursements to have been $19,369.19, the accounts of which are properly vouched and correctly cast, leaving a balance in the hands of the Treasurer, of $8,641.09."

When you have something good why mess around with it!

CHAPTER THREE

MUNICIPAL ACCOUNTING IN THE PLYMOUTH COLONY -- 1657 TO 1686

Linda H. Kistler

Introduction

The struggle by the Pilgrims to establish the first New England settlement in 1620 has been well documented by historians beginning with William Bradford, second governor of the Plymouth Colony. Published information on the financial affairs of the Pilgrims is relatively rare. Two exceptions are the analysis of the group's financial problems during the colony's first two decades by McIntyre[1] and an earlier article in this volume by Stone.[2] Both papers graphically portray the economic and financial burdens, skullduggery, mismanagement, and outright fraud that plagued the Pilgrims during the crucial early years as the colony began to gain a foothold in the new land.

This paper traces the evolution of a municipal accounting system used by the Pilgrims through an analysis of the records of the colony treasurer from 1657 to 1686.[3] The treasurer was charged with maintenance of all financial records of the colony and with periodic reporting of his stewardship of public funds. The treasurer's accounts were reviewed annually by an audit committee chosen by the General Court (the Pilgrims' administrative, legislative, and judicial body).

The annual reports of the Plymouth Colony audit committees beginning in 1658 provide useful insights into the economic development of the Plymouth Colony. These early records also reveal the importance placed on the enforcement of the Pilgrims' religious and ethical beliefs. The imposition of fines against people found guilty of misconduct was very common, and examination of the Treasurer's Accounts provides a rare glimpse of the customs and mores of our Founding Fathers. Finally, the Treasurer's Accounts reflect the beginnings of municipal accounting in the United States. By the 1680s, the budgets and reports of the treasurer begin to resemble modern municipal accounts in several fundamental respects.

Financial records for the years prior to 1658 are very rudimentary and provide few details of transactions. A fragmentary record of activities for 1648 was located; and in 1653, an audit committee reported receipts of 143 pounds and disbursements of some fifty pounds, leaving a balance in the treasury of about ninety-two pounds. These simple records indicate that the colonists recognized the importance of maintaining financial records, at least in summary fashion. Unfortunately, details of the years before 1657 have not survived.

Although complete records are not available before 1658, evidence exists that the Pilgrims understood the importance of auditing the treasurer's accounts much earlier than 1658. A review of the General Court records of the Plymouth Colony indicates that an audit committee was appointed as early as March 1645, when the Court selected Miles Standish, John Done, and John Dunhame to "take the account of Thomas Prence, Treasurer." Similarly, the rival Massachusetts Bay Company in Boston appointed an audit committee as early as 1629, according to records of that larger and more prosperous colony.

Historical Setting

Following the extraordinarily difficult task of establishing a foothold in New England during the winter of 1620-21, the Pilgrims experienced a series of misfortunes that would have defeated all but the most stouthearted of settlers.

The dangers associated with carving a viable settlement out of an inhospitable wilderness were compounded by the financial naivete of the colonists, by an accumulation of enormous debts to the original adventurers who financed the colony, and by some highly questionable actions of the Pilgrims' business agent, Isaac Allerton. The colony's early misfortunes are discussed in Stone's paper and McIntyre's book and need not be reviewed further.[4]

By 1646, twenty-five years after the colony was founded, the Plymouth settlers finally freed themselves of debts to both the original adventurers and to the undertakers who succeeded the earlier group of backers. The colony began to concentrate on developing its modest resources and to establishing new settlements on Cape Cod.

<u>Population Growth</u>.[5] Pneumonia and scurvy had exacted a terrible toll during the first winter on Cape Cod, and the original group of 102 settlers declined to only eighty-six men, women, and children. By 1624 the population had increased to 180 persons, and in 1630 the Plymouth Colony is thought to have risen to approximately 300 settlers.

The middle years from 1630 to 1650 in Plymouth were characterized by modest growth in population, including the establishment of several towns, and by the development of agriculture, cattle raising, and by the inception of trade and commerce among the other New England colonies at Boston, Rhode Island, and Connecticut. The population may have increased to as many as 3,000 inhabitants by 1644, although that figure is thought to be too high; and in 1693, when the Plymouth Colony and the Massachsuetts Bay Company merged, the Cape Codders were credited with a population of 17,000 people.

<u>Government</u>. The Mayflower <u>Compact</u>, signed in 1620 prior to the Pilgrims' landing on Cape Cod, established the foundation for administration of the colony.

Certain fundamental operating principles such as equal rights, administration of justice, law, and order, and communal safety were carried forward from the Compact. During the early years, the governor and his assistants comprised the administration, having been elected by the freemen at an annual town meeting. Freemen were individuals who had originally signed the Compact as well as other settlers who were subsequently voted to membership by persons already designated freemen.

By the late 1640s, the colony's voting requirements were tightened to include a minimum age (21 years), endorsement or sponsorship by local townsmen, an estate of twenty pounds, and a religious faith, although formal church membership apparently was not necessary.

During the late 1630s, the settlers began to establish satellite towns within the colony. Duxbury, Barnstable, Scituate, Taunton, Sandwich and Yarmouth were founded, thereby necessitating a change in government. The first representative assembly (called the General Court) was held in Plymouth in 1639. The General Court met four times a year. The governor, his assistants, and the treasurer were chosen annually at the June session. In 1636, the General Court completed a major revision of the forty statutes then in force, and the revised laws became the Pilgrims' colonial laws.

Economic Development. The Plymouth Colony never achieved the wealth and economic success enjoyed by the larger Massachsuetts Bay Colony at Boston. Plymouth settlers were burdened during the early years by huge debts, while their larger, wealthier colonial neighbors quickly engaged in fur trading, fishing, shipbuilding, trade and commerce as well as agriculture and cattle raising. The Boston colonists proved to be much more successful financially than the Pilgrims of Plymouth.

Despite difficult beginnings, the settlers slowly attained economic self-sufficiency. Initially, the Pilgrims concentrated on farming, fishing, and hunting. The settlers were not particularly experienced in these activities; and the harsh climate, mediocre soil conditions, and a labor force weakened by disease did not produce bounteous crops during the first years. Indeed, were it not for the assistance and counsel of friendly Indians, the Pilgrims might not have survived. The settlers imported cattle soon after 1620, but the introduction of sheep was hindered by both the harsh climate and by the presence of wolves which ravaged the sheep and small animal population.

Forest products were harvested for both domestic use and export. Lumber for homes, pine and other woods for shipbuilding, and tar, turpentine, and resin were common forest products. Animal trapping and fishing also occupied the early settlers together with the production of cloth from wool and flax.

One of the most serious obstacles to economic development was the scarcity of money. For many years the Pilgrims resorted to barter for trading and the settlement of debts. As will be shown later, the major grains, beef, pork and other commodities were assigned monetary values by the General Court. Taxes, fines, and other debts could be discharged by payment in commodities. Moreover, wampum (the Indian bead money) was accepted as legal currency until 1661.

The public tax system was simple and effective. An excise tax on real estate and personal property was the principal source of revenue, although an income tax supplemented the property tax, and a poll tax also was imposed. Because currency was scarce, the General Court at Plymouth annually established a schedule for payment of taxes in commodities. Finally, substantial public revenues were raised through imposition of fines. Minor offenses and unseemly conduct such as working on the Sabbath, swearing and drunkenness were heavily penalized, reflecting the importance the Pilgrims attached to their religious and ethical principles.

Public expenditures primarily were used to pay the salaries and expenses of the governor, his assistants, and the treasurer, and to provide military protection for the colony. The threat from unfriendly Indians was a continuing source of anxiety. For example, colony records in 1645 provided the details of costs of an expedition against the Narragansett Indians.[6] Expenses for the two week period totalled nearly seventy pounds and involved some forty militiamen. Each town was charged a portion of the total cost; and the Genral Court specified the wages to be paid each town's soldiers. The rest of the assessment was forwarded to the colony treasurer to defray the joint costs of the expedition. The cost of military protection from the Indians and occasionally from the French unquestionably was an important colonial expense.

This rather lengthy historical perspective of the Plymouth Colony has described the economic and social conditions during the early decades of the colony's existence. In the next section, the Treausrer's Accounts of the colony are analyzed for selected years between 1657 and 1686. The objective of the examination is to learn more about the Pilgrims' growth and development, to trace the early beginnings of municipal accounting, and to examine the sources and uses of public funds in the 1600s.

Treasurer's Account - 1657

Except for the references noted in the introduction, the financial records of the Plymouth Colony's very early years have not survived. In 1658, the General Court (the governing body of the colony) ordered an audit committee to examine the treasurer's records and to report their findings for the year 1657. The committee's tasks were to verify revenues and expenses, to provide details of accounts receivable and accounts payable, and to compute the ending balance owed to (or owed by) the treasurer.

The 1658 audit committee consisted of Captain Josias Winslow, Lieutenant Thomas Southworth, Edmond Hawes, and Josias Cooke. Normally, audit committees comprised from three to six men, selected annually by the General Court. With a few exceptions, different people were selected for service on the committee each year.

The treasurer of Plymouth Colony during most of the period under study was Mr. Constant Southworth, who served for more than twenty years. Southworth was succeeded by Major William Bradford during the period 1679 through 1686. Constant Southworth made an extraordinary contribution to Plymouth Colony during his lifetime, and his accomplishments merit closer examination. On January 2, 1637, he was admitted a freeman of the Plymouth Colony along with a group of ten other men. Court records show that he was first granted a parcel of land in 1636. During subsequent years, he acquired substantial additional acreage in the town of Duxbury. In 1637, Southworth married Elizabeth Collyer, and he proceeded to establish a reputation for service that few settlers could equal. In 1640 he was a surveyor of highways in Duxbury; and he became a constable in 1641. The records indicate that Southworth became a volunteer soldier in 1637 and served as "ensigne bearer" of the Duxbury Company from 1646 to 1653.

In 1645 Constant Southworth served with Miles Standish and John Alden on a committee appointed by the General Court to apportion among the settlers a four square mile parcel of land in Duxbury. Southworth and John Alden represented the town of Duxbury at the General Court during the late 1640s and early 1650s. Among the services he performed for the colony were: Administrator of an estate and later guardian of the orphaned children of James and May Lendall; member of a committee to build a house of correction adjacent to the Plymouth prison in 1658; member of a council of war in 1653; and deputy of Duxbury. Clearly, Constant Southworth was a man of unusual ability, and his fellow colonists must have appreciated both his recordkeeping ability and his personal integrity because they returned him to the office of treasurer of Plymouth Colony for more than twenty years.

The report of the audit committee in 1658 is shown in Exhibit I. Although details of receipts and expenditures are omitted, a crude picture of the colony's public activities can be developed. Several aspects of the report are noteworthy. All debits (revenues) to the colony are listed first, followed by a summary of disbursements. The amount owed to the country by the treasurer for collections made was seventy-nine pounds, sixteen shillings. In the following section, the accounts receivable are listed. Unpaid fines totalling nearly 175 pounds are reported, including miscellaneous fines of thirty pounds. Fines for refusing to take the oath of fidelity were levied against thirteen men at ten pounds each. Note that George Webb was fined five pounds for refusing to take the oath of fidelity, but the penalty was remitted because Mr. Webb agreed to "depart the govment." Gorg Allin, who also refused to take the oath within the alloted time, was fined five pounds, but the Court required him to pay only one-half the levy. The oath of fidelity related to the annual requirement that all freemen in the colony pledge their fidelity to the king and colony. Failure to take the oath was a serious offense, and persons were fined accordingly.

In June, 1658, the settlers at Kennebeck (Maine) still owed more than four pounds from 1656, and additional rent of some fifty-two pounds was due for the year 1657. Exhibit I also shows that the colony was owed eight pounds for four barrels of oil. Note also that selling guns to Indians was forbidden. Anthony Loe

EXHIBIT I

TREASURY ACCOUNTS OF THE COLONY OF NEW PLYMOUTH IN NEW ENGLAND

For the Year 1657 - 1658

*CAPT: JOSIAS WINSLOW, Leiftenant Thomas Southworth, Mr Edmond Hawes, and Josias Cooke, being ordered to take an account of the Treasurer this 10th of June, 1658. 1658. 10 June (*1)

It̄, the Treasurer is debter by money of the countrey, alreddy receiued,	79 : 16 : 00
It̄, by fines not yett levied,	30 : 06 : 00
It̄, p^r more, four barrells of oyle,	08 : 00 : 00
It̄, by money due on Kenebecke, it the yeare 1656	04 : 07 : 03
It̄, more, for one yeare and an halfe rent now dew,	052 : 10 : 00
In totall due,	174 : 19 : 06

We haue not heerin meddled with fines about the oath of fidelitie, nor any fines condemned by this p̄sent Court, held June the fift, 1658. Att which Court, Rob Harper, Ralph Allin, Seni^r, Jolin Allin, Thomas Greenfeild, Edward Perrey, Richard Kerbey, Juni^r, Willam Allin, Thomas Vre, Willam Gifford, Mathew Allin, Daniell Wing,Francis Allin, and John Jenkens, all of Sandwich, for refusing to take the oath of fidelitie, fined eucry of them the som̄e of Ł10, in all, 130 : 00 : 00

1658 10 June	George Webb, for refusing to take the oath of fidelitie within the time prefixed, fined	05 : 00 : 00

The said Gorge Webb engageing to depart the goument, in case hee soe doe, the other fiue pound is remitted.

Gorḡ Allin, takeing the matter about the oath into considerat̄, is likewise for p̄sent not required to pay the one halfe of his fine, which is five pound; neverthelese, for his refusing to take the said ōth within the time p̄fixed in the order, is fined 05 : 00 : 00

Anthony Loe, of Warwick, for selling a pistoll to an Indian, was fined the sum̄e of	03 : 00 : 00
Moses Rowley and Robert Parker, for striking each other, fined each,	00 : 03 : 04
*The Treasurer is p[r] contra credit by seuerall disburs̄ments,	69 : 10 : 11

By debts now owing.

Imp[r], to the Gou[r], by the appointment of the countrey,	10 : 00 : 00
To M[r] John Howland	01 : 00 : 00
To the marshall	02 : 00 : 00
To Mistris Bradford	15 : 01 : 04
To Capt̄ Winslow	04 : 10 : 00
To M[r] Constant Southworth	04 : 00 : 00
To M[r] John Barnes	04 : 07 : 06
	40 : 18 : 10
It̄, more to bee alowed to him for his two yeares seruice	12 : 00 : 00
	52 : 18 : 10
	69 : 10 : 11
The totall of the Tresurers creditt	122 : 09 : 09

Rest to the countrey on ballence due from the Tresurer	52 : 09 : 06
It̄, by mistake in one barrell of oyle, lesse	02 : 00 : 00

This is a trew account, errors excepted.

The countrey haue alowed more to the Tresurer	04 : 00 : 00
Soe that now remaines due to the countrey	46 : 09 : 06

was fined three pounds for that offense. Finally, Moses Rowley and Robert Parker were fined three pounds each for fighting.

The disbursements portion of the report for 1657 does not itemize specific expenses paid by the treasurer, who had disbursed more than sixty-nine pounds during the year. The schedule of accounts payable totalled more than forty pounds, and here also, few details are reported. The ending balance in the treasurer's account was further reduced by an error in the oil debit and by an allowance of four pounds to the treasurer, leaving a net balance carried forward to the next year of more than forty-six pounds.

During the period under study in this paper, delinquent tax levies and fines comprised a significant portion of the colony's accounts receivables. A study of the Treasurer's Account in subsequent years indicates that the General Court was not always successful in collecting some of the fines. Several fines were carried on the records for eight to ten years before they eventually disappeared from the audit reports. One may conclude that delinquent taxes and fines are not merely a twentieth century phenomenon.

One of the most significant aspects of this early record is the sentence near the end of the report: "This is a trew account, errors excepted." This phrase, or similar wording, was very commonly found above the signatures of the audit committee. The statement is akin to a one sentence auditor's opinion, and it represents the audit committee's attestation of the report's accuracy and the treasurer's stewardship. The phrase, "errors excepted," implies that the auditors did not rule out the possibility of error in the treasurer's accounts. Modern auditors also very carefully do not attest as to the accuracy of financial statements, merely to their overall fairness. One concludes that even seventeenth century "citizen" auditors recognized the risk of attesting to the complete accuracy of the accounts they were charged with examining.

The documentation of audit committees existing and functioning in a relatively sophisticated manner in the mid-1600s represents a contribution to the literature on the history of accounting in the United States. The evidence of ongoing analyses of the treasurer's stewardship on an annual basis and reporting the results of an audit to third parties indicates that the colonists understood the importance of the safeguarding of public funds. Clearly, the Pilgrims made a significant contribution to the development of municipal accounting practices in the United States and they also contributed to the development of auditing more than 250 years before public accounting was recognized as a profession.

A study of General Court proceedings of the Massachsuetts Bay Company confirms similar audit practices within that colony as early as the 1630s. Audit committees fulfilled a very important function in these Massachusetts colonies, and their contribution to the evolution of accounting should not be overlooked..

Treasurer's Accounts -- 1665

The audit committee's report of June, 1666, for the year 1665 is interesting in several respects. First, the colony's economic progress is reflected in the substantial increase in revenues and expenses; second, specific tax levies for each town are summarized; third, detailed procedures for payment of taxes are set forth; and finally, unpaid fines continued to comprise a lengthy list of receivables. The audit report for 1665 is shown in Exhibit II.

On June 7, 1665, the General Court set the tax levy for the following year: "A rate of one hundred and fifty pounds being agreed on to be levied on the seuerall townshipps of this jurisdiction, warrants were forthwith issued forth for the sume of forty pounds thereof to bee paid in money." Note that only about twenty-five percent of taxes were payable in currency. This is significant in that it reflects the

EXHIBIT II

TREASURER'S ACCOUNT -- 1666

*June the 8th, 1666.

THE account giuen in by the Treasurer vnto Mr Paine, Mr Nathaniel Bacon, and Josias Cooke.

	li s d
The Treasurer is debter to the countrey, as appeers by his accounts, the sum̄e of	188 : 10 : 09
The Treasurer is p contra creditt to the countrey by disburs̄ments and debts, as appeers by his accounts the sum̄e of	205 : 16 : 09
Soe that there aresteth due to the Treasurer, to ballence the account, the sum̄e of	17 : 06 : 00

Debts due by rates to the countrey from these p̄ticulars townes of the last yeare.

			li
Item, Sandwich,	00 : 17 : 08		
Item, Scittuate,	00 : 02 : 00	in all,	5 : 14 : 02
Item, Bridgwater,	04 : 14 : 06		

Debtes due by fines and otherwise to the countrey.

	li
Kanelme Winslow, Junior,	00 : 10 : 00
Ralph Earle,	01 : 00 : 00
Thomas Pope,	00 : 03 : 04
Timothy Hallowey,	00 : 10 : 00
John Bayley,	00 : 03 : 04
Richard Willis,	00 : 13 : 04
Thomas Cushman, Juni^r,	03 : 00 : 00
Thomas Totman, for committing fornication, fined,	05 : 00 : 00
Thomas Little,	01 : 10 : 00
Samuell Norman,	00 : 10 : 00
John Barnes,	01 : 00 : 00
Thomas Lucas,	00 : 10 : 00
Thomas Phelpes,	00 : 10 : 00
Abraham Jackson,	05 : 00 : 00
Francis Baker,	00 : 03 : 04
John Barrow,	00 : 10 : 00
Gorge Barlow,	00 : 10 : 00
James Cole, Seni^r,	00 : 05 : 00
Nathaniel Church,	05 : 00 : 00
Sarah Barstow, allies Sarah Church,	05 : 00 : 00
John Carsley,	00 : 03 : 04

The countrey is debtor, vpon old account, a barrell of powder to the countrey.

	li
The countrey is debtor to Thomas Sauory,	7 : 1 : 1

In reference vnto the paines and charge the Treasurer hath bine att in the countreyes busines this last yeare, hee is alowed the sum̄e of twenty fiue pounds.

importance of the colony's highly developed barter system as well as the scarcity of hard cash in Plymouth.

An entry in the records dated October 3, 1665, indicates that the rest of the 1665-66 levy was due in commodities: "Warrants were issued forth to levy the hundred and ten pounds remaining, which was to bee paid, one third pte in wheat, and the other two thirds in either wheat, pease, barly, or Indian corne." The 1665 records do not show specific rates established for each commodity. However, in 1666 the record does report rates to be used for fiscal 1667 (see Exhibit III), and it may be assumed that a similar set of rates for commodities existed in 1665.

Examination of Exhibit II for 1665 shows receipts and expenditures were summarized without presenting details. The balance of 17:01:00 is an amount due to the treasurer, who had paid expenses in excess of his collections and beginning balance. Note also that several towns were delinquent in payment of their 1665 taxes. Further, the audit report lists more than twenty-eight pounds due to the colony for unpaid fines; and accounts payable of some thirty-two pounds, including twenty-five pounds owed the treasurer "in reference unto the paines and charge the Treasurer hath bine att in the countreyes busines this last year. . ." During the period examined in this paper, the treasurer typically received from twenty to thirty pounds annually for his services in maintaining the colony's financial records.

The increase in revenues and expenditures from 1657 to 1665 is interesting. Expenses increased 68 percent, while receipts rose 88 percent. However, analysis of audit reports during the eight year period revealed wide fluctuations in both receipts and disbursements. For example, in 1659 receipts were more than 749 pounds and expenses and accounts payable totalled nearly 495 pounds. In 1660 receipts and beginning balance were nearly 670 pounds, while payments and accounts payable totalled more than 632 pounds. Receipts and expenditures

EXHIBIT III

PLYMOUTH COLONY TAX LEVY BY TOWNS - 1666-1667

*June the 9th, 1666.

WARRANTS was issued forth from the Court to leuy by rate the sume of two hundred and thirty pounds, for the publicke charges of the countrey for this yeare, besides the sume of seauen pounds to pay for certaine law bookes belonging to the countrey; the said sumes to bee payed in speeye, as followeth, vizS: To bee payed one third therof in wheat, or porke, or both; one third in butter, or barly, or both; and the other third in beife, Indian corne, peases, or rye, or any of these, or some tarr, prouided it exceed not one third pte of the last third.

The wheat att four shillings and sixpence a bushell.
The porke att three pound and ten shillinges a barrell.
The barly att four shillings a bushell.
The butter att thirty shillings a firkin, if sizable.
The beife att forty fiue shilling a barrell.
The Indian corne att three shillinges a bushell.
The pease att three shillinges and sixpence a bushell.
The rye att three shillinges and sixpence a bushell.
The tarr att three shillinges a barrell.

To bee deliuered to the Treasurer, or att Boston or att Plymouth, as hee shall appoint, and the charge of transportation defrayed by the first weeke in Nouember next.

The proportions of the surerall townes to the said rate are as followith: -

Plymouth,	19 : 08 : 06
Duxburrow with Bridgwater,	17 : 11 : 09
Scittuate,	31 : 15 : 03
Sandwich,	17 : 11 : 09
Taunton,	17 : 11 : 09
Yarmouth,	15 : 04 : 00
Barnstable,	19 : 08 : 06
Marshfeild,	15 : 04 : 00
Rehoboth,	26 : 05 : 03
Eastham,	14 : 03 : 06
Sowams,	07 : 17 : 06
Dartmouth,	10 : 10 : 00

The pticulares for which this rate is

Item, to the Goū,	50 : 00 : 00
Item, to the other majestrates,	50 : 00 : 00
Item, to the Treasurer in debt, &å,	42 : 06 : 00
Item, to the majestrates table,	40 : 00 : 00
Item, for law bookes,	7 : 00 : 00
Item, for Sauory,	6 : 13 : 04

Memorandum, that the ten pounds alowed to each of the Assistants to bee payed in specye, according to the two last thirds aboue expressed.

declined to only 211 and 208 pounds respectively in 1661. During the next two years receipts and expenses fluctuated between 300 and 400 pounds. Clearly, the colony's needs varied from year to year, as reflected in the variation in budgets from year to year.

Exhibit III, which reports the anticipated revenues and the proportion due from each town for fiscal 1667, is particularly significant because prices are established by the General Court for each commodity. Moreover, specific instructions for delivering commodities to either Plymouth or Boston are given. Perhaps most significant is the budget for fiscal 1667 which is part of the exhibit.

The information displayed in Exhibit III may be viewed as the Plymouth Colony's 1666-1667 budget, complete with anticipated revenues and their sources, and an itemized list of budgeted expenses. Notice that the General Court did not estimate any revenues from imposition of fines, nor did they provide any funds for military protection, possibily because of the uncertain nature of these two items. These records provide a relatively complete example of municipal accounting in Massachusetts, and their historical value should not be minimized.

<u>Treasurer's Account</u> -- <u>1685-1686</u>

The Treasurer's Accounts for the fiscal year 1685-86 are shown in Exhibits IV and V. During the twenty years from 1666 to 1686, the Plymouth Colony continued to expand and prosper. In 1666, taxes were assessed against twelve towns. By 1685, twenty-one towns were taxed a total of 346 pounds, a fifty percent increase over the 230 pounds raised by taxation in 1666 (see Exhibit IV). One is struck by the relative stability of tax collections in the colony. The Pilgrims' public needs were being met by the individual towns in the colony.

During the twenty years from 1666 to 1686, the salary of the Governor of Plymouth Colony continued to be fifty pounds annually, and each of the five

EXHIBIT IV

PLYMOUTH COLONY BUDGET FOR 1685-86 AND TAX LEVY ASSIGNED TO EACH TOWN

*Jun 1685

MONEY to be raised to defray the charge of this colony for this year, so far as at present apears, & for what was expended extraordinary in the yeare past.

For the Gouer[r] & Magistrats salery,	100 : 00 : 00
For the Treasurers salery,	020 : 00 : 00
For officers sallery,	35 : 00 : 00
For the magistrats table,	45 : 00 : 00
For Nathaniell Hall, in siluer 30; in prouission 6,	36 : 00 : 00
For William Clarke, for seuerall disbursm[tts] as p[r] note of perticulars apears, siluer,	48 : 00 : 00
For the Gourer[rs] man & horse, to comission,	04 : 00 : 00
For the secretary for writting ouer the new lawes, for paper & wax for the comisions, & for writting 10 or 12 dayes for the Courte	03 : 10 : 00
Towards printing the lawes,	30 : 00 : 00
For the comittee that spent a months time about reuiueing the lawes	20 : 00 : 00
For a barell of powder spent when King James the 2 was proclaimed,	05 : 00 : 00
Totall,	346 : 10 : 00

THE proportions of the rate of the seuerall towns are as followeth: -

Plimouth,	31 : 00 : 00
Duxbury,	14 : 10 : 00
Bridgwater,	14 : 19 : 00
Scittuate,	49 : 18 : 06
Sandwich,	31 : 01 : 00
Taūton,	30 : 03 : 00
Yarmouth,	23 : 09 : 06
Barnstable,	31 : 00 : 00
Marshfeild,	23 : 19 : 06
Rehoboth,	26 : 04 : 06
Eastham,	21 : 12 : 06
Swansey,	14 : 01 : 00
Dartmouth,	13 : 03 : 06
Midlebery,	04 : 03 : 06
Manomoy,	03 : 12 : 08
Free town,	03 : 12 : 08
Litle Compton,	03 : 12 : 08
Accord Pond,	01 : 16 : 06
Nanaquakett,	01 : 01 : 08
Punkatest proprietors,	02 : 06 : 08
Fords Farme,	01 : 01 : 08
Totall,	346 : 10 : 00

EXHIBIT V

ACTUAL DISBURSEMENTS OF PLYMOUTH COLONY - 1685-1686

*June y^e 5th, 1686.

THE Generall Court made choyce of Barnabas Lothrop, Esqr, Capt Joseph Lothrop, Capt Jonathan (Sparrow), and $Leiv^{tt}$ Isaac Little, to take the Treasurers (accompt).

*June y^e 5th, 1686, P^r contra.

To the $Govern^r$ & Magistrates,	100 : 00 : 00
To Mr Clarke for their table,	045 : 00 : 00
To the Treasurers salliry,	020 : 00 : 00
To the under marshall,	006 : 13 : 04
To Nathaniel Hall,	036 : 00 : 00
For the comittee,	020 : 00 : 00
To the $Govern^r$, man & horse,	004 : 00 : 00
For a barrel of powder expended at the proclamation of King James,	005 : 00 : 00
For printing y^e law books, 36^{ll},	036 : 07 : 00
For bringing home the law books,	000 : 07 : 00
To William Voabes, p^r order of the Court,	001 : 05 : 00
To Saml Sprague,	000 : 05 : 00
To the under marshall for whipping,	000 : 10 : 00
For repairing irons for the prisoners,	000 : 03 : 06
To Mr Russell,	001 : 00 : 00
For the officers sallirv,	035 : 00 : 00
To Mr William Clarke,	048 : 00 : 00
To the secretary for writing paper & wax,	003 : 10 : 00
For the rates of Accord Pond, remitted,	001 : 16 : 06
For the rates of Anaquakett Neck, not paid,	001 : 01 : 08
For the rates of Puncateast, not paid,	002 : 06 : 08
For ye rates of Foords Farme, not paid,	001 : 01 : 08
For Simeon Stoddard, warr accompt, due to Mr Smith,	006 : 06 : 03
Sum,	375 : 13 : 07
The ballance due from the Treasurer,	037 : 03 : 05
	412 : 17 : 00

This accompt taken by us,

BARNABAS LOTHROP,
JOSEPH LOTHROP,
JONATHAN SPARROW,
ISAAC LITTLE.

magistrates was paid ten pounds a year. The treasurer was paid twenty-five pounds in 1666 and only twenty pounds in 1686. A comparison of estimated expenditures and actual expenditures offers few surprises. Several extraordinary expenses from 1685 were budgeted for payment, including expenses for writing and printing the laws. Also, the committee that had spent a month reviewing the laws was to be paid twenty pounds for its labors. Finally, a payment of forty-eight pounds was authorized to Mr. Clarke for several disbursements and Mr. Hall was authorized payment of thirtysix pounds, both payments to be made in silver.

Based upon a review of anticipated expenditures, the Plymouth Colony apparently was enjoying a relatively prosperous and crisis-free period. This contrasts markedly with the difficult decades from 1620 to 1640 when the Pilgrims nearly failed in their efforts to make a home in the new world.

An assessment of the Pilgrims' improving financial sophistication may be obtained by comparing the colony's budget of anticipated expense as shown in Exhibit IV and the actual revenues and expenditures for the year as shown in Exhibit V. Estimated expenses of 346 pounds proved to be a reasonably accurate projection. Actual expenses of 275 pounds included debits for taxes either remitted or still unpaid, and a charge of six pounds to Simeon Stoddard. The printing of law books proved to be more costly than anticipated, but most of the remaining epxenses had been estimated correctly.

An analysis of taxes levied against the colony's towns in 1666 and 1686 reveals some interesting data on the relative wealth and growth of each town. Recall that taxes were based upon assessments of real estate and personal property, including livestock.

Villages whose taxes were highest may be presumed to have possessed relatively more real estate, livestock, and other taxable property than other settlements. For example, the wealthiest town in 1666, as measured by taxes assessed, was Scituate. This town retained the distinction of wealthiest settlement in 1686 (see Exhibits III and V).

Sandwich, Barnstable, Plymouth, and Taunton were substantial towns by 1685, while Yarmouth and Eastham also appear to have experienced significant growth. On the other hand, Rehoboth's tax assessment was nearly the same in 1686 as in 1666, implying some stagnation in that town's development. In 1686, the numerous smaller and newer settlements were assessed almost no taxes, an indication of their recent founding and their presumably modest economic base. Comparison of taxes levied in 1666 and 1686 may provide clues to population growth patterns within Plymouth Colony as well as comparative wealth.

Conclusion

In December, 1620, the Pilgrims of Plymouth Colony established a tenuous foothold in an inhospitable land. After enduring extraordinary natural disasters, these naive and financially ignorant settlers finally managed to free themselves of the burdensome debts incurred during their formative years. In fewer than seventy years, the Pilgrims progressed from recording their financial transactions in the most rudimentary manner to developing and implementing a relatively sophisticated financial system that included the preparation of annual budgets, establishment of tax levies and collections from towns within the colony, and annual formal evaluations of the treasurer's stewardship by independent audit committees. The evolution of a funancial system designed to serve the needs of a prospering and expanding colony is a tribute to the intelligence and ingenuity of the Founding Fathers whose lack of financial acumen had nearly doomed the colony to failure during the early years.

This paper has examined the Treasurer's Accounts of the Plymouth Colony for selected years from 1657 to 1686 in order to trace the development of accounting practices during the earliest years of America's colonization. Among the findings of this study are: (1) Evidence of an evolutionary process from simple bookkeeping to a relatively complex system of budgets. (2) Municipal accounting practices in the United States can be traced to the 1600s in Massachusetts. (3) Audit committees were established as early as 1629, reflecting an understanding of the desirability of third party attestation of financial data when public funds are involved. (4) The imposition of numerous fines against colonists found guilty of misconduct provides evidence of the importance the Pilgrims placed on enforcement of their religious and ethical principles.

FOOTNOTES

[1]See McIntyre, Ruth A. Debts Hopeful and Desparate, Plimoth Plantation, Inc., 1962.

[2]See Chapter 1, Williard Stone, "Accounting Woes, Pilgrim Style."

[3]The Treasurer's Accounts are contained in Miscellaneous Records Volume V, Records of the Colony of New Plymouth, edited by Nathaniel Shurtleff, Boston, Mass. Authorized by the Commonwealth of Massachusetts 1855. The financial information discussed in this study was obtained from this transcript of the original records of the Plymouth Colony. The original manuscript contained about 112 pages, with a large portion of the writing being on one side of the paper. The Treasurer's Accounts originally were found in a volume of the Plymouth Colony records which contained a portion of the laws, the Indian deeds, the Treasurer's Accounts, and the fourth volume of Court Orders. The financial data were gathered by Shurtleff and put in chronological order in Volume V.

[4]See Willard Stone, op, cit., and Ruth McIntyre, op. cit.

[5]For an excellent summary of the history of the Plymouth Colony, see Commonwealth History of Massachusetts, edited by Albert Bushnell Hart, published by the States History Company, New York, 1927-1928. See also Wiliam Bradford, History of Plymouth Plantation, Boston, by the State, 1898.

[6]See Records of the Colony of New Plymouth, op. cit., Volume II, pp 8993.

CHAPTER FOUR

JOINT VENTURE ACCOUNTING IN EARLY COLONIAL AMERICA

William Holmes

Historical Background

In 1636 King Charles I by royal decree, tried to make good Episcopalians out of the Presbyterian Scots. In doing so, he inadvertently caused an economic crisis in the Massachusetts Bay Colony five years later. The Scots would have none of his Bishops or Book of Common Prayer - they still won't - and in 1638 put an army of 20,000 men in the field to prove it. Charles was forced to recall the Parliament he had been doing without to raise money to fight the Scots, but found Parliament thoroughly unsympathetic. The face off between king and parliament resulted in the Cavalier v Roundhead wars shortly after and the English Puritans, instead of emigrating to Massachusetts in boatloads, as they had been doing during the 1630's, stayed home to fight. The economy of the Massachusetts Bay Colony had flourished during the 1630's as the earlier arrivals disposed of their surplus cattle, corn, lumber and provender to each boatload of new arrivals. When the supply of newcomers dried up there was no immediate market for the surplus and the local economy got sick. Luckily for them, the early colonists had no economists around to confuse them and didn't know about Federal help or the International Monetary Fund. They just got busy on their own to do something about it. They had surplus beef, pork, lumber, and dried fish and there was a developing market for these things down in the West Indies. They had, of course, to get the goods down there. So they went into the shipbuilding business. The Boston merchant seatrader was born and the first leg of what later became the triangular trade to the West Indies and Europe was established. Thomas Dewer was one of these Boston merchants in 1666. He had recently voyaged to Barbados, made some good friends among the merchants there, most of whom had Scottish surnames like himself - Scott, Grant, Maxwell, Riddock, Reid, and Thompson. His friend Robert Scott owned a quarter interest in a ship - the Thomas and Sarah, originally out of Boston - and sold half of his share to Thomas. The other partners were Barbados merchants. In August 1666 the Thomas and Sarah was caught in a hurricane, badly damaged and driven ashore on Carlisle Bay in Barbados. Repairing the ship was a costly business and two of the original partners - Mr. Hooper and Mr. Barksdale - decided to sell out their shares at this time. The 3/8 owned by them was taken up 1/8 by Lt. Colonel Riddock and 1/4 by Captain George Thompson. The partnership interests were then as follows:

Lt. Colonel Alexander Riddocke	1/4
John Reid	1/4
Captain George Thompson	3/16
William Bosman	1/16
Robert Scott	1/8
Thomas Dewer	1/8

The new partners renamed the ship "Katherine".

The Katherine was eventually ready for sea again and Thomas Dewer in a letter to his friend Mr. Scott says "Mr. Bartholomew (the master) tells me y^{t} now she is girdled, sheathed and masted she is an everlasting ship". Thomas in the meantime had given Mr. Scott and Mr. Riddock his Power of Attorney to act for him in either repairing or selling the ship.

However, when he found out the cost of the repairs Thomas was in a mood to get out of the partnership and wrote several letters to Mr. Scott urging him to find a buyer for his share, which Scott was apparently unable to do.

The Katherine in the meantime got back to sea, voyaged to Boston to pick up beef, pork, mackerel, horses, masts and on up to "Piscataqua" - which is modern Kittery, Maine - to load with lumber and barrel staves. She also made at least one trip to the Cape Verde Islands.

Mr. Scott died in 1669 and Mr. Brown his administrator had accounts prepared of the trading results to date that indicated Thomas Dewer owned the estate the equivalent of 11,530 1/2 lbs. sugar. Dewer ignored the claim and the matter dragged on for years until finally in 1683 Brown was successful in getting the claim before the Courts of Massachusetts. The court called for an accounting. The accounts submitted and found in the State House archives of judicial proceedings are shown as Exhibits 1 and 2.

Thomas Dewer

Thomas Dewer seems to have been a typical, but not prominent merchant in Boston in the period from 1650 at least through 1677. He is listed in the Town Officials of Colonial Boston 1634-1775 (Robert Francis Seybolt, Harvard University Press, 1939) as holding the following offices in the town -

1657/58	Surveyor of Highways	(one of five elected)
1659/60	Clerk of the Market	(one of two elected)
1663/64	Constable	(one of six elected)

In addition he is listed as one of the 129 signatories to a petition in 1677 from the "Handycraftsmen", comprising merchants and craftsmen, to the General Court "to control admission of inhabitants" and require that "Tradesmen shall fulfill a sufficient apprenticeship before they set up Trade". (History of Boston, Caleb H. Stone, M.D. - 1828)

In one of his letters to Mr. Scott he mentions his wife and children. His sons David and Sampson both made trips to Barbados on his behalf, and in a letter to Mr. Scott in 1668 he mentions the death of David "whom the Lord hath taken to Himselfe".

An interesting sidelight is that he was one of the founding members of the Scottish Charitable Society in Boston in the 1650's. The Society was still hale and hearty and in business in Boston in the 1950's.

Legal Arguments

Mr. Browne, the Administrator of Robert Scott's estate introduced the accounts into the Boston court to substantiate his claim for 11,530 1/2 lbs. of sugar. He offered as further evidence what purported to be Dewer's Power of Attorney, given to Messrs. Scott and Riddocke in August 1666. I think the form of this document will be interesting to modern readers.

Power of Attorney

Barbados 27 August 1666

> Know all men by these presents that I Thomas Dewer of Boston in New England do make, constitute ordein and appoint my loveing and honored ffriends Alexand^{r} Riddocke Esquire and Mr Robert Scott jointly and severally my true and lawful Attorny's for me in my name to use to aske demand implead for and recover all debts dues sum or sums of money merchandizes or whatever is else due unto me the said Thomas Dewer either by bill books specialty or contract bargain or otherwise and in a special manner to act and do concerning my eight

part of the ship Thomas and Sarah of Boston now ashore on Carlisle Bay, either to recover and set to sea or else to make sale of as they think best for my benefit and behoofe, and what my s[d] Atturny's shall do in and about the ꝑmisses I do engage myself to make firme in law as amply as I myself were ꝑsonally present to all respects and purposes and construction. Ratifying allowing and confirming whatsoever my said Attorny's shall lawfully do in about the ꝑmisses. As witness my hand and Seale the day & year above said.

Sign'd Sealed and Deliv'd
in the presence of
Alexander Nicoll
Tho Bossack

Memorandum

That I Thomas Dewer do engage my self to pay what my said Attory's shall expend about the selling out of my 8th pte. As witness my hand

Tho Dewer

The Ship

Samuel Eliot Morison in his "Builders of the Bay Colony" tells us that much of the coasting and West Indies trade in the 1650 period was carried on small, decked ketch-rigged vessels about fifty feet long, with a square rigged mainsail and a triangular lateen sail on the mizzen. I have a feeling the Katherine was a little bigger than this, perhaps a pinnace. One of her voyages was to the Cape Verde islands - a long haul for a ketch - and the repair items listed on Folio 2 include "1 maine topmast", suggesting the possibility of a main topsail. The repair items also include:

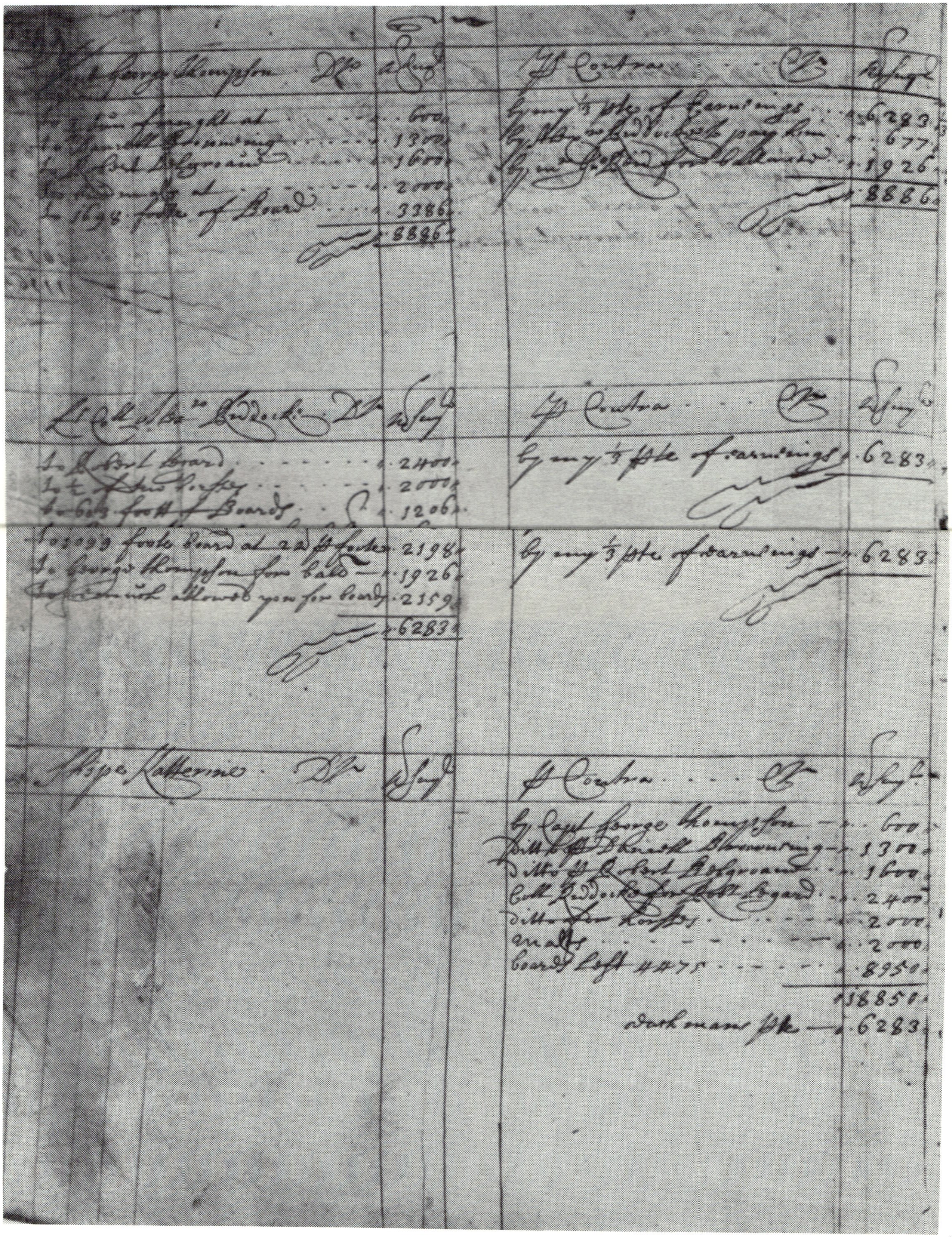

Original page forming part of Folio 4.

5 boatloads of ballast
70 ydds canvas
21 ydds canvas
2 anchors
1 lanthorne
119 lbs roapp
compass glasses

THE ACCOUNTS

Samuel Eliot Morison in his "Builders of the Bay Colony" remarked that the 1650's were a period ripe for economic expansion in Massachusetts and that fortunately the right men were there to take advantage of the situation. He lamented, however, the sparsity of accounts from the period. In this respect I think the accounts are important. It should be noted, of course, they were prepared in Barbados. However, the ties between Barbados and New England were already strong through family and mercantile connections, and I believe the accounts are probably typical of those prepared for the average joint venture. The court in Boston was perfectly willing to accept them, and the jury reached a verdict based on the accounts as submitted.

The court found for Mr. Browne in the case and Mr. Dewer thereupon appealed the case to the Court of Assistants (the Upper House). The Court of Assistants upheld the decision in favor of Browne, but the grounds for his appeal make interesting reading.

Thomas Dewer's Appeal

Mr. Brown plf.	Thomas Dewer his reason of Apeals from a judgment against him (at the instance of the plt) at ye County Court
Tho. Dewer Def.	held in Boston in July 1683, to ye hon^{ble} the Court of Assistants ensuring.

1st ly. I am sued by Mr Browne pretended Adm^{r} to ye estate of Robert Scott Deceased, but no legall Administration advised as I humbly conceive, neither legally proven to be signed by the president, nor attested under the seale of office, only by one naming himself deputy secretary, and may be a counterfeit for ought I know; it being usuall for such Instruments that are to be carry^{d} to and made use of in other parts of the world or else attested by a Public Notary.

2ly. The Letter of Attorney produced is not at all proved to be my Act and Deed which the law requires in such cases and I hope the hon^{ble} Court will consider and relieve the oppressed who hath not only lost the Shipp but brought sixty pounds more in Debt.

3ly. Admitt it had been my Act wh I cannot owne, such laime atto^{y} drawn upp by others whom ꝑhaps have been interested to my Disadvantages, besides it is of soe ancient standing th^{t} I humbly concieve it not actionable. Wherever he dost humbly prays the assemblie for being yor most obed^{t} humble serv^{t}.

Thomas Dewer

Boston 30 Aug 1683
These Reasons Rec^{d}
J. S. Addington Scty.

Tho. Dewer his Reasons
of Appeal

The Accounts

To facilitate reference, I have labelled the two principal attachments Exhibit 1 and Exhibit 2. Exhibit 1 is the "account current" of Robert Scott against Thomas Dewer and the balance of this account - 11,530 1/2 lbs. of sugar - was the amount being sued for. Exhibit 2 gives the details of the various expenses to repair and operate the Katherine and shows the partnership accounts allocating the costs and credits to the partners.

The Folio references appeared on the original manuscripts and help cross reference the amounts in the accounts back to the supporting detailed accounts of the individual partners.

Note that there are three distinct "sets" of partnership accounts, covering three distinct "ventures" and that the partnership interests vary with respect thereto. The "venture" following Folio 4 involved only Thompson, Riddocke, & Reed in equal "thirds". The other two "ventures" involve Reed, Riddocke, Thompson, Scott & Bosman in the more normal distribution of 1/4, 1/4, 3/16, 1/4, and 1/8 set forth on the frontispiece to Exhibit 2. I know no reason for this unless a partner had the right to abstain from a particular voyage if he so desired.

Dewer is, of course, not specifically mentioned in Exhibit 2, but owned 1/2 of Robert Scott's share.

Currency

The accounts provide for both a currency column (£ s. d.) and a "lbs. of sugar" column. Note that in all instances the "lbs. of sugar" column is the basis of the accounts, currency being translated into sugar at the rate of 100 lbs. of sugar for 10 shillings of currency. Sugar was introduced into Barbados in 1645 and by 1666 had taken over as the real medium of exchange, including the apparent extensive use of "sugar notes". This was obviously due to the shortage of real currency - a common problem in the history of the Colonies.

Exhibit 1

With respect to the debits in the "account current" note the following:

Item 1 - The 20,046 is 1/2 the 40,092 comprising the total debits in Robert Scott's account in Folio 7.

Item 2 - The 4,920 is 1/8 of 39,359 which is the sum of the 39,159 plus 200 shown among the credits on the first page of Folio 6.

Item 3 - The 4,030 1/2 is offset by a contra credit entry.

Item 4 - Apparently no tie in to Barbados accounts in Exhibit 2.

Item 5 - The 2,010 is 1/2 the 4,020 total debits in Robert Scott's account in Exhibit 2.

With respect to the credits in the "account current" -

Item 1 - The 10,000 is 1/2 of Robert Scott's "1/4" share as shown on the frontispiece to Exhibit 2.

Item 2 - The "9,786 lbs. eowed by Coke" appears as a debt on the first page of Folio 6.

Exhibit 2

(a) The 40,720 on Folio 1 consists of 23,303 + 17,417, the two numbers shown in the first two debits in each account in Folio 7.

(b) The totals of Folios 2,3,4, and 5 can be traced to the corresponding accounts in Folio 7.

Notice the LAUS DEO salutation at the head of each page. This or a similar religious invocation was common in Europe - See Pacioli's comments in the Summa Arithmetica - but was already going out of style in Europe by the 1600's.

Mr. Thomas Dewer of New England his accompt Currant

		Dr. L	s	d	Lbs. Sugar
	To yor 1/8 part of Shipp Katterines disbursm^{ts} as appears in folio 7	-	-	-	20,046
	To yor 1/8 of seamens wages from New England as in folio 6	-	-	-	4,920
	To profitt and loss p Mr. Coke being 8061 lb short of frau^{t}	-	-	-	4,030 1/2
10^{s}pct	To yor 1/8 pairt of Ŀ 373.19.8 disbursm^{ts} in piscataqua yor pte being	46	14	10	9,347
	To yor 1/8 of 16080 lbs disburst on ye Capdebarde voyage	-	-	-	2,010
10^{s}pct	To yor pts of Ŀ 92.10 8 pd seamens waiges being	11	11	3	2,312
	To 240 lb paid seaman boswon	-	-	-	240
	To horse hyer and attendance as p my expenses for hyring	-	-	-	1,500
		58	6	1	44,405 1/2

Barbados

We whose names are heirwith subscrived have fully examined the above accompt Currant of Mr. Thomas Dewer of New England and do find the same to be just and agreeable to the annexed accompts with expenditures by us the 20th of June 1668 as owners of the shipp Katterine Joseph Bartholomew Comander
Certified by:

John Reid
Alex^{r} Riddocke
Wm Boseman
George Thompson
R^{o} Scott

Exhibit 1

Laus Deo in Barbados Anno 1669

1669	P Contra	Cr.	L	s	d	Lbs. Sugar
	By yor 1/8 pte of the shippe Katterine sold		-	-	-	10,000
6	By yor pairte of 9789 lbs eowed by Coke and pd Capt. Bartholomew		-	-	-	4,894 1/2
	By profitt & loss yor 1/2 of 8065 sugar Mr. Coke haith not paid		-	-	-	4,030 1/2
	By yor 1/2 4000 lb sugar exspended on shipp wracke		-	-	-	2,000
	By yor pte of fraight for 13mo to Capdebarde Islands		-	-	-	6,000
	By yor disbursmts in N. F. L 29.15 s. you pd Capt. Bartholomew		29	15	-	5,950
10pct	Ballance on Mr. Robert Scott this 24th June 1669		-	-	-	11,530 1/2
			-	-	-	44,405 1/2

Barbados

By the Deputy Governor

Personally appeared before me Capt. George Thompson & Willm Boseman and made Oath upon the holy Evangelist that the foregoing acctts proper and true to the best of their knowledge. Sworne before me this 17th day of May 1670 and Mr. John Reid Esq. likewise appeared on the day and years aforesaid and made oath to the truth of the foregoing acctts.

This 17th day of May 1670 John Reed Esqr. Capt. George Thompson and Mr. William Boseman and made other that they being part owners of the Ship Katherine had past this a true accompt relating to said ship.

C. D. Codington

August 9, 1670

This day appeared before me Luft Coll. Alexander Riddocke partt owner of the sd shipp and made oath that the abovesaid actt was past as A true acco relatting to the sd shipp above mentioned.

C.D. Coddington

Exhibit 2

Laus Deo in Barbados anno 1666

A Booke of Accompts In ye prnershipp
with Mr. John Read and Company Relateing
to the shippe Katterine of Barbados

Each mans part In the Ships Katterine

Lt. Collonell Alexander Riddocke	1/4 pte	20,000
Mr. John Reid	1/4	20,000
Capt. George Thompson	3/16	15,000
Mr. William Bosman	1/16	5,000
Mr. Robert Scott and Company	1/4	20,000
The whole value at		Lbs 80,000

Laus Deo In Barbados anno 1666

An accompt of disburments upon the Ship Sarah alias Katherine from the tyme she was wrackd till the first of X[ber] yt 3/8 was sold by the Candell.

	£	s	d	lbs. Sugar
To Jonathan Gotlioew for his disbursments & Wages	-	-	-	17,417
To Robert Scott for his disbursments	17	5	4	7,424
To ditto Scott for his paines on said shipp	-	-	-	1,500
To Charles Barksdale as pr his accompt	-	-	-	3,116
To John Reid as pr his accompt	-	-	-	2,721
To John Headsbrok as pr his accompt	-	-	-	3,458
To Captan Terry for his paines	-	-	-	500
To Jonathan Gotlioew for his and servants waiges	-	-	-	3,000
To Alexander Reid his accompt of disburments	1	7	6	100
paid Mr. Scott pr severalls	18	12	10	39,236
appears to be	11	4	6	
Sugar 10/s p 100 lb	7	8	4	1,484
				40,720

18:12:10
11:04:06

7:08:04 = The above written article given in by Mr. Jonathan Gotloiew of seventeen thousand four hundred & seventeen pounds of sugar is a true charge as y[d] Jon Gotloiew certified upon oath

October 30th 1669 before
Edward Sym. Officer

Each mans pte of ditto disbursments

Mr. X[tian] Hooper	1/4	10,180
Lt. Collonell Alex[er] Riddock	1/8	5,090
Mr. John Reid	1/8	5,090
Mr. Robert Scott and Comp[y]	1/4	10,180
Capt. George Thompson	1/16	2,545
Mr. William Bosman	1/16	2,545
Mr. Barksdale	1/8	5,090
	Lbs.	40,720

Laus Deo In Barbados anno 1666

Shipp Katterin to Capt. George Thompson		Dr.	L	s.	d.	Lbs. Sugar
Xber 2	To cash for soemuch Mr. Reid		2			400
	To ditto for soemuch ~~dd~~ ditto		9	6	8	1,867
	To ditto for soemuch ~~dd~~ Mr. Bartholomew		7	17		1,570
	To soemuch paid for Jack and beins		-	-	-	400
	Brought over		-	-	-	25,624

Item	Amount
To 6 gallons ruhm	72
To 12 pewter spoones	45
To 1 springlocke	50
To 2 lb 6d + 2lb 8d naills	34
To one tankard at	50
To sug^{r} for punch	30
To soemuch pdJn^{o}	84
Longe	84
To soemuch pdJn^{o} Alisson	254
To 5 lb of 2d naills	15
To one hammer	25
To one ditto for	14
To soemuch pdJn^{o} Long	74
To 4 wooden plaits and two bowls	120
To 12 wooden plaitts	45
To 4 wooden dishes	24
To 18 wooden spoones	18
To wooden ladells	6
To one brass candestick	45
To one p^{r} scissors	16
To 3 brushes	18
To one saltcellar	6
To one gall of oyll	70
To 4 axes & 1 hatchett	120
To 24 lb oackam	72
To sugar for punch	86
To 146 lb pitch at 4 lbs	584

Item	Amount	L	s.	d.	Lbs. Sugar
To one gallon sweitt oyll	70				
To 5 jars ditto oyll	600				
To 25 yds 1/2 of bittern at 30 lb	735				
To 34 gall ruhm at 12 lb	408				
To frau^{t} of one Cable	100				
To ye hyrer of one horse	50				
To 6 lb of powder	150				
To 2 sling leads	30				
To soemuch ~~dd~~ Wm Pillington	160				
To severall naills pr order	71				
To 70 ydds canvas at 24 lb	1,680				
To 21 ydds ditto at 30 lb	645				
To 2 ydds of wood	180				
To William Gibbs for naills	620				
To soemuch pd Wm Day	20				
To soemuch pdJn^{o} Weedge	433				
To soemuch pd for Oars	250				
To pd Sam Baker, smith	429				
To paid carpenters	815				
To pd Daniell ye Carpenter	285				
To bill of Joseph Bartholomew his accompt	3,804				
To 15 qt jair of oyll	200				
To divers ~~dd~~Jno Rotheridge	332				
To 2 lb 20d & 2 lb 2d naills	44	-	-	-	12,111
To soemuch disburement on acc^{o} of the voyage					18,866

Folio 2 cont

Laus Deo In Barbados anno 1666

Shipp Katterine to Capt. George Thompson		Dr.	L	s.	d.	Lbs. Sugar
To 5 boateload ballast	1,000					
To divers ~~dd~~ ffra Boult	298					
To one gallon of Oyll	70					
To one barrell mollasses	100					
To one ditto lyme	25					
To 114 lb candles at 10 lb	1,140					
To paid Mr. Gotham	3,000					
To 5/8 pd Mr. Batholomew	60					
To one cable at Mr. Bond	9,100					
To John Rawlings, Blockmaker	1,017					
To Sam Hoshamp occ^{o}	3,501					
To Charles Collings	500					
To Joseph James	456					
To pd for Compass glasses	200					
To Daniell Browning pr acc^{o}	1,683					
To 2 coard of woode	180					
To one bush of salte	50					
To Randall Brant Exspenses	150					
To one gall sweet oyll	70					
To divers p Jno Weederougnon	260					
To ditto for Jno Rotheridge	251					
To ditto p Wm Day	152					
To ditto p Edw Oyon	74					
To ditto Jno Weedgerougnon	168					
To 1 Hhd for water	125					
To soemuch p Jno Weedge	16					
	25,624					
To Thomas Coke, Cooper		828				
To one jair of sweet oyll		200				
To divers ~~dd~~ Jno Rotheridge		332				
To naills for Severalls		212				
To sum pd Sam Jones		246				
To divers for Thomas Drake		1,922				
To divers for Sam Jones		48				
To Sam Baker, Smith		130				
To severall naills		343				4,261
Somme Totall						65,099

Folio 3

Laus Deo In Barbados Anno 1666

	Shipp Katterine to Mr. John Reid merchant Dr.	£	s.	d.	Lbs. Sugar
Xber 2	To John Jonston for naills				180
	To one barrell barmindoli beafe				875
	To soemuch paid p Mr. Downs carpenter				600
	To soemuch paid Capt. Webster doctor				60
	To soemuch paid John Headsbrok smith				300
	To Richard Rumney for naills				50
	To John Riddock paid Steaphen a seaman				400
	To soemuch paid for 119 lb roapp at 5 lb				595
	To soemuch paid Capt. Camos seaman				1,000
	To soemuch paid ye Boatswain				1,000
	To one Jarr of oyll				70
	To John Johnstown p Capt. Bartholomew noate				1,715
	To Samuell Connor for two Anchors				2,809
	To soemuch paid the Spanish Carpenter	2	5	-	
	To Edward Bodkin for 1 maine topmast	3	10	-	
	To one barrill of beafe				300
	To Capt. Camos for his assistance				1,000
	To Thomas Read for his boate & hawser				600
	To Samuell Prim p Mr. Bartholomews noate				507
	To three barrills of beafe				990
	To soemuch pd p. Mr. Bartholomews noate	7	2	-	
	To Mr. Hobbs for 10 galls rhum at 14 lbs p gall		11	8	
	To 481 pound biskett at 2lb p pound				967
	To 3 tun of watter cask				900
	To soemuch p noate of Mr. Bartholomew				200
	To John Headsbrok smith				5,010
	To ballance of one on accompt as appears	22	18	11	13,968
	To soemuch pd Capt. Camos Carpenter	6	-	-	
	To soemuch pd Capt. Chinalls Carpenter				200
	To two Carpenters 9 days worke	3	12	-	
	To Mr. Alex^{r} Read his accompt of disbursements	1	7	7	100
	To 4 pound sterling paid Mr. Scott for acc^{o} of ye Shipp	4	-	-	
	To John Holland Carpenter	3	-	9	
	To Daniel Horne Carpenter				550
	To John Ruderidge Boatswaine				900
	To Boards and Ioyrn				706
	To two barrills of beafe				800
	To one barrill of pease				148
	To one lanthorne at				70
	To John Headsbrok his half accompt				1,344
	To sugar paid seamen				210
	To Mr. Kingsffish for one phunnell and one Rundhett				200
	To Jonathan Rainsfoord				360
	To Thomas Revill p Mr. Bartholomews noate				3,673
	To John Cooke for one share				200
	To Mr. Ponniston for his paines				400
	To the Boatswain of Capt. Camos shipp				800
	To Abraham Tilliard for timber and one sparr				816
	To Nicholas Browne for hier of his boate				5,200
		54	7	11	50,744
	Money laid out = 54:07:11				
	Money remained = 14:13:04 dew £ 39:14:07 Sugar - 10/s pc 100 lb.				7,946
	= 39:14:07				58,720

Laus Deo In Barbados anno 1666

Shipp Katterine to Lt. Coll Alex[r] Riddocke		Dr.	Ł	s.	d.	Lbs. Sugar
Xber 2	To John Riddocke paid Mr. Gottliewe					2,000
	To Mr. Gottliew being my 1/8 pt. of fraught					3,000
	To money paid Mr. Reid, Mr. Scott and Mr. Bartholomew					2,000
	To divers p. ord[er] Mr. Bartholomew etc pro wages					7,308
	To soemuch on accompt of the voyage from N. E.					17,220
	To soemuch p. Mr. Bartholomew noate			13	4	133
	To soemuch pd by my brother in N. E.		18	-	-	3,600
	To soemuch paid towards seamens waiges					9,554
	To soemuch paid for roaps					100
						44,915

Shipe Katterine to Mr. William Bosman		Dr.	Ł	s.	d.	Lbs. Sugar
Xber 2	By an Accompt of particulars amounting too					6,203 1/2

Folio 5

Shipp Katterine to Mr. Robert Scott		Dr.	Ł	s.	d.	Lbs. Sugar
June 20	To one firkin butter waight nett 138 lb at 6 lb. p pound		-	-	-	828
	To 6 gallons ruhm p Joseph Bartholomew		-	-	-	72
	To 6 gallons ditto p John Ridderidge		-	-	-	72
	To one empty barrell worth		-	-	-	60
	To his pticular accompt given in		-	-	-	10,132
						11,164

1668 Capt. George Thompson Dr.	lbs. Sugar	Per Contra Cr.	lbs. Sugar
To 3/4 run fraught at	600	By my 1/3 pte of Earnings	6,283 1/3
To Daniell Browning	1,300	By Alex[r] Riddocke to pay him	677
To Robert Belgreave	1,600	By Mr. Jn[o] Reid for ballance	1,926
To two masts at	2,000		
To 1698 foot of Board	3,386		
	8,886		8,886

Lt. Co[ll] Alex[r] Riddocke Dr.	lbs. Sugar	Per Contra Cr.	lbs. Sugar
To Robert Legard	2,400	By my 1/3 pte of earnings	6,283
To 1/2 of two horses	2,000		
To 603 foott of boards	1,206		
To Geo. Thompson for ball[ce]	677		
	6,283		

Mr. John Reid Dr.	lbs. Sugar	Per Contra Cr.	lbs. Sugar
To 1099 foote board at 2 lbs. p foote	2,198	By my 1/3 pte of earnings	6,283
To Beo. Thompson for ball[c]	1,926		
To soemuch allowed you for boards	2,159		
	6,283		

Shipe Katterine Dr.	lbs. Sugar	Per Contra Cr.	lbs. Sugar
		By Capt. George Thomspon	2,600
		Ditto p. Daniell Browning	1,300
		Ditto p. Robert Belgreave	1,600
		Coll Riddocke for Robt. Legard	2,400
		Ditto for horses	2,000
		boards left 4475	8,950
			18,850
		each mans pte	6,283

An Accompt of fraught from N. E.

Barbados:

Goods consigned:

		Tun	lbs. Sugar
To	Pastor Sallmon	6 at 719 lb p tun	4,500
	Steaphon Evans	1/4	200
	Robert Belgreave	2	1,600
	James Hayman	1	800
	Bushell and Bond	3 3/4	2,850
	Alex McGaskill	1/4	200
	Richard Rumney	11 2/3	8,850
	Daniell Browning	1 7/8	1,300
	John Williams	5 1/4	4,200
	Robert Logard	3	2,400
	John Stosher	4	3,200
	Symon Lambarte	1 1/2	1,200
	William Dean	1 3/4	1,425
	Capt. George Thompson	3/4	600
	William Gibbs	1 1/2	1,200
	Thomas Dowdin	2 1/4-1/3	1,866
		47 1/8	36,391
	Mr. William Coke	18	

Remember 4 fraught
dew to Mr. Wm. Coke

Memorandum

2 horses
2 masts
7 M boards
a parcell of stands and heading
a parcell of planks
8 bundles of hoops at 2/3 our fraut rened
7 bundles ditto on Josepth Bartholomew's acct.

Capt. Joseph Bartholomew is Dr		Per Contra is	Cr
To fraught 10 bar^ll makerall	900	By 2 masts cost 3:0:0	
To James Hayman & Stea Evans	1,000	By 7 M boards 46/8 p M 16:5:0	
To William Dean	1,455	By 7 θ of hoops 2:9:0	
To Capt. Dowdin paid you	1,866	By a parcell of stands heading & planks cost	
To Coll Syman Lambart	1,200	By acc^o seamens waiges	39,159
To pd per Wm. Gibbs fraut	1,125	By soemuch pd seamen allow^d him	200
To Mr. Shoster	3,200	By his pticular acc^o of disbursements	1,504
To severall boards sold by you	4,570	By soemuch allowed him on makerall	375
To Lt Coll Riddocke pd seamens waiges	9,553		
To Mr. Coke pte fraut	9,789		
To Capt. Geo Thompson pd seamen	1,970		

1668	Lt. Collonell Alexander Riddocke Dr.	lbs. Sugar	1668	Per Contra is Cr.	lbs. Sugar
	To your 1/8 pairte of 23303 lbs sugar is	2,913		By what is allowed you on ye 17417 lb yor pairte being	3,000
	To yor 1/8 pairte of 17417 lbs sugar is	2,177		By your disbursments as appears in folio 4	39,915
	To yor pte of the whole disbursments	41,898		By Mr. John Reid for ballance	4,073
		46,988			46,988

1668	Captain Geo:ge Thompson Dr.	lbs. Sugar	1668	Per Contra is Cr.	lbs. Sugar
1/16	To 1/16 pairt of 23303 pound sugar and is	1,456		By soemuch paid Mr. Gotliew	3,000
1/16	To 1/16 of :7417 pounds ditto and is	1,089		By yor disbursments as appears in folio 2	62,099
	To yor pairte of the whole disbursments	31,425			
	To Mr. Robt. Scott for ballance	24,310			
	To soemuch which Mr. Boseman allowed you and is	6,819			
		65,099			65,099

1668	Master John Reid Dr.	lbs. sugar	1668	Per Contra is Cr.	lbs. Sugar
	To yor 1/8 pairte 23303 pods sugar is	2,913		By yor disbursements in folio (3) and is	58,720
	To yor 1/8 pairte 17417 pounds Sug^{r} and is	2,177			
	To jor pairte of ya whole Disbursments	41,898			
	To Mr. Alexander Riddocke for ball^{c}	4,073			
	To Mr. Robert Scott for balance	615			
	To Mr. Alex Riddocke on his pticular accompt	1,761			
	To Mr. Robert Scott on his pticular accompt	1,761			
	To Capt. George Thompson his acco^{tt}	1,320			
	To Mr. William Bosman for	445			
	To profitt and loss for soemuch you are willing to allow on your pairte	1,761			
		58,720			58,720

1668	Mr. Robert Scott Dr.	lbs. Sugar	1668	Per contra is Cr.	lbs. Sugar
	To yor 1/4 pairte of 23303 pounds Sug^r and is	5,826		By yor disbursments as appears in folio 5	11,164
	To yor 1/4 pairte of 17417 pounds ditto and is	4,354		By soemuch allowed you: on ye 17417 and is	4,003
	To yor pte of all disbursments whair you are consearned	29,912		By Capt. George Thompson for	24,310
				By Mr. John Reid for ballance	615
		40,092			40,092

1668	Mr. William Bosman Dr.	lbs. Sugar	1668	Per Contra is Cr.	lbs. Sugar
	To 1/16 pairte of 23303 pounds Sug^r and is	1,456		By yor disbursments as appears in folio (4)	6,203
	To 1/16 pairte of 17417 pounds ditto and is	1,089		To Capt. George Thompson for ball^c and is	6,817
	To yor pairte of disbursments q^r in you are consearned	10,474			
		13,020			13,020

1668	Mr. John Reid is	Dr.	Lbs. Sugar
	To yor pairte being soemuch you are to the Cappdeberde voyage and is		
			2,951 3/4

1668	Per Contra is	Cr.	Lbs, Sugar
	By severally you disbursed on Cappdeberde voyage and is		225
	By Capt. George Thompson for		97
	By Mr. Robert Scott for ballance		604 3/4
			2,951 3/4

1668	Lt. Collonell Alexander Riddocke	Dr.	Lbs. Sugar
	To what your part is to allow		
			2,951 3/4

1668	Per Contra is	Cr.	Lbs. Sugar
	By soemuch being short on credit pd a cooper fortrimming water cask		445
	By soemuch you disbursed out of yor New England voyage and is		2,159
	By Mr. Robert Scott for ballance and is		347 3/4
			2,951 3/4

1668	Captain George Thompson is	Dr.	Lbs. Sugar
	To yor pte disbursed on said voyage and is		2,213
	To Mr. Bosman for		738
	To Lt. Coll. Alexand^{r} Tiddocke for ball^{c}		97
			3,048

1668	Per Contra is	Cr.	Lbs. Sugar
	By severally yor acco^{t} and have disbursed and is		
			3,048

1668	Mr. Robert Scott	Dr.	Lbs. Sugar
	To yor pairte of the smith accompt and is		115
	To pairte of disbursments on said voyage		2,951 3/4
	To Mr. John Reid for		347 3/4
	To Lt. Coll. Alex^{r} Riddocke for ball^{cc}		605½
			4,020

1668	Per Contra is	Cr.	Lbs. Sugar
	By severally you disburst and is		
			4,020

1668	Mr. William Bosman is	Dr.	Lbs. Sugar
	To yor pairte you are to allow on said voyage		737 3/4

1668	Per Contra is	Cr.	Lbs. Sugar
	By Capt. George Thompson for ball^{cc}		737 3/4

CHAPTER FIVE

ACCOUNTING FOR WITCHES

William Holmes

Witches are back! Bookshop shelves are full of witchcraft paperbacks - historical, hysterical, psychological, and do-it-yourself. Covens of them cavort in California, and the Old Sturbridge Village craft shop in Massachusetts is selling rush broomsticks as fast as they can make them. Don't tell me people use these things to sweep with!

I suppose each of us has his own image of a typical basic witch. There is the common, everyday Halloween variety with hooked nose, pointed hat, and a Sturbridge broomstick. If, on the other hand, you favor the dramatic, you probably see them as Shakespeare did in Macbeth -

> "Round about the cauldron go
> In the poison'd entrails throw..."

As a Scot, I lean towards the Robbie Burns "Tam o'Shanter" variety, revelling in old Kirk Alloway on a stormy night, with the devil - auld Nick, himself - playing the bagpipes.

> "He screw'd the pipes and gart them skirl
> Till roof and rafters a' did dirl."

and Cutty Sark, the youngest witch, chasing Tam on his horse to the very keystone of the auld Brig o'Doon.

These literary phantasmagoria have one thing in common. They entertain but do not frighten us.

However, if your ancestry is old New England you are troubled by a vision of a different calibre. You know about Macbeth's beldams, of course. You may even know that Cutty Sark was originally something other than a popular brand of Scotch whisky. But over your shoulder a blurred kaleidoscope of sad faces out of the past haunts you and reminds you of the communal madness that took hold of your ancestors in 1692. When it was over, more than one hundred and fifty neighbours - children and adults - had been arrested, nineteen of them hung, and one abdurate old man pressed to death beneath a pile of rocks. It is this reality, conjured out of a weird mixture of medieval superstition and religious bigotry, that makes us shiver.

The New England witches' trials of 1692 is of particular interest to the accountant for another reason. The whole process, in all its various phases, was well and truly "accounted for". Furthermore, a large part of the accounts were duly audited according to the standards of the times.

A good place to start looking at the records is the Account of Charge and Discharge which John Phillips, the Treasurer of Massachusetts, submitted to the Great and General Court for the fiscal year 1692/1693. The details of the account deal mainly with the raising by taxes of approximately 30,000 pounds to pay the soldiers and sailors "Imployed in their Majesties Service against the French and Indian Enemy" - the so-called King Williams' war. However, two entries relate directly to the witches' trials -

1692		Ł	s.	d.
Aug the 1°	Paid Capt Stephen Sewall, Clarke of the Special Court of Oyer and Terminor for the Necessary charges of s^{d} Court	0040	"--"	-
1693				
Febru 20th	Paid Mary gedney for the Entertainment of Jurors & Witnesses at a Special Court of Oyer and Terminor held in Salem for the County of Essex	0040	"--"	-

The "Special Court of Oyer and Terminor" was an English legal institution called "to hear and determine" the circumstances surrounding any unusual matter. And the unusual matter in this instance was the trial of the accused witches following their preliminary examination before the local magistrates.

Every schoolboy knows - as Macaulay used to say - that the story started when two little girls, nine year old Betty Parriss, and her eleven year old cousin, Abigail Williams, came down with a sickness that was beyond the comprehension of Dr. Griggs, the local doctor. Two women, Sarah Good and Sarah Osborne, were accused of practising witchcraft against the girls. Warrants were issued and preliminary examinations made in Salem Village before two magistrates, John Hathorne and Jonathan Corwin, sent out by the General Court.

The two Sarahs were completely unalike. Sarah Good was shrewish, idle, slovenly and pregnant. Sarah Osborne was well-to-do, but had earned the ill-will of the community by being "uppity" and slack in her church attendance. Both were "examined" on March 1 along with Tituba, a woman slave the Parriss family had brought with them from Barbados. Tituba "confessed" for three days, holding her audience spell-bound with tales of red cats and red rats who could talk to her. She implicated the two Sarahs as the ones who "forced her to obey" in tormenting the

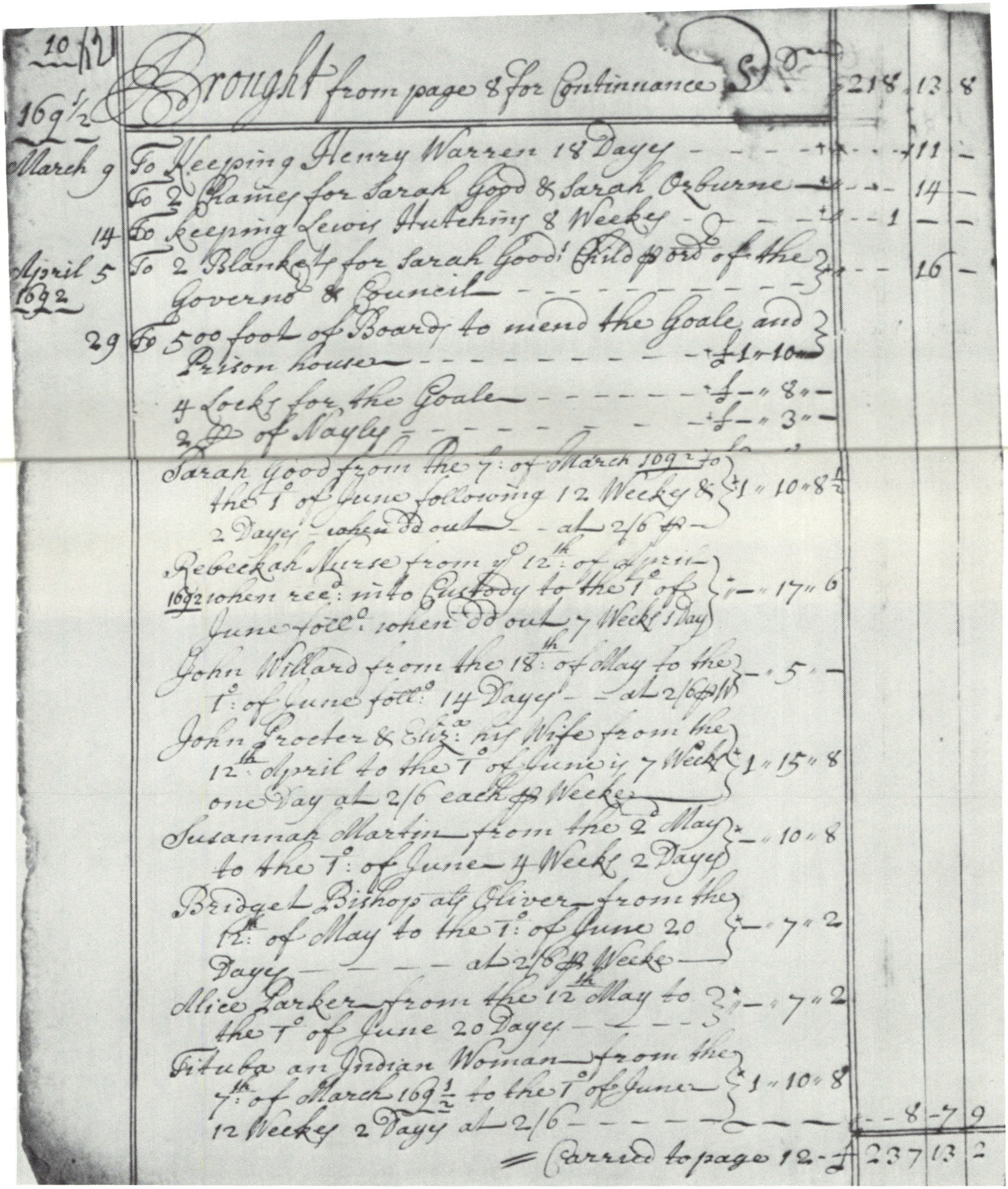

10 [12]

Brought from page 8 for Continuance £ 218 . 13 . 8

		£	s	d
169½ March 9	To Keeping Henry Warren 18 Dayes		11	—
	To 2 Chaines for Sarah Good & Sarah Ozburne		14	—
14	To keeping Lewis Hutchins 8 Weekes	1	—	—
April 5 1692	To 2 Blanketts for Sarah Good's Child by ord of the Governo & Council		16	—
29	To 500 foot of Boards to mend the Goale and Prison house — £1"10 4 Locks for the Goale — £—"8"— 2 … of Nayles — £—"3"— Sarah Good from the 7: of March 169 2 to the 1 of June following 12 Weekes & 2 Dayes when dd out — at 2/6 — £1"10"8½ Rebeckah Nurse from ye 12th of April 1692 when rec: into Custody to the 1 of June foll: when dd out 7 Weeks 1 Day — £—"17"6 John Willard from the 18th of May to the 1: of June foll: 14 Dayes — at 2/6 — £—"5"— John Procter & Eliza: his Wife from the 12th April to the 1 of June is 7 Weeks one Day at 2/6 each Weeke — £1"15"8 Susannah Martin from the 2d May to the 1: of June 4 Weeks 2 Dayes — £—"10"8 Bridget Bishop als Oliver from the 12: of May to the 1: of June 20 Dayes — at 2/6 Weeke — £—"7"2 Alice Parker from the 12th May to the 1 of June 20 Dayes — £—"7"2 Tituba an Indian Woman from the 7th of March 169½ to the 1 of June 12 Weekes 2 Dayes at 2/6 — £1"10"8	8	7	9

Carried to page 12 — £ 237 . 13 . 2

Excerpts from Accounts of John Arnold, the Keeper of the Boston jail.

sick children. Not content with this, she told of the"The Tall Man" who appeared to her in her visions with a book containing names of nine witches. The hunt was on! The magistrates and the community must determine the identity of the nine names. Obligingly, several other teenage girls, notably the precocious twelve-year old, Ann Putnam, came to the aid of the magistrates and took over the role of accusors.

Sarah Good, Sarah Osborne and Tituba were removed to Boston prison for safekeeping, pending trail, on March 7.

Four days later Ann Putnam named Martha Cory, a respectable matron and pillar of the church, as the next witch. She was arrested March 21, duly examined and joined the two Sarahs in the Boston jail.

The day Martha Cory was arrested, the "afflicted children" implicated poor, deaf, inform, seventy-one year old Rebecca Nurse. A few days later they switched to the other end of the age spectrum and accused Dorcas Good, the five-year old daughter of Sarah Good. Rebecca and Dorcas joined the others in Boston prison. And so the horrible business ground on. Which leads us to the 1692 accounts of John Arnold, the keeper of the Boston jail.

Boston 1692 The Countrey is		D^r
March 9	To Chaines for Sarah Good & Sarah Osborne	£ - "14" -
14	To Keeping Lewis Hutchins 8 weeks at $2^s.6^d$	1 "--"
April 5	To 2 blanketts for Sarah Good's Child p order	- "10" -
29	To 500 footboards to mend the Goal and prison house	1 "10" -
	To 4 locks for the Goal	- " 8" -
	To 2^c Nails	- " 3" 0
	To repairing the prison house	2 " 8" -
May 10th	To 3 large Locks for the Goal	- " 9" 9
23	To Shackles for 10 prisoners	2 "--"
29	To 1 p^r of Irons for Mary Cox	- " 7" -
	To Sarah Good of Salem villedge from the 7th of March to Ditto 1st June 12 weeks at $2^s.6^d$	1 "10" -
	To Rebecca Nurse of same place from the 12th April 7 weeks and one day at $2^s.6^d$	- "17" 10
	To George Jacob 6 week & 4 days from y^e 12th May	- "16" 4
	To John Proctor & Elizabeth his Wife from the 12th April to the 1st of June at 5^s	1 "15" -
	To Susanna Martin of Amsbury from y^e 2^d May to the 1st of June 4 weeks & 2 days	- "10" 8
	To Bridget Bishop als Oliver of Salem from y^e 12th May 20 days at $2^s.6^d$p week	- " 7" -
	To Alice Parker of Salem from y^e 12th of May to the 1st of June 20 days at $2^s.6^d$	- " 7" -
	To George Burroughs 7 weeks from 9th of May	- "17" 6
	To Sam Passanauton an Indian 8 weeks & 4 days from the 28th of April at $2^s.6^d$p week	1 " 1" 5
	To Roger Toothaker of Salem villedge)5 weeks & 5 days To John Willard of Salem villedge)from 18th May)at $2^s.6^d$p week	1 " 8" -
	To the Keeping of Sarah Osborne from the 7th of March to the 10th of May when she died being 9 weeks & 2 days	1 " 3"
	To yearly Salery	20 "--" -
	To mending the Prison	- "13"
		£ 40 "16" 6

John Arnold

The boston jailer's account, with its precise enumeration of weeks and days at two shillings and sixpence per week, its chains and irons and locks, draws a pathetic picture of the prisoners shivering through the waning days of a cold New England winter in a draughty Boston prison, patched together with footboards and nails. Hogarth could not have drawn it better. The one touch of charity in the whole account - "2 blanketts for Sarah Good's Child p order" - serves only to emphasize the contrasting grimness of the whole scene.

However, we should be cautious about passing 20th century judgments on 17th century behaviour. To the average man in Boston and Salem in 1692 these prisoners were suspected witches who had been practising their black arts on children. They were capable of all sorts of tricks. The could, for instance, easily shrink themselves to Lilliputian dimensions, slip through a keyhole, and be back in Salem on their broomsticks in a trice tormenting more victims. To them this was not fantasy! The point was made forceably by the people of Salem to Sir William Phips, the new Governor, almost as soon as he landed from England on May 14, 1692. Sir William solved the problem very neatly: each prisoner should fitted with a set of chains. Nobody, not even a witch, could shrink cold iron! Solomon himself could have ruled no better!

Faced with jails overflowing with suspected witches in Boston, Salem, Charlestowne, Amesbury, Andover, and half-a-dozen other towns, Sir William and the Council moved fast to get the trials under way. They appointed a Court of Oyer and Terminer which met for the first time in Salem on June 2, 1692. The first prisoners examined were the original group from Salem now in Boston jail, which explains why most of those on the Boston jailer's list were "delivered out" on June 1.

The Boston jailer's account is of prisoners languishing in chains and irons, their preliminary examination over and waiting for their formal trials to begin. The account of the sherrif for Charlestown paints a livelier picture.

Midd^{x} "An Account of Charges Expended upon Prisoners Accused for Witchcraft and tryed att Charlestowne

1692/3

		£ : s : d
	To Carying Elizabeth Coleson to Salem by warant from Charlestowne	
Jany 3rd	Expenses & Assistance	3 : 01 : 00
	To removing 6 prisoners from Cambridge to Salem by habeas corpus 5 men & 5 horses Vitewalls & drink upon ye Road	9 : 08 : 00
	To Expenses for prisoners when Brought by habeas corpus from Salem to Charlestowne for Tryall, for Victewalls, Drinks & a keeper for them at Charlestowne	2 : 04 : 00
	To Mony for Wood when in Charlestowne Prison	00 : 09 : 00
	To 8 persons Tryalls for my ffees as alowed att Salem 15s per piece	06 : 00 : 00
	To Transporting of them after Tryall to Camebridg with cart & 4 men to guard	03 : 00 : 00
	To 7 dayes mySelf Spent with a guard to Seize and pursue with huencry after them	1 : 00 : 00
	To the County Prison Keeper for Diott as appears in peticules	13 : 07 : 08
	To Mr Henry Summers Money Due for ye Prisoners	00 : 09 : 08
	To ye Keeper 6 Bushells of Corn at 2^{s} pr bushell	00 : 12 : 00
	To ye Cryers fees and to ye Constables Ringing ye bell	03 : 02 : 00
		42 : 13 : 10

Sim^{o} Phillips Sherriffe

March 22^d 1696 Read

26⅟ Read a Second time

on Decem^r 17, 1697

Voted, that the Consideration hereof by referred to the next Quarter Sessions in the County of Middlesex. That if anything be their due, it be discharged as the Law provides

Sent-up for Concurrence

Penn Townsend, Speaker

This is livelier scene, with the jailer seizing and pursueing "with huencry after them", the town Cryer broadcasting the latest developments, and the constable "Ringing ye bell". And through it all accused witches are being shuttled in carts between Salem, Cambridge, and Charlestowne under writes of habeas corpus with mounted escorts, while the panoply of English justice, one step removed from the middle ages, goes to work on the American continent. When it was over, nineteen people had been hung. In addition, the indomitable 80-year old Giles Cory, had been pressed to death beneath a pile of rocks for remaining mute under examination - a medieval form of the Fifth Amendment - to prevent the court from confiscating his estate.

Four years later, in 1696, John Arnold still had not been paid for housing the prisoners in his Boston jail in 1692. Not only that, he was also still waiting to be paid for 1689, 1690, and 1691. So he lodged a petition with the Great and General Court and resubmitted all his accounts for the total period 1689/1691. The petition is an interesting document and the second half has special significant in the matter of the witches.

Petition of John Arnold - Submitted 1696

The Humble Petition of John Arnold to y^{r} Excell^{cy} & C

Humbly Sheweth

That yor Petitioner (in the late Happy Revolution in the year 1689) being then Keeper of his Maj:^{tys} Goal for the County of Suffolk in Boston in the Province afores^{d} ....: AND WHEREAS in the year 1692 Sundry & divers persons were by the Pulick Authority of s^{d} Province comitted into the Custody of yr Petitioner as being Witches & possess'd with that Diabollicall Sin of Witchcraft for wch s^{d} Crimes Severall of them were convicted & suffered condign punishment according to the Laws of the s^{d} Province in that case made & provided: for all wch s^{d} Prisoners as also for many other poor & Duepe^{d} & disable persons your s^{d} Petitioner hath been at an Extrordinary charge & Expense in mending repairing & securing the s^{d} Comon Goal of s^{d} Disbursements & Expense sy^{r} s^{d} Petitioner hath greatly lessen'd & impaired his Estate to the great impoverishing of ye s^{d} Petitioner & his Family

Wherefore ye Petitioner Humbly implore this Honble House to take this his Case into your most mature & Serious Consideracon: that Expended by yr Petitioner as in & by the s^{d} Account doth appear by Such ways & means as to your Excell^{cy} & etc shall seem most convenient & meet so he will as in Duty bound

For Ever pray & c^{a}

The original account for 1692 ended with Arnold's expenses for those prisoners "delivered out" of his prison prior to June 30, 1692. This late account went beyond that date and listed many more of the witches who were still in his custody as of that date. The General Court got round to considering his petition on

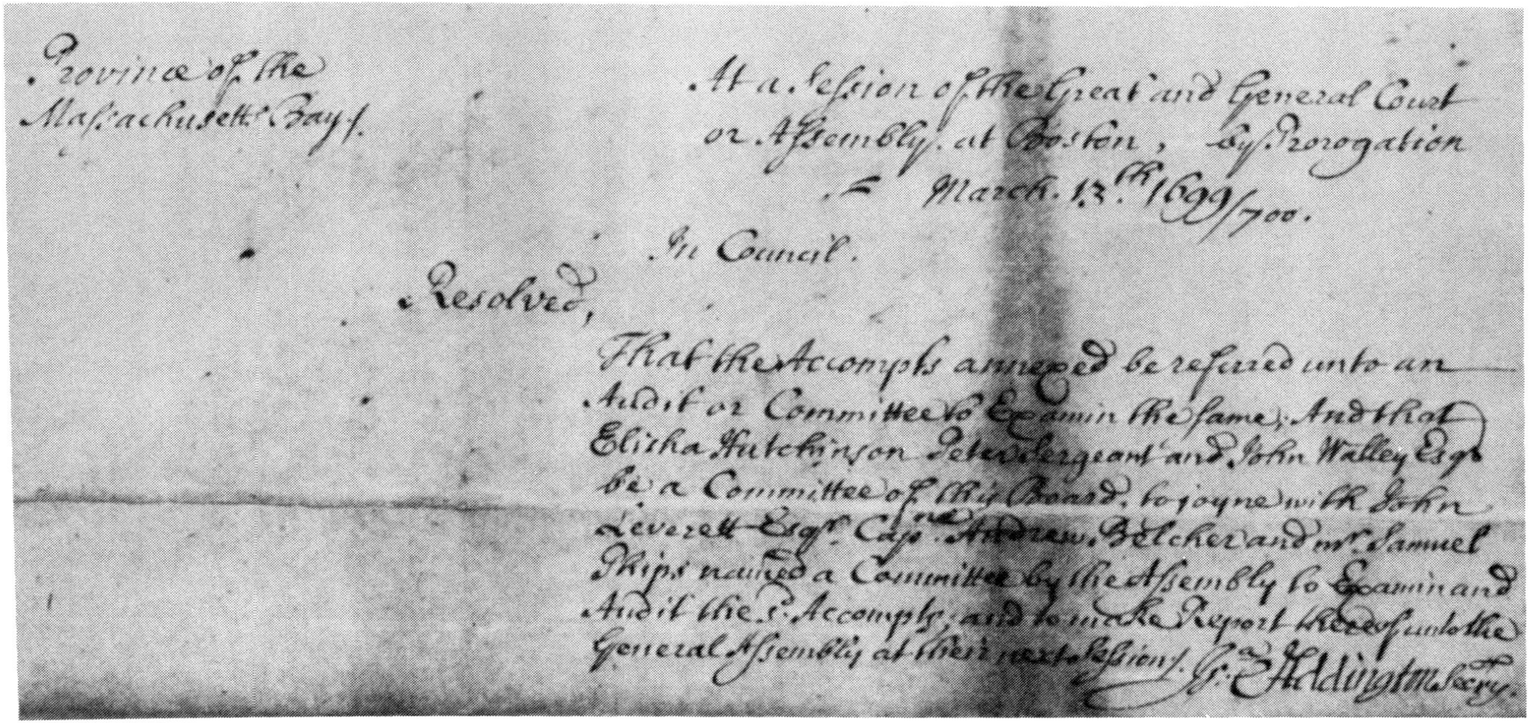

Province of the
Massachusetts Bay.

At a Session of the Great and General Court
or Assembly at Boston, by Prorogation
— March 13th 1699/700.

In Council.

Resolved,

That the Accompts annexed be referred unto an
Audit or Committee to Examin the same; And that
Elisha Hutchinson Peter Sergeant and John Walley Esqs
be a Committee of this Board, to joyne with John
Leverett Esqr Capt Andrew Belcher and Mr Samuel
Phips named a Committee by the Assembly to Examin and
Audit the sd Accompts, and to make Report thereof unto the
General Assembly at their next Session. Is. Addington Secry.

Resolution appointing Audit Committee to audit accounts of Keeper of the Boston jail for his expenses in connection with witches trials.

March 13, 1700 and reacted like careful Puritan keepers of the public purse. They appointed an audit committee!!

Province of the
Massachusetts Bay

At a Session of the Great and General Court
of Assembly at Boston, by Prorogation
- March 13th 1699/700

In Council

Resolved,

That the Accompts annexed by referred unto an Auditor Committee to Examin the same; And that Elisha Hutchinson Peter Sergeant and John Walley Esqr be a Committee of this Board, to joyne with John Leverett Esqr, Cap^{n} Andrew Belcher and Mr. Samuel Phips named a Committee by the Assembly to Examin and Audit the s^{d} Accompts; and to make Report thereof unto the General Assembly at their next Session.

Issac Addington
Secry.

Considering poor John Arnold had now been waiting about seven years to be paid, the audit committee went to work with commendable speed and on June 27, 1700 rendered their report as follows:

Boston June 27, 1700

Wee the Subscribers being a Committee appoynted by the great & General Court at their Session the 13th March 1699 to Examine & Audit the acco^{t} of Jn Arnold Prison Keeper in Boston & to make a Report unto the General Assembly

In Obedience to said Order we have carefully examined said acc^{t} & find that at two shillings & Sixpence per weeke there is due to said Arnold the sum of thirty eight pounds eleven shillings Sixpense for the keeping the Prisoners committed at the time of the Revolution, wch Sum^{e} he saith hath not been yet allowed him; and by Ord^{r} was to release s^{d} Prisoners wthout Saying the paying of fees - So that he could not detain them for there diett; representing as aforesaid, he is ready to give his oath if required that he was never paid the two shillings Sixpence per weeke for their dyett neither by them not the Publick.

We also find that in his acco^{t} presented to the Honble Assembly in Nov 20th 1693 amounting to ₤ 350 the court see cause to Ord^{r} that he should have by 320^{d} & that it should be in full, wch Sume he saith his necessity was such that he was forced to take that money; he saith the only reason of the abatement of the s^{d} was upon the acco^{t} of the prisoners Sent from Salem that could not be kep there - Boston being then a Prison for the Whole Province and the said Arnold affirms he was never yet paid for their dyett neither by the publick nor the perticular persons, & it lieth only wth this Court to relieve him

We further find an Article in the last acco^{t} presented to this Court of Sixteen pounds for Blanketts ye wch was an Article not charged in the former acco^{t}. For Consideration of the premisses humbly offer to the Consideration & Determination of this Honble Assembly

Elisha Hutchinson
Peter Sergeant
John Walley
John Leverett
Saml Phips

There was one further matter on the business of accounting for the witches.

Puritan conscience will not leave you alone, and within a few years of 1692, many Massachusetts citizens were wishing there was some way to unhang the victims, not to mention removing the rocks from old Giles Cory. But is was not until 1709 anything effective got done. In that year the relatives of twenty-three of the victims petitioned the Government for some financial damages and formal clearance of the stains on their family escutcheons. The General Court on October 1710 reversed the attainders on those victums whose relatives signed the petition but granted no general absolution for others.

In December 1711 the Governor and council authorized payment of Ŀ 598.12s to surviving children and relatives who had entered claims. In these modern days of malpractice suits and million dollar settlements the accounts accompanying the claims are interesting - and pathetic. The two following are typical:

> The Honorable Committee now
> Sitting at Salem Sept 13, 1710
>
> Whereas my mother Anne Foster of Andover suffered imprisonment 21 weeks and upon her Tryall was condemned for Supposed witchcraft upon which evidence as is now generally thought insufficient of And died in prison I being well persuaded of my mother's innocency of the crime for which she was condemned, Humbly Desire that the Attainder may be taken off -
>
> The Account of my charges and expenses for my mother during her Imprisonment is as followeth.
>
> The money which I was forced to pay the Keeper before I could have dead body of my mother to bury 2-10-0
> Money & provisions expended while she was in prison 4- 0-0
> Per Abraham Foster
> The Son of the Deceased

An account of what was seized and taken away by the sherriffe of his Deputy and assistants out of the estate of Samuel Wardwell late of Andover. Deceas'd who suffered the paines of Death under condemnation, on the sorrowful tyralls for witchcraft in the year 1692

Was seized and taken away

5 cowes at 2p	10-00-00
1 Heifer & a yearling	2- 5-00
1 Horse	3- 0-0
9 Hogs	7- 0-0
9 Load of Hay	4- 0-0
A set of Carpenters Tools	1-10-0
6 Acres of Corn upon the ground	9-00-0

Sarah Wardwell the wife of Samuel Wardwell aforesaid was condemned upon her Tryall for witchcraft at Salem in 1692

I being well satisfied in the Innocency of my father and Mother of the Crime for which they were condemned humbly desire the attainder may be taken off

per Samuel Wardwell eldest son of the Deceased

It was mentioned above that those victims not included in the 1709 petition were not covered by the absolution. In 1957 some descendants of Ann Pudeator, one of the condemned witches, petitioned the General Court in Massachusetts and introduced an Act to "Reverse the Attainder, Judgments and Convictions for Witchcraft of Ann Pudeator and Others". What a chance for New England to admit its mistake and redeem itself in a grandiloquent gesture of charity spanning more than two and a half centuries of American history! A few well chosen words adopted by unanimous voice acclaim by the House and Senate was all that was needed. Some latter day Oliver Wendell Holmes or Longfellow could have delivered a suitable oration from the State House steps and the Ancient & Honorable Artillery could have paraded in full uniform and fired their gun.

Massachusetts did none of these things. In a situation demanding simple Justice the Great and General Court settled rather for cold hearted jurisprudence. See what the lawyers wrought.

"Resolve Relative to the Indictment, Trial, Conviction and Execution of Ann Pudeator and certain other persons for "witchcraft" in the year Sixteen hundred and ninety-two.

"Whereas One Ann Prudeator and certain other persons were indicted, tried, found guilty, sentenced to death and executed in the year sixteen hundred and ninety-two for "Witchcraft" and

"Whereas Said persons may have been illegally tried, convicted and sentenced by a possibly illegal court of oyer and terminer created by the then governor of the Province without authority under the Province without authority under the Province Charter of Massachusetts Bay; and

"Whereas, Although there was a public repentance by Judge Sewall, one of the judges of the so-called "Witchcraft Court", and by all the members of the "Witchcraft" jury, and a public Fast Day proclaimed and observed in repentance for the proceedings but no other action taken in regard to them; and

"Whereas, The General Court of Massachusetts is informed that certain descendants of said Ann Prudeator and said other persons are still distressed by the record of said proceedings; therefore be it "RESOLVED, That in order to alleviate such distress and although the facts of such proceedings cannot be obliterated, the General Court of Massachusetts declares its belief that such proceedings, even if lawful under the Province Charter and the law of Massachusetts as it then was, were and are shocking, and the result of a wave of popular hysterical fear of the Devil in the community; and further declares that, as all the laws under which said proceedings, even if then legally conducted, have been long since abandoned and superseded by our more civilized laws no disgrace or cause for distress attaches to the said descendants or any of them by reason of said proceedings; and be it further

RESOLVED, That the passage of this resolve shall not bestow on the commonwealth or any of its subdivisions, or on any person any right which did not exist prior to said passage, shall not authorize any suit or other proceeding nor deprive any party to a suit or other proceeding of any defense which he hitherto had, shall not affect in any way whatever the title to or rights in any real or personal property, nor shall it require or prompt the remission of any penalty, fine or forfeiture hitherto imposed or incurred."

Reduced to simple words, the General Court finds the 1692 shenanigans "shocking" but refuses to pass on their legality. However, the Court officially informs the descendants they don't really have to feel ashamed; but nobody can sue anyone for their having said so.

The voting on the Resolution added insult to injury. It was rejected four votes to twelve on the third reading, but adopted ten votes to four on a motion to reconsider.

But rest in peace Ann Prudeator - and you other tormented ghosts. The rest of us New Englanders eschew the carping caution of lawyers and politicians. Unanimously and unequivocally we "reverse the attainder, judgments, and convictions," - and the devil take the legal consequences.

> "Faith, Hope and Charity, these three;
> but the greatest of these is Charity."

CHAPTER SIX

ACCOUNTING AND ACCOUNTANTS IN MASSACHUSETTS - PART ONE

William Holmes

Prior to 1800

Ethel S. Kingman's "Accountancy in Massachusetts," published in 1952, had much to do with the birth of my interest in accounting and accountants in bygone days. Her "brief study" offers a solid foundation to build upon and is particularly useful with respect to the formative days of organized public accounting from about 1890 to 1910.

From the start, however, I was somewhat puzzled by the sparsity - almost absence - of any accountants mentioned in her chapter on "The Pioneers" practising the art prior to 1850. She lists Thomas H. Leavitt in business in 1847, G. N. Comer, accountant and teacher who founded Comer's commercial college in Boston in 1840, and Benjamin Franklin Lord, who conducted a commercial school from 1834 to 1837. She makes note of the fact that Richard Brown, FCA, of Edinburgh, stated in his "History of Accounting and Accountants" (Published in 1905) that one gentleman, then still living, who had commenced business in Boston in 1847, for a year or two "was the sole representative of the profession in that city, and it was many years before it was regarded with much favour."

The impression is of a city of businesses sailing aimlessly on an unledgered sea, hoping for some latter day Pacioli to come along with a modicum of Italian

View of Long Wharf and part of the harbor in 1764 from a painting by Lt. Byron of the British navy. Lt. Byron was a great uncle of Lord Byron. (Courtesy of Bostonian Society)

method bookkeeping to prescribe for them their proper course and speed -debits to port, and credits to starboard. But this view of things just doesn't make sense to anyone who has read his New England history and enjoyed, for instance, Professor Samuel Eliot Morison's "Maritime History of Massachusetts."

Morison quotes an English observer who stated that by 1676 Massachusetts had thirty merchants worth ten to twenty thousand pounds, was feeding itself and exporting its surplus to Virginia and the West Indies, and that 430 vessels between thirty and two hundred tons burthen were "built in and belong to that jurisdiction." Morison goes on that Thomas Boylston was supposed to be worth about $400,000 just before the Revolution "and Colonel Elisha Doane was a good second."

Anyone who has enjoyed looking at old maritime engravings will have been pleasantly surprised at the variety of shipping shown in Boston Harbor by the early 1800's, and Morison paints a vivid verbal picture of the rivalry between Salem and Boston for the Far East trade in the early 1800's, Salem trading via the Cape of Good Hope and India, Boston via Cape Horn and the Canadian Northwest. These were the ventures of substantial busienssmen who must have required a fair amount of reasonable accounting to help them in their endeavors. And help they had! Morison in a later chapter tells us "Central Wharf, built in 1819, with fifty-four brick stores running down its center for a quarter of a mile, was a fitting companion to India Wharf. In its upper stories were three great halls for auction sales, and in its octagonal cupola the headquarters of the "Semaphore Telegraph Company......" Below, as on India Wharf, were warehouses, wholesale stores, and counting-rooms of leading mercantile firms. Here cargoes from all parts of the world were bought and sold and accounted for. Respectable male clerks on high stools were constantly writing in the calf-bound letter-books, ledgers, and waste books, or delving in the neat wooden chests that enclosed the records of each particular vessel." Ledgers and waste books were the tools of trade for the old time Italian method bookkeeper who, with his "To's" and "By's" and copperplate curlicues often managed to create a ledger page as pleasing to the eye as a scroll of Japanese or Chinese caligraphy.

From time to time one of the old high desks from these counting rooms, turns up on the city's antique shops. I saw one fairly recently in the Green Dolphin down on old Long Wharf and was tempted to purchase it. After all, Chief Justice Holmes, by his own preference, wrote many of his famous briefs and opinions at such a desk, which had belonged to his grandfather, and attributed some part of their brevity and clarity to the fact that he stood while doing so. In his own words - "Nothing conduces to brevity like caving in of the knees."

With this feeling of certitude that the bookkeepers were there, I went looking to the old Boston city directories, the earliest dating from 1789 when Boston boasted a population of about 18,000 souls, and there along with a variety of merchants, shipwrights, and mariners, plus a few fencing masters and dancing masters, alphabetically arranged, I found the following:

Burroughs, William	accomptant	Federal street
Lowell, John	accomptant	Cook's Court
Winnet, John	accomptant	Bowdoin Square

These men were in business seven years before the first American textbook was published in Philadelphia by William Mitchell and just about the time American maritime trade began to recover from the embargoes and unsettled conditions brought about by the revolution. Having found them, the next question that came to mind was where they had learned their "accompting" and from what textbooks? They could, of course, have been late emigrants from Britain who brought their knowledge with them, but their names have an old New England flavor that suggested otherwise. Harry Bentley, in his excellent "A Brief Treatise on the Origin and Development of Accounting" (published in 1929) quotes from a 1928 article "Commercial Education in Retrospect" by Louis J. Fish, included in the Annual Report of the superintendent of Boston Public Schools as follows:

> "There was a little trace of commercial education in the American colonies, although at that time it did not play an important part in the school system. With the rising importance of trade in the eighteenth century 'writing schools,' so called, came into prominence. Young men of good families who showed more aptitude for money-making than for learning Latin were sent to the writing schools to learn 'good hands and accounts.' These writing schools taught an elaborate system of penmanship, arithmetic in forms somewhat fantastic, and the science of bookkeeping complicated and made intricate by the multitude of varying monetary and metrical systems.
>
> Writing and ciphering schools had been a part of the Boston public schools since 1682. In 1740, however, writing schools under private auspices were established in Boston."

The last paragraph indicated private writing schools which might have taught bookkeeping as far back as 1740, and it seemed worthwhile to pursue this line of thought. A friend suggested the library of the Bostonian Society in the Old State House on Washington Street as a likely source - a quiet lunch-time haven, ably administered by the Society's curator.

The Boston Town Records for 1660 - 1701 gives the earliest reference to teaching accounting in Massachusetts. It reads as follows -

> 1667
>
> "Mr. Will Howard hath liberty to keep a wrighting school, to teach children to write and to keep accounts."

I doubt if the kids worried very much about deferred taxes and capitalized leases, but at least it was a start.

Although not directly related to the teaching or practice of accounting, I believe the following from the Boston Town Records is worth including here-

> March 10 1689/90
>
> At a publique meeting of the inhabitants of Boston "Voted that Mr. Peter Sergeant, Mr. Benj Alford, and Mr. Samson Sheafe be desired to Audit the Townes Acct with ye Selectmen for the two years past."

The auditors apparently went at the task with due deliberation and raised enough questions that only an interim report could be made a year later, for at the meeting of March 9, 1690/91 they were "desired to perfect what remaines to be done of the Accts of those 2 yeares, as also to audit the accompt of the Selectmen in the year 1690."

They finally got the first two years out of the way at the meeting on March 14, 1691/92 when their report was unanimously adopted. In 1695 the meeting voted "that the Treasurer's accompt be audited once in every year." Peter Sergeant was again one of the three auditors chosen and by that time had about five years experience in the busienss. The town apparently was satisfied with the results of these audits and on June 7, 1697 appointed a special three-man audit committee "to audit the acct of the Expence about the Fortifications, and also an acct given in by Mr. Arthur Mason."

This habit of auditing public accounts was in the English tradition. We remember, for instance, that on May 27, 1663 Samuel Pepys, when Clerk of the Acts to the King's Ships, confided to his Diary -

> "With Pett to my Lord Ashley, Chancellor of the Exchequer; where we met with the auditors about settling the business of

the accounts of persons to whom money is due before the King's time in the Navy, etc., etc."

Francis Pixley, one of Britain's best authorities on Auditing in the 1880's, in the preface to his "Auditiors, Their Duties and Responsibilities," points out that the post of Auditor to the Exchequer was established in 1314 and continued till 1834 when the duties were taken over by the Office of Controller - General of the Exchequer.

So much for tradition! I still wonder why the inhabitants of Boston in 1690 suddenly decided they needed an audit! Perhaps they suspected a modicum of Puritan hanky panky with the public funds.

The search for references in the 1700's was not so difficult after all. The Bostonian Society library shelves produced Robert Francis Seybolt's "The Private Schools of Colonial Boston," published in 1935 by Harvard University Press. Amoung other things, Mr. Seybolt had searched the old Boston weekly newspapers published in the eighteenth century extracting the advertisements relating to private schools. The list covered schools for dancing, fencing, music, elocution, singing, etc., but also included a significant number of the "writing schools" mentioned above by Mr. Fish teaching "good hands and accounts." I think all of those relavent to our search are worth reproducing, and they are listed below chronologically.

1709

Reading, Writing, Aritmetick, Merchants Accompts, Geometry, Trigonometry, Plain and Saphaerical, Dyalling, Gauging, Astronomy and Navigation are Taught: And Bonds, Bills, Indentures, Charter-parties, & c. are Drawn; and Youth Boarded, in Cross-street, Boston. By John Green.

B. N. L., Mar. 21-28, 1708/9.

1718

Mr. BROWNE TYMMS Living at Mr. Edward Oakes Shopkeeper in Newbury Street, at the South End of Boston, Keeps Merchants & Shopkeepers Books, Also Writes Bills, Bonds, Leases, Licences, Charter-parties, & c. for any Person that may have Occasion, at reasonable Rates. And Likewise teacheth Young Men Aritmatick and Merchants Account.

B. N. L., Feb. 17-24, 24-Mar. 3, 1717/18.

1720

AT THE HOUSE formerly Sir Charles Hobby's are taught Grammar, Writing after a free and easy manner, in all the hands usually practiced, Arithmetick Vulgar and Decimal in a concise and practical Method, Merchants Accompts, Geometry, Algebra, Mensuration, Geography, Trigonometry, Astronomy, Navigation and other parts of the Mathematicks, with the use of the Globes and other Mathematical Instruments, by Samuel Grainger.

They whose Business won't permit 'em to attend the usual School Hours, shall be carefully attended and instructed in the Evenings.

B. G.,Mar 21-22 (S.) 1719/20. "Samuel Grainger Late of London Admitted an inhabitant and Licensed to Keep School to teach writeing Logick and Merchants Acco^{ts} in this Town," Jan. 27, 1719/20 (B.R., XIII, 65).

1730

WRITING, Aritmatick, Merchants Accompts, Foreign Exchanges, eith in French or in English, are taught at the Widow Copps, at the Lower End of Prince-street, Boston, by Charles Lewis.

W.N.L., Mar 5-12, 12-19, 19-26, Apr. 3-9, 1730.

1738

THESE are to Notify all Gentlemen, Ladies and others, who have Children of fit Age, and are disposed to give them Instruction in Writing, Aritmetick, or Merchants's Accompts, that the Subscriber (Having the Approbation of the Select Men) has opened a School for that Purpose in the Room over which Mrs. Brownell now dwells, at the Head of Queen Street, where he will receive and instruct Children at the Customary Price, and give Attendance at the usual School Hours.

Ebenezer Swan

B.E.P., Sept. 18, 1738. Licenced, Aug. 16, 1738 (B.R., XV, 129).

1752

THIS is to inform the Publick That the School Lately Kept by Mr. John Leddel, now deceas'd, is Still Kept by Richard Green, where may be taught Writing in all its usual Hands, Also Arithmetick, in all its Branches, Algebra, Geometry, Trigonometry apply'd to Navigation, and Book-keeping after the Italian Method, & c. & c.

N.B. Youth may be boarded at Mrs. Leddel's, as formerly.

B.E.P., June 1, 15, 1752. Licensed "to Open a School in this Town" July 30, 1753 (B.R., XVII, 298).

1753

FOR THE BENEFIT of Persons confin'd in Business in the Day-Time, Notice is hereby given, that they may be taught Writing, Arithmetick, Algebra, Navigation, Gauging, Book-keeping, & c. & c. in the best Manner during the Winter Season, from Candle-Light till Half an Hour past Eight o'Clock in the Evening,

By Richard Green

At his School, at the South-End opposite Mr. Church's Vendue, - To begin the First of Next Month.

B.W.N.L., Sept. 13, 20, 27. Oct. 4, 1753.

1755

SAMUEL HOLBROOK

WRITING-MASTER, Keeps his School in Court-Square; teaches Writing, Arithmetick and Reading; also Merchants Accompts; with whom Youth may Board. Opens his School this Week of Evenings, and Keeps till April, for those who can't attend any other Time.

B.G. or C.J., Sept. 22, Oct. 6, 13, 1755.

1761

JOHN VINAL

Hereby informs the Publick,

THAT HE intends to open an Evening School at the South Writing-School as usual the 28th Instant, where Persons may be instructed in Writing, vulgar and decimal Arithmetic, several Branches of the Mathematics, and Book-Keeping after the best Methods. -N.B. Persons of but ordinary Capacities may be taught book-keeping in so plain a Manner, that they may be able to Keep their own Accompts in a short Time, and at a small Expence.

B.N.L., Sept. 10, 17, 24, Oct. 1, 1761.

1763

THIS is to give Notice to any Gentlemen who want a Person that understands the following Sciences of the Mathematics, viz. vulgar and decimal Arithmetic, Mensuration, Gauging, Surveying, Dialing, Mair's Italian Method of Book-Keeping, Geometry and Theory of Navigation, and the Use of Gunter's Scale and Sliding Rule.

N.B. The above Sciences will be taught in the newest and best Method now used in Europe by

Cornelius Hogan.

The said Hogan will serve either in the Capacity of a School-Master or a Clerk; Any who will employ him may be sure of sufficient Security for his Honesty and Industry. Inquire of Green & Russell for further Intelligence.

B.P.B. & A., Oct. 10, 17, 24, 1763.

1767

ARITHMETIC

AND various branches of the Mathematicks taught by William Corlett, at his Apartment in Capt. Beach's House near the Rev. Mr. Checkley's Meeting-House, where any one of a moderate Capacity may Learn the first five Rules of Arithmetick in 40 hours, Navigation in 48 hours, Surveying in 48 hours, and Book-Keeping after the Italian Method in one Month.

N.B. He Lives near the Rev'd Checkley's Meeting House, South End, Boston.

B.E.P., Aug, 10, 17, 24, 31, 1767.

1769

A GENTLEMAN well versed in Learning, will, upon proper Encouragement, teach Reading, Writing, Spelling and Arithmetick, Merchants Accompts, Book-Keeping after the Italian Manner, and the Course of the Classicks, either private or publick; he'll observe good Order and Dicipline essentially necessary to virtuous Education; His wife would engage in a good Family as House-Maid, or Child's Maid, she is a good Seamstress, can read and write and understands House-work extremely well: She can spin Woolen & Linen from 3 to 8 or 9 Dozen.. They came here in quest of Mr. John Walters, who writes from Boston to Ireland, for some of his Family to come to him to enjoy his Estate; they can't gain any Intelligence of him, and would be greatly obliged to any Person who would give them any Account relative to him; For Further Particulars enquire of the Printer hereof.

B.W.N.L., May 4, 11, 18, 1769.

ABBREVIATIONS

B.N.L.	THE BOSTON NEWS-LETTER
B.G. or C.J.	THE BOSTON GAZETTE OR COUNTRY JOURNAL
B.R.	BOSTON RECORDS, i.e. REPORTS OF THE RECORD COMMISSIONERS OF THE CITY OF BOSTON
W.N.L.	THE WEEKLY NEWS-LETTER
B.E.P.	THE BOSTON EVENING POST
B.W.N.L.	THE BOSTON WEEKLY NEWS-LETTER
B.P.B. & A.	THE BOSTON POST-BOY & ADVERTISER

What do the advertisements tell us? We have no information prior to the 1752 advertisement of Richard Green whether "Merchants Accounts" included double entry bookkeeping. However, his reference to "Book-keeping after the Italian Method" clearly indicates instruction in double entry bookkeeping, and we note this reference in several of the later advertisements. Hogan's 1763 advertisement mentions "Mair's Italian Method of Book-keeping" so we know the text-book being used. John Mair was a Scottish schoolmaster, who published his "Bookkeeping methodiz'd; or a methodical treatise of merchants accompts according to the Italian form" in 1736. His textbook was something of a best seller and reached its 9th edition in 1817, and it is of interest that William Mitchell who published the first American textbook in 1796 also pays tribute to Mair's textbook.

We note that Mr. Browne Tymms "keeps Merchants and Shopkeepers Books" - in 1718. He may well be Boston's first public accountant! Samuel Granger may have operated the first evening school in "The House formerly Sir Charles Hobby's" in 1720 and we get some idea as to the hours kept by those evening schools in Richard Green's 1753 advertisement where he mentions "from Candle-Light till Half and Hour past Eight o'Clock in the Evening." It is comforting to note in William Corlett's 1767 advertisement that while navigation took only 48 hours to teach, book-keeping after the Italian Method took all of one month. The balance of the curriculum in almost all the advertisements is worth noting - the common factors in many cases including arithmetic, geometry, trigonometry, astronomy and navigation. Early documents from Scotland mirror the same subjects. For example, in 1695 a teacher of the art of navigation, bookkeeping, and arithmetic was appointed by the Town Counsel of Glasgow. In this respect also we should remember that the earliest known treatise on double entry bookkeeping was a chapter in Lucas Pacioli's "Summa de Arithmetica, Geometria, Proportione, et

Proportionalita." The early Italian businessman, as were many of his later European and New England counterparts, was a sea trader and this might explain the coupling together of accounting and mathematics useful to the art of navigation.

A rough comparison between the scope and number of the above advertisements with the situation in Scotland during the period 1700 to 1800 (as brought out in David Murray's "History of Bookkeeping and Accounting" published in Glasgow in 1930) indicates Boston was reasonably well served. However, the fact that several books were published in Scotland on the subject of bookkeeping during this period, of which Mair's was probably the best, might indicate a higher degree of expertise in the application of the art.

In any event, Boston had its Colonial accountants. We know some of their names, their addresses and something of their work. It is possible a Boston accountant was present at the Boston massacre. One may even have helped Paul Revere keep his books straight - according to the Italian method. What else would he use living in the North End!

CHAPTER SEVEN

ACCOUNTING AND ACCOUNTANTS IN MASSACHUSETTS - PART TWO

William Holmes

1800 - 1850

Some have said that accounting is more art than science. If so, it would seem to be more a responsive than a creative art; business creates a need for change in the art, and accounting moves to fill the need. I would suggest that at any point in time business gets the accounting it needs, and very little more! In appraising the accounting art in any period, therefore, it is useful to scan broadly the overall business backdrop against which the accountant plays his part.

In 1800 Boston was a town of 18,000 souls, with about 900 children attending seven "Free" schools. It was basically a maritime trading port, heavily involved for a long period of years with its West Indies trade, and just beginning to profit from its new routes to the Orient, via the Cape of Good Hope and Cape Horn. It boasted three banks, and its principal manufactures consisted of "rum, loaf-sugar, beer sailcloth, cordage, wool and cotton cards, playing cards, pot and pearl ashes, paper hanging, hats, plate glass, tobacco and chocolate." It had "thirty distilleries, two breweries, eight sugar houses, and eleven ropewalks." It was small, busy, and in a sense merely an extension of its own waterfront - and apparently thirsty.

In 1850, on the other hand, Boston was a city of 140,000 souls, supporting about 75 newspapers and periodicals. It was served by eight railroad stations within the city limits, with lines reaching out to Portland, Lowell, Fitchburg, Worcester, Providence, Fall River, and Plymouth. Its foreign trade, served by its expanded system of wharves and warehouses, grew ever greater. Frank H. Forbes, speaking about the old Boston Water Front to the Bostonian Society in the early 1900's said, "With many of the leading ports in Europe, Asia, Africa, South America, the West Indies, and the West Coast, Boston fairly had the monopoly of trade. The decade from 1844 to 1854 witnessed the culmination of old Boston's prosperity as the leader of foreign trade." In 1850 Boston supported 30 banks with total resources of $42,000,000. Its businesses were bigger, more complex, and obviously had a need for more and better accountants.

The Boston Directory for 1789 listed three "accomptants." The number is small, but by way of comparison, Lawrence Dicksee, the doyen of English auditing, tells us in his "The Student's Guide to Accountancy," published in 1897, that the London Directory for 1799 listed only eleven "accomptants."

The 1810 Boston Directory lists only three references to accountants as follows:

Elisha Penniman	compting room,	22 Marlboro st, house S. Bennet st.
Joseph Lovering	compting room,	49 State st, house Hollis st.
Samuel Alden	compting room,	21 Merchants row.

In addition it lists -

Nathaniel Furness, accountant, Massachusetts Bank, house Purchase st.

The Directory does not tell us directly whether the three "compting room" references relate to three early accountants offering accounting services, or are merely three individuals employed in compting rooms of private business. I believe

---

B

Boston Directory - 1822

the former to be the case. To begin with, there must have been considerably more than three "compting rooms" belonging to businesses in the city, and there would seem to be no reason to single out these three for special mention. In addition the Directory lists no house address for Samuel Alden, and it is most likely the address given was both his office and his home. The town was full of small buisnesses, which undoubtedly needed bookkeeping services, and it would seem reasonable to assume we are dealing with three early public accountants. Joseph Lovering was listed at the same address from 1809 to 1816. Elisha Penniman was at the same address for a number of years, but in 1816 gave up the "compting room" and opened a shoe store on the same premises - a further indication he was running a private business as an accountant.

The 1820 Directory shows considerable expansion in the list of accountants, as might be expected as the city grew. The following accountants are listed:

William Abrams, Jr.	Accountant	29 Middle st, house Sun court st.
John Bray	counting room,	13 Bray's Wharf
Peter C. Brooks	counting roon,	17 Kilby st, house - Atkinson st.
Andrew Campbell	Teacher of bookkeeping	6 North Russel st.
John Cannada	counting room	on the T (Wharf)
Gilman Collamore	counting roon,	48 Marlboro st, house 50 Beach st.
Joseph H. Dorr	counting room,	11 Central wharf, house Batterymarch
Samuel Greenleaf	counting room,	32 Broad st, house Somerset court
Eliphalet Hale	counting room,	32 Broad st, house 2 Federal st.
Jonathan W. Lillie	accountant	14 Vine st.
Charles Vose	counting room,	30 State st.
James White	counting room,	94 Court st.

We regretfully note the change to modern spelling - I would prefer to be a Certified Public Accomptant - and the pattern mentioned before of some men apparently working from their homes. A significant number of the counting rooms are located right on the wharves, the remainder within a block or two. And one wonders if perhaps Greenleaf and Hale were in some sort of partnership since they are both located at 32 Broad Street.

I noticed two entries - there may have been more - that reinforce to some extent the idea that the "counting rooms" mentioned above represented accountants in business for themselves. These are:

Abel Hall, wnarfinger - counting room Tileston's wharf, house South st.
Putnam and Pratt, distillers - counting room 18 Central wharf.

These entries indicate to some extent that when a counting room was attached to a business the style of the listing was different, and it is noticeable neither address is duplicated in the list of counting rooms above.

We get out first real idea of the scope of services some of these men possibly offered in 1822. The Boston Directory in that year started printing advertisements and one of the first is the following:

Book-keeping & Stenography
Upon the Most Modern and
Approved Systems
taught by
Frederick Beck
In Congress Square

"Books commenced, closed or posted and monthly and intricate accounts adjusted for a moderate compensation. Monthly or Quarterly Statements and Trial Balances, either on single sheets, or books neatly ruled, at short notice."

Mr. Beck is listed in the body of the 1822 Directory as:

Beck Frederick, accountant, Congress square, house 43 Warren

He ran a school in Cornhill square from 1818 to 1820, changed his listing to "accountant" in 1821, and is so listed in the Directories through 1831.

My guess would be that the type of work mentioned in his advertisement might be somewhat typical of that performed by some of the other people listed in the 1820 listing.

We notice also in the 1820 list another teacher in Andrew Campbell. He is listed as a "Schoolmaster" in the 1789 Directory and was still teaching school in 1833 - a span of 44 years.

I think it is worth mentioning also at this point that during those first 20 years of the 19th century the American accountant began to have access to American textbooks. The first four writers were:

(1) William Mitchell (Bookkeeper).
"A New and Complete System of Bookkeeping; being an Improved Method of Double Entry." (Philadelphia, 1796)

(2) Rev. Richard Turner, LL.D.
"A New Introduction to Bookkeeping after the Italian Method of Debtor and Creditor." (Salem, Massachusetts, 1801)

(3) Thomas Turner (Professor and Teacher of Bookkeeping).
"An Epitome of Bookkeeping by Double Entry." (Portland, Maine, 1804)

(4) James Bennett (Teacher of Bookkeeping and Mathematical Science).
"The American System of Practical Bookkeeping by Double Entry." (New York, 1814)

We can take pride in the fact that a Massachusetts writer produced the second book, and another New Englander the third book. Of these early books Mitchell's is probably the best. During the period 1750 - 1800 in Europe and America some individual businesses were getting larger and more complex, and the old pure "Italian method" procedure of journalizing every transaction was becoming increasingly burdensome. The answer was the adoption of specialized journals in the form of Sales, Purchases, Cash, and Bills day books, coupled soon after with multi-columnar analysis sheets. Mitchell's book deals directly with those problems and indicates some American accountants were keeping abreast of advances in the art in Europe. The best proof that the Boston accountant was on top of the situation is probably the advertisements by the town's booksellers and stationers for special day books and rulings of which the following example from the Boston Directory of 1825 is typical.

1825

Stationary and Account Book Warehouse

No. 94

Washington - Street (Cornhill) Boston

Leonard C. Bowles

Importer of

Stationary, Cutlery and Fancy Goods;

and

Manufacturer of Account Books

"Current books, of every description, viz: Legers, Journals, Waste, Invoice, Sales, Cash, Letter, Day Books, Memorandums, etc, made of the best Paper, bound in superior style, in Russia Leather, Sheep, and Morocco, with elastic spring backs, and ruled to any pattern."

The year 1830 was also a vintage year in the Boston Directory. Accountants continue to thrive with some interesting individual entries.

William Appleton	counting room	54 State	house	51 Beacon
Frederic Beck	accountant	Congress sq.	house	64 Warren
Amos Binney	counting room	33 Long wf.	house	17 Summer
Amos Binney, Jr.	Long wharf		house	21 Summer
Charles Binney	33 Long wharf		house	Allen
John Binney	counting room		house	29 Green
Peter C. Brooks	counting room	10 Court		
William Francia	accountant	81 Court		
Jonathan French	counting room	31 S. Market	house	722 Washington
John B. Hilliard	accountant	Church		
Thomas Kendall	counting room	28 Kilby,	house	53 Chambers
Thomas H. Kimball	bookkeeper		house	Stillman
Henry Lewis	counting room	31 India		
John Liscom	counting room	Brown's wh, Lynn		
Joshua Moss	counting room	70 State		
Samuel Newell	counting room	7 Chatham		
John Odin	counting room	40 State,	house	Beach
Benjamin Sewall	counting room	State,	b'ds	Commercial
Thomas Tremlett	counting room	Foster's wf		
Moses Whiting	counting room	36 Washington		

BOOKS POSTED, &c.

AND taken charge of, by yearly contract, on moderate terms. COMPLICATED ACCOUNTS ADJUSTED, DEEDS, CONTRACTS, &c. faithfully drawn up—COPYING and all kinds of WRITING executed with fidelity and despatch, by **G. N. COMER**, ACCOUNTANT, 17 State street.

Mr. COMER respectfully announces that he continues to receive into his office, Students of all ages, for instruction in Commercial

WRITING,

BOOK-KEEPING,

and the PRACTICAL DUTIES OF THE COUNTING ROOM, upon as moderate terms as those of the "Academies."

☞ Each Pupil is taught by himself, and *not in a class.*

No Stenography, Card Marking, or twelve lesson humbug!

MERCHANTS supplied with competent Clerks.

The Subscribers have their Order Boxes at G. N. Comer's, 17 State street.

Horn, Sinclair & Co.	*Lumber Dealers.*
T. L. Rayner & Co.	*Slaters.*
West & McIntyre,	*Lumber Dealers.*
Luther Barnes,	*Composition Worker.*
Gillum Barnes,	" "
Paul & Wilson,	*Housewrights.*
Thomson & Jenkins,	*Builders and Plasterers.*
R. W. Turner,	*Painter and Glazier.*
John V. Ford,	*Paper Hangings.*
John W. Rollins,	*Builder.*
William Jordan,	*Dealer in Scythes.*
Edward B. Parshley,	*Builder and Contractor.*

We note the appearance of the Binney family all working out of 33 Long Wharf. One or more of the group was in business from 1826 to 1835. I was down on Long Wharf recently and noted two old advertisements still quite visible on the end of the old Custom House Block. They read:

"Established 1831
Martin L. Hall Co.
Shapleigh Coffee Co.
Coca Tea Coffee"
and

"Boxell's School of Navigation"

Maybe the Binneys kept the books for Martin L. Hall Co.

The other interesting item in the 1830 list is the repeat performance of Peter C. Brooks who was also listed in the 1820 list - the second entry to appear as in business more than a decade, Frederick Beck being the first.

We note also three descriptive terms now appearing - namely counting room, accountant, and bookkeeper - with no clear indication of the relative differences in these terms except that Frederick Beck, referred to in the 1820's, labelled himself "accountant" and his advertisement in 1822 suggests a broad degree of proficiency.

The 1840 Directory continues a representative list:

Samuel Baker	bookkeeper	house 19 Warren
Daniel A. Brown	counting room	31 India
Samuel Cleland	bookkeeper	39 S Market
J. M. Colburn	accountant	house 2 Sewall pl.
Gardner Greenleaf	counting room	Broad cor Pearl
Samuel Greenleaf	counting room	51 Kilby, house 16 Winthrop pl.
Calvin S. Lane	accountant	34 Union, house 6 S Cedar
Melvin Lord	counting room	131 Wash house 37 Bowdoin
George W. Pearson	bookkeeper	Pavilion
T. M. Pettingill	bookkeeper	45 Kilby, boards 24 Howard
A. Pope	bookkeeper	house 3rd street near Dorchester
John C. Tebbets	counting room	14 Water
Nathaniel Tracy	counting room	17 Central wharf
Thomas Tremlett	counting room	28 Fosters wf.
Henry Van Wart, Jr	counting room	91 Kilby

Samuel C. Ware	bookkeeper	boards 1 Acorn
Benjamin F. White	counting room	77 Milk, house 133 Tremont
Moses Whiting	counting room	6 Cornhill court
Horatio B. Wilbur	bookkeeper	house 5 Vernon

Again we see the mix of counting room, accountant and bookkeeper with "bookkeepers" beginning to proliferate. Thomas Tremlett and Moses Whiting are new additions to the ten year list, both appearing also on the 1830 list, and Samuel Greenleaf was listed in the 1820 list.

The 1840's also give us a closer look at the day to day work of the public accountant of the times. George N. Comer appears in the 1842 Directory as:

Comer. Geo. N. broker & account. Wilson la h 65 Myrtle

He operated a school and for a time acted as an accountant. Later the school was expanded to a full-blown "Commercial College," which, operated in later days probably by his son, was still going strong in 1900. He also wrote a text book which was published in 1844, with later editions at intervals. His advertisement in the Boston Directory of 1845 is interesting -

HAND WRITING

BOOKS POSTED, &c

> And taken charge of, by yearly contract, on moderate terms. COMPLICATED ACCOUNTS ADJUSTED, DEEDS, CONTRACTS &c faithfully drawn up-
>
> COPYING and all kinds of WRITING executed with fidelity and despatch, by G. N. COMER, ACCOUNTANT, 17 State Street
>
> Mr. Comer respectfully announces that he continues to receive into his office Students of all ages, for instruction in Commercial -

WRITING

BOOK-KEEPING

and the PRACTICAL DUTIES OF COUNTING ROOM, upon moderate terms as those of the "Academies"

Each pupil is taught by himself, and not in a class

No Stenography, Card Marking, or twelve lesson humbug!

MERCHANTS supplied with competent Clerks.

The advertisement also lists twelve small businessmen who kept their "Order Boxes" at G. N. Comer's. George was a busy fellow, and his advertisement tells us a lot. His daily work is the usual mixture of accountng and semi-legal work, but his remarks about his teaching methods are interesting - especially the bit about "twelve lesson humbug." He evidently had a low opinion of the level of instruction in the so called private academies. We note also his final "Merchants supplied with competent Clerks." From this we surmise that listings in the Directories referring to accountants, compting rooms, or bookkeepers indicate something above the level of the many "clerks" listed in the Directories. I estimated about 500 "clerks" listed in the 1840 Directory.

Another advertisement for a school appears in 1842 as follows:

L. KENT'S (Commercial) School
(Over 23 Harvard Place, opposite the Old South Church)
for
PENMANSHIP, BOOKKEEPING &c
BOSTON, July 4, 1842

In 1844 Lewis Kent moved the school to 35 Beach Street with "Accommodation for Permanent and Transient Boarders" and added an evening school.

The list of accountant and "counting rooms" culled from the 1846 Boston Directory continues to grow-

Joseph H. Allen	accountant	h 306 Washington
Israel W. Bourne	accountant	boards U. S. Hotel

Charles Brentnell	accountant	h 4 McLean court
George N. Comer	counting room	17 State
William C. Fay	accountant	49 India wf, h 454 Washington
B. Wood Foster	accountant	109 Wash h 21 S. Bennet
Elisha V. Glover, Jr	accountant	h 20 Bridge
Samuel Jones	accountant	h 6 Oneida
Charles B. Locke	counting room	428 Washington
Melvin Lord	counting room	131 Wash, h 37 Bowdoin
George Patterson	accountant	h 20 Purchase
Thomas Tremlett	counting room	28 Foster's Wf.
Andrew E. Turner	accountant	475 Wash. h West RR Ho.

The years from 1840, however, showed a veritable explosion in "bookkeepers." The 1840 Directory listed 7 bookkeepers. The 1846 Directory listed 53. Apparently Goerge Comer's "no humbug" methods, or perhaps those of Lewis Kent, were beginning to have an effect.

Of the 1846 accountants, Melvin Lord was in the 1840 list and Thomas Tremlett gets the long service award. He was working out of Foster's wharf in 1830. We note the term "counting room" gradually falling into disuse apparently in favor of accountant. B. Wood Foster joined the list of Massachusetts authors with a rather ordinary little textbook published in 1843. Like many of his contemporaries, he wanted to do away with the Journal.

So much for the men. But what of their endeavours? Of the books written during the period, Harry Bentley has said - "On the whole, our writers of 1800 to 1850 were more experienced and scholarly than those of the following fifty years, and their books were superior in scope and treatment." I would add that in my opinion, Mitchell's book, the first published, was probably the best. The accountant of 1850 was familiar with accounting for proprietorships, partnerships, and joint ventures; with accounting for retailers, wholesalers and commission agents; with consignments, bills of exchange, and foreign exchange. He regularly accrued interest, and some of them recognized the need to set up reserves for bad debts.

The textbooks recognize the need for periodic inventories, but cannot decide whether these should be at cost or at selling price. In general, property, real and personal, was treated as just additional inventory to be valued on some basis each year.

The principal advances since 1800 were the adoption of specialized Day Books, use of columnar analysis sheets, and the gradual recognition of the role and importance of financial statements - not a great step forward. But the average business was still small, still a proprietorship or partnership, and still made use of little in the way of machinery.

There was one outstanding exception during the last decade prior to 1850 - the railroads. Construction of the first lines in Britain and America got under way in the early 1830's and from the start required large amounts of capital which could only be obtained from large numbers of investors who expected some form of an accounting. Furthermore, the long construction period meant there could be no regular earnings in most instances for several years. Early rolling stock was subject to rapid obsolescence, and wear and tear and heavy maintenance charges became obvious facts of doing business. So the railroad accountant between 1835 and 1850 was face to face with bewildering new problems including a corporate form of doing busines, stock subscriptions, sinking fund debt, interest during construction, the need to distinguish between capital and other expenditures, and depreciation. By 1850 he was a long way from solutions, but in grappling with them the accountant began to attain status.

Also, within the railroads, the complexity of administration which had to provide for obtaining state charters, negotiating rights of way, raising capital, constructing and maintaining lines, acquiring and repairing equipment, establishing passenger and freight business and setting rates - all created a need for strong centralized fiscal control in a Treasurer's department, backed up by an internal "audit department" which "audited" all receipts and expenditures passing through the system.

Speaking of conditions in England, Lawrence R. Dicksee in 1897 said --"It was not until the middle of the present (nineteenth) century that any real vitality existed in Accountancy as a profession, but a great impetus was given about this time by the application of the recent discovery of steam as a motive power to railways, and during the railway mania (1841 - 1857) there arose a considerable demand for persons skilled in accounts which gave a great fillip to the profession."

This was as true of New England as of old England, and the annual reports of, for instance, the Massachsuetts Western Rail Road Corporation prior to 1850 are surprisingly detailed, well designed, and provide a wealth of meaningful monetary and statistical information.

Modern financial and cost accounting, and much of today's auditing techniques can be traced to experience with these early railroads. The British public accountants, backed by early Companies Acts, used these experiences to blaze a trial to the broad highway of modern accounting. Without such legislation the American and New England accountant continued to meander in the accounting byways of an earlier age for almost fifty more years.

Boston Shipbuilding and Buildings - 1850 (Courtesy of Bostonian Society)

CHAPTER EIGHT

ACCOUNTING AND ACCOUNTANTS IN MASSACHUSETTS - PART THREE

William Holmes

1850 - 1890

The population of Boston in 1850, including East and South Boston, was approximately 140,000. During the four decades through 1890 the city expanded both in physical size and in the number of people calling it home. Land filling went on almost continuously. Old Fort Hill was leveled in the late 1860's and the soil used to fill in the waterfront and to provide the foundation for Atlantic Avenue and what became the market district. The Back Bay was in process of filling throughout most of the period, adding 570 acres to the city by 1890. In addition, during the period Roxbury, West Roxbury, Dorchester, Brighton, and Charlestown became officially part of Boston, which in 1890 could boast a population of approximately 450,000 souls - a threefold increase in forty years.

This same period saw the City and State surge ahead economically. The 1850's was the decade of the Clipper ships with Donald McKay, Samuel Hall, and R. E. Jackson bringing glory to East Boston with clippers like "Gamecock," "Stag Hound," and "Flying Cloud." Their owners - the Forbes, Russells, and Danas -added to their already considerable fortunes servicing the California goldrush trade and it has been said that the entire $70,000 to $80,000 cost of one of these ship could be recouped from one successful California voyage.

The railroads pressed ahead also during this period. Early State legislation gained for Massachusetts railroads a reputation for sound finance and after the early years of building, the latter years of the period saw a drive for consolidation of smaller railroads into larger units. However, the New England railroads could not provide wide enough horizons for her thriving bankers and merchants who funneled their resources into ventures further afield. Francis R. Hart, Vice Chairman of the Board of Directors of the Old Colony Trust Company, in an article written about 1915 tells us that between 1850 and 1890 Boston capital made possible the Union Pacific, the Atchison, Topeka & Santa Fe, Chicago, Burlington & Quincy, the Oregon railroads, the Mexican Central, and many others.

This period also saw the founding of many of the State's shoe and leather companies, of the expansion of its textile businesses, the continued growth of printing and publishing, and the establishment of a wide diversity of other industries.

Surely with all this economic hustle and bustle the state of accounting in Massachusetts might have been expected to surge ahead. Similar conditions in Britain about this time provided the necessary impetus and nudged accountants towards professionalism. In early 1950's the Scottish accountants petitioned Victoria, Queen of all the Britons, Empress of India and Defender of the Faith, and obtained her Gracious consent to form an Institute. The Scottish Chartered Accountant thereupon waded into the stormy seas of industry and finance, and fifty years later was second only to whisky in that country's exports. After a decent interval of about fifteen years, the English Institute also tried the waters. The American accountant was well aware of these happenings and might have been expected at least to wade a little. He didn't! -Neither in Massachusetts, nor elsewhere in these United States.

THE PROFESSION - 1850 - 1865

In Massachusetts, for some reason I have not been able to determine, the number of what might be called public accountants, at least in the first fifteen of this forty year period, shrunk almost to nothing. In Part Two of this three part series we noted thirteen "accountants" or "counting rooms" listed in the 1846 Boston Directory, including several established in business ten to twenty years. The 1850 Directory, in its new classified Business section, under the heading ACCOUNTANTS AND COPYISTS lists only two names that would seem to qualify as public accountants. These are -

Comer, G.N. 139 Washington St.

Leavitt, T. H. 15 Merchants Ex.

Comer is our old friend George, whom we met in Part Two - still busy with his college which kept growing in size and probably not too interested in "adjusting complicated accounts" except as a side line. That leaves T. H. Leavitt. Ethel Kingman in her "Accountancy in Massachusetts" made note of this and suggests he was the gentleman referred to in Richard Brown's "History of Accountants" (1904) as having commenced business in Boston in 1847 and who "for a year or two was the sole representative of the profession in that city." This would appear to be true, at any rate in 1850.

Things weren't much better in 1855 when the only public accountants appear to have been -

Holbrook, Geo. 75 State St. Accountant

Leavitt, T. H. 1 Phoenix Building, Notary public, accountant, and adjuster of marine losses

May, Geo. P. 31 Exchange Accountant

- and the number stayed at about three through 1865 with Holbrook and Leavitt the anchor men.

However, if Boston and Massachusetts were lacking in professional accountants during these fifteen years, they were not remiss in turning out bookkeepers. It was as though the American genius for mass production which developed in the next century decided to have an early trial run with accounting. Instead of developing a "few good men," to quote a modern advertisement, they produced a plethora of merely adequate bookkeepers. They created not a profession but a profusion! - and the medium was a new style "Commercial college."

THE BUSINESS COLLEGES

There is some controversy over just who started the first "business college" in America. We have made various reference to teachers of bookkeeping in Boston during the 1700's and early 1800's, but most of their ventures seemed to have been on a small scale and comparatively short-lived. Harry Bentley in his Brief Treatise on the Origin and Development of Accounting (1929) recorded his vote for James Arlington Bennett who published his own textbook on bookkeeping and conducted public lectures in New York City in 1818. The New York City directories still list him as "teacher in bookkeeping" until 1835. The tenth edition of his textbook, issued in 1828 listed 1,500 names of people who had attended his courses.

Boston's George Comer started his school in 1840, and we have seen his 1845 "no twelve lesson humbug" advertisement in Part Two of this series. The college continued to flourish, was in due course handed over to his son, and was in business as Comer's Commercial College as late as 1917. The school was originally operated from 17 State Street, George Comer's business address as an accountant. The

COMER'S

COMMERCIAL COLLEGE,

BOSTON.

Granite Building, No. 666 Washington Street,

(CORNER OF BEACH STREET.)

FOUNDED A.D. 1840.

GEORGE N. COMER, A.M., President.

Open every business day (six days in the week) throughout the year, from 9 to 2 o'clock. Evenings between 1st October and 1st April, from 7 to 9 o'clock.

Specimens of styles of handwriting taught, will, on request, be sent by mail with this Register, or may be had FREE at the College.

☞ **Please circulate this among your neighbors.** ☜

location was moved several times as the school expanded, but in 1874 it was settled into the Granite Building at the corner of Washington and Beach streets. In the 1874 Annual Register of the college George tells us the new premises constituted "eight elegant rooms, all on one floor, lighted on three sides by twenty-seven large plate-glass windows, up only two flights of an extra broad stairway.....with accommodations for three hundred students at one time without the slightest crowding." The enrollment for that year included 455 gentlemen and 105 ladies, and a review of the Catalogue of Students shows students in attendance from Norway, England, Russia, Sweden, Germany, and Ireland. The large majority were, of course, from New England with a fair sprinkling from other Eastern states and Nova Scotia.

The courses offered included a general Commercial Course, Bookkeeping, Banking, Penmanship, Commercial Correspondence, Arithmetic and Commercial Computations, and Practical Navigation. The principles of double-entry, according to the curriculum "can certainly be learned in thirty working-days." A working day was "four or five hours per day," so George was figuring on about 120 to 150 hours of effort - an improvement certainly on "twelve lesson humbug."

There were ten listed Rules and Regulations for students and numbers five and six are worth noting as signs of the times.

> 5. No talking, whispering, laughing or other improper noise, grimacing or gesticulating, lounging, or collecting in groups, is permitted.
>
> 6. No spitting on the floor, walls or furniture allowed. Students using tobacco, and those having occasion to spit, must provide themselves with pocket handkerchiefs to spit into. If such people are compelled to carry about them the

unnecessary filth they create, it may help to abolish a vile habit.

George was obviously out to run a high-toned college fit for his "eight elegant rooms" and worthy of his "105 ladies."

I have written at some length on Comer's college to give some idea of the size and scope of these schools as they were operated during these forty years from 1850 to 1890. Comer was not the only fish in the Boston pool. Hanaford & Payson's College, Spears and Sawyers Mercantile and Nautical College, and A. D. Bill's Boston Commercial College were all operating in the 1860's and offering curricula similar to Comer's.

In the meantime, down in Rhode Island three gentlemen - H. B. Bryant, H. D. Stratton, and James W. Lush in 1853 got a lead of about a century on Mr. Donut, Kentucky Fried Chicken, and other latter day franchise operators by establishing the first chain school movement, prescribing their own text books and granting operating rights to suitable licensees around the country. They did well! They also wrote suitable textbooks for use in public schools and academies. Bryant and Stratton didn't move into Boston until 1874 and one suspects they deliberately chose greener pastures elsewhere during the early years rather than tackle the well established competition in Boston.

THE PUBLIC SCHOOLS

Long before the business colleges, bookkeeping had been taught in the public schools of America. Most of the early writers in America, including Turner, Bennett, Preston, and Comer, had the school market very much in their minds. However, indications are that the quality of the teaching was somewhat limited at least in the early 1800's. Preston, for instance, divides his Treatise on Bookkeeping (1831) into two parts, the first a forty page dissertation on single entry bookkeeping and designed "with a view not only to make it useful as a school book, but with a particular desire also to adapt it to the business of Mechanics." And it is likely that in the early days of this century the number of teachers in the common schools capable of teaching a full course in double entry was small.

Harry Bentley in his "Brief Treatise," mentioned previously, quotes a number of authorities on the subject, including the following from "The History of Education," by Cubberley--

> "The first high school in the United States was established in Boston, in 1821. For three years it was known as the 'English Classical School,' but in 1824 the school appears in the records as 'English High School'......The real beginning of the American high school as a distinct institution dates from the Massachusetts Law of 1827, enacted through the influence of James G. Carter. The law is significant in that it required a high school in every town having 500 families or over, in which should be taught United States history, bookkeeping, algebra, geometry, and surveying.'

So Massachusetts was to the fore in introducing its young into the mysteries of accounting in the public school system and the number of qualified teachers undoubtedly grew as the city grew and the number of high schools multiplied. As time went by the standard of teaching must also have improved. It is interesting that Charles C. Kurtz (1828-1918) who, at age 83, was honoured at a special meeting of the Incorporate Public Accountants of Massachusetts in 1910 as 'Dean of the Profession,' learned his bookkeeping, according to the minutes of the meeting, "at school in 1841 at the English High School in this city."

The city's schools maintained the tradition into the 1850-1890 period were are now considering. I have in my collection a copy of Bryant and Stratton's

Common School Book-keeping, the 1878 edition, inscribed by the owner in a fair round hand "Mary G. Harkins, Ninth Grade." Like the earlier text books it is in two parts, single entry and double entry, and Mary's homework tick marks come to a sudden stop at the end of Part One. Double entry was presumably reserved for the tenth and later grades. So the school system started the mass production system carried further by Comer's, Bryant and Stratton and the other business colleges around town.

I believe the real training ground for a better grade of accountant during the period was neither the school system nor the business colleges. The graduate of these institutions who became a bookkeeper in a small local business would have little to excite his imagination. The "action" was elsewhere - in the railroads.

THE RAILROADS

I have occasionally tried to visualize myself as chief accountant for one of the early railroad corporations - say about 1835. To begin with I was probably coming face to face with the corporate form of doing business for the first time, with no textbooks and no precedents to guide me. If I was in New England my capital was probably a mixture of local capital, long-term sinking fund debt raised in England, some local privately placed debt, and a little later on, possibly some State funding. My share capital was subscribed for and was collected through a succession of "calls." The debt was entitled to interest from the day borrowed, but during a long initial construction period I had no income. So willy-nilly, I capitalized the interest during construction. So much for the source of my funds.

On the disbursement side I was dealing with a variety of local contractors building roadbeds, laying lines, and bridging rivers over a long stretch of miles, all the construction designed by engineers who were not at all sure of the problems involved. At the same time I was placing orders for new fangled locomotives and rolling stock. As the line stretched out I was trying to determine how much to charge for passenger service, and how much for freight, and to collect money all up and down the line, with no real price guides to help me. I was almost forced into developing some measuring standards - ton miles, passenger miles, locomotive miles, as guides to measure my progress along the way. And my schooling was probably somewhat limited to begin with.

Initially, both in the United States and England, the whole thing was a mess.

In his article "Aspects of Railway Accounting before 1868" Harold Pollens, commenting mainly on British railroads, but mentioning parallel conditions in America, says -

> "Many of the companies were large; some in the 1860's had a paid-up capital of as much as $30 - $40 million. They needed highly elaborate systems of accounting and financial control to avoid misappropriation of resources. Not all of them had the necessary safeguards. Several published Reports and accounts reveal that the secretary or treasurer had absconded with the funds, and registrars misappropriated dividends by forging stock..... A study of the methods adopted by the companies to prevent financial irregularities would usefully add to our knowledge of the history of financial administration in business concerns." (underlines added)

Another quote from the same article says-

> "In 1850 the Times referred to the financial affairs of the Caledonian Railway Company in these terms. 'The Caledonian Railway Company, the work neither of Lawyers, nor of old women, nor spendthrifts, but of shrewd middle-aged mercantile men, is just such a tangle as one might dream of after supping on lobster salad and champagne.'"

The problem to some extent was that accounting, like nature, "abhors a leap." It took time to develop new ideas, new systems, and new techniques to meet the new circumstances. However, by the 1850's obvious signs of progress - and progress in New England - are there.

To overcome the problems of control, remarked on by Polens, New England railroads created divisional and functional control. The line itself was divided into sections each under a superintendent. Each section was responsible for its repairs and maintenance of the line and rolling stock. The superintendent was responsible for dealing with the local contractors and subcontractors. Each section had its "accountants" who reported to a central Treasurer's office. At the same time an Auditors' department was formed which vouched all bills prior to payment, checked section and divisional payrolls, audited passenger and freight receipts, and reported to the Directors on the correctness of the Treasurer's accounts. Their reports were included in the Annual Report to the stockholders. Here is an example taken from the 1856 Annual Report of the Western Rail Road Corporation whose headquarters were in Springfield, Mass.

AUDITOR'S REPORT

To the President and Directors)
of The Western Rail Road).

GENTLEMEN:

In discharge of my duties as Auditor, I have once each month during the past year, thoroughly examined the Books of the Treasurer, ascertained that the amount of moneys received and paid out, were correctly entered upon his books from the proper vouchers in his possession, and that the balance represented to be on hand by his cash book, was actually on deposit in various Banks, as shown on the first day of each month by their accounts current and books of deposit.

A statement of transfers made and a balance sheet of the Stock Ledger has been handed in to you monthly by the Treasurer, examined and certified by me as correct. Having been engaged in making up the dividends for the past three years, I can with confidence assert that the whole number of Shares issued by the Western Rail Road Corporation on which Dividends have been paid is 51,500.

The accounts of the Treasurer have been compared with those of the Cashier at Springfield and found to agree.

The books of the different Departments at Springfield and at the Stations on the Road are well kept, and written up to the end of the year.

Annexed you have a list of the uncollected freight at Stations for the year ending November 30, 1855, showing the amount unpaid on the 15th day of December to be $448.92.

Yours, Very Respectfully,

WILLIAM RITCHIE, Auditor.

Boston, Dec. 27, 1855.

An even more interesting example is that included in the Annual Report of the Boston & Worcester Railroad for 1857. The entire Auditor's Report is spread over four full pages but the following excerpts will give the flavor of it.

Boston & Worcester Railroad,
Auditor's Office, Jan. 14, 1857

To the President and Directors:

Most prominent among the duties of this office, is that of examining and approving all the bills, payrolls, or other claims against the Corporation, prior to their payment by the Treasurer.

In order to perform this duty satisfactorily, the Auditor ought to know personally the value of all articles purchased, or services rendered..........

As an additional protection against error, and to insure the means for immediate reference to the original account which has in any case been allowed, I have adopted a plan by which all the bills are retained in this office, and in their place a certificate sent to the Treasurer, which describes each one in a few words, and upon being receipted, serves every purpose as proof of payment.

These certificates, as well as all other vouchers in the

Treasurer's hands for charges on his books, have been examined both by the Auditor and Committee on Accounts, and found uniformly correct and satisfactory.........

Another and important portion of an Auditor's duty should be to inform himself as to all the sources of revenue, and see that each produces its proper amount.

PASSENGERS

The amount to be received from Passengers and Freight constitutes the great bulk of income on all roads, and is affected primarily by the schedule of prices charged, that being determined by the Directors through the Superintendent.

Each of the departments is in charge of an efficient head, and in their respective offices it is ascertained whether the several agents on the road account for all the tickers or the freight bills with which they stand charged.

So far as the sale of tickets is concerned, there is no difficulty in imposing a sufficient check. But all passengers do not purchase tickets, and I believe their number increases year by year, and that the rule which has been made in regard to such is either of no use or not enforced.

In this respect I think there should be a change.

FREIGHT

The quantity and price of freight to each station having been properly billed, the agent is charged therefor, and then as the several sums due are collected and returned, they are checked off and the charge cancelled.........

It is very clear that a short road, at the terminus of a long line, cannot afford to incur large risks in the collection of monies of which so small a portion comes for its own service.

Such risk should either be avoided altogether, or shared by other parties to the same business.

MAIL, RENTS, ETC.

The amount received for mail service is determined by contracts with the government, and requires but little notice.

The income from rents is becoming more and more important, and requires constant care.

A schedule of all property under rent is kept in this office, with which the collections are from time to time compared.

SALES OF OLD MATERIALS

These sales are made only by the Superintendent, or under

his direction.

The amount is returned through this office to the Treasurer, and by him credited to the proper accounts.

TRANSFERS OF STOCK

All stock certificates signed by the President, are recorded in the Auditor's office, and copies kept of all transfers of stock by the treasurer.

The stock ledger and dividend books have been carefully compared and found correct.

I annex the Treasurer's trial balance at the close of the month of November 1st, and a condensed statement of the financial condition of the Corporation on that day........

All which is respectfully submitted,

DAVID WILDER, Jr., Auditor.

As can be seen, this is not only an "Auditor's Report" on the Treasurer's accounts but an early form of Auditor's Letter to Management on weaknesses in control with recommendations for improvement, and indicative of a sophistication entirely absent from accounting texts of the times.

Depreciation was a knotty problem for these early railroad accountants. They argued over it, scorned it, denied it, anatomized it, and misused their own concepts. But in the end it was from the very ashes of their disagreements that out modern concepts of depreciation rose Phoenix-like fifty years later.

The railroad accountant did something more. He gradually standardized his practice. The ICC did not get round to prescribing a uniform chart of accounts for the railroads until 1906, but the Railroad Gazette in 1876 published a 265page book entitled "Railway Disbursements and the Accounts into Which They are Naturally Divided" which is indicative of the state of the railroad accountant's art at that time. It gives excellent instructions as to the proper use of "betterment" accounting, lucid examples of the distinction between construction and repairs and maintenance, a complete chart of accounts, instructions for the proper charges to each account and a complete set of divisional reporting forms. It also gives instructions to the auditors how best to audit each account.

Some of the instructions bring a nostalgic tear to the eye. Included under "Furniture and Fixtures for Cars" are the following:

> "bulls-eye lamps, curtains, dippers, fire buckets, feather dusters, lamp chimneys, pokers, stoves, stove fixtures, spittoons, waste buckets, wash basins, etc."

It is a sobering thought when we listen to the old railroad folk songs of Casey Jones and the "Wreck of Old 99" that somewhere, sometime a railroad accountant had to decide how to account for the repair of "Old 99" and turned for guidance to this little book. It didn't fail him. Rule 16 reads --

> "When an engine is rebuilt wholly or in great part, an account should be opened with it, as, say, "Rebuilding Engine No. 25", and the total cost of rebuilding should be charged up under such heading."

The rebirth of "Old 99!" - and the birth most probably of job order cost accounting.

THE PROFESSION - 1865 - 1890

So much for the business colleges, the public schools and the railroads. What of our erstwhile public accountants while all this was going on? We looked at them last in 1865 when only Holbrook & Leavitt were holding the fort. By 1870 the garrison could muster eight names. A. R. Turner joins the ranks, arriving on the parade ground in 1868, and from the first describing himself as an "Auditor of Accounts," a description he retained throughout his working life. His initial advertisement in the Boston Directory in 1868 reads -

A. R. Turner
Auditor of Accounts
No. 30 Court Street
Boston

> Will attend to matters pertaining to the Arrangement, Examination and Settlement of Accounts; act as Treasurer, Secretary, Auditor and Transfer Agent of Corporations, Corporation Accounts being a specialty.

I like this advertisement! It has a much more professional ring to it than the old "complicated accounts adjusted" of the 1840's. We note too the Corporation taking over as the medium for doing business.

Charles C. Hurtz, whom we mentioned earlier as being recognized in 1910 at the age of 83 as "Dean of the Profession" also makes his bow in 1870. His bookkeeping teacher at English High in 1841 would have been proud.

By 1875 the platoon increased to eleven names, including all those mentioned by name above. Turner's address is now given as "Treasurer's office B&MRR." In light of the earlier discussions of railroad accounting problems, I believe it likely he was rendering some special service to the Boston & Maine.

Charles T. Plimption is listed as at "accountant" in 1878. He has the honor to be the first auditor of the American Bell Telephone Company, which commenced business in 1880. I think the first audit certificate of this great corporation is worth printing.

> Boston, March 21, 1881
>
> I hereby certify that I have audited the books and accounts of the Treasurer of the National Bell Telephone Company, from March 1, 1880, and of the books and accounts of the American Bell Telephone Company from their commencement in May 1880, to March 1, 1881, as follows:-
>
> The cash books, their debits and credits, journalizings,

postings, stock ledger, bank accounts, trial balances and cash on hand.

In my investigations have found everything in connection with the above correct, and that all disbursements as entered in cash books are sustained by approved vouchers, and that the books are kept with accuracy.

Charles T. Plimpton, Auditor

In 1880 Plimpton was working out of 40 Water Street, Room 60, which he shared with Henry A. Piper who joined the club about that time. They may have carried on some kind of partnership, although until 1898 Plimpton's name alone appears on the audit certificates of the Telephone Company. He appears to have retired in that year and the audit was then taken over by his room-mate, Henry A. Piper. Piper, is, of course, one of the early members, although not a charter member, of the Incorporated Public Accountants of Massachusetts.

By 1880 nineteen "Account and Book Adjusters" were listed in the Directory plus our old friend Turner, still the sole name listed under the heading Account Auditors. The list includes another founding member of the Society in George T. Stoddard. One address is noticeable. Gustavus V. Hall operated out of "35 Old State House." The Old State House was a business building until aobut 1882 when it was turned into the museum most of us fail to notice every day. Room 35 may be the last address of a public accountant from the 1880's we can still visit.

The number of public accountants continued to grow, and the title of the Directory listing changed to the more modern "Accountants and Auditors" in 1881. By 1885 thrity-four names were listed. The most significant addition in that year was Rodney McLaughlin, one of the incorporators in 1887 of the Amercian

Association of Public Accountants, the first national organization and later to become the American Institute of Accountants. McLaughlin became a member of its first council.

Beyond 1885 there seems little point in further "numbering" the accountants listed in the Directory. The profession was well established and moving quickly towards a higher standard of professionalism. Most of the founding members of the Incorporated Public Accountants of Massachusetts were on board and advertising their expertise in a thoroughly competitive and uninhibited American Style. The first British accountants on the scene appear to have been Edmund Willcox and W. Norton-Reed & Co., who are listed in the Directory in 1890. They also were not modest about peddling their wares. One advertisement reads-

> W. Norton-Reed & Co.
> Public and Consulting
> Accountants and Auditors
> Yearly Contracts for Auditing
> Experts specially experienced in Partnership and Corporation work; Arbitrations and References; Marine, Stockbrokers' and Fire Insurance accounts and claims; also English methods and trade customs. Conditions of Firms and Corporations examined and certified to for Banks, Investors, or Creditors, Accounts made of for Assignees, Trustees or Executors in due form for filing in Courts or otherwise. Negotiations privately advised and conducted for firms requiring additional capital
> 21 Pemberton Square

SUMMARY AND CONCLUSION

The tantalizing question is the reason for the near disappearance of practising public accountants between 1850 and 1865. One possible reason is the general upgrading of the city's bookkeepers as a result of the school and business college programs. The role of many of the older "accountants" prior to 1850 seems to have been as experts who helped their lesser trained bookkeeper brethren unravel the tangled webs they had woven. They advertise themselves as "adjusters of complicated accounts." As the supply of competent bookkeepers increased the need for such assistance declined. And there was as yet no real demand for purely auditing services. Furthermore, at about this time the railroads were looking for all the expert accounting assistance they could find, but as employees and not as consultants. Competent men who might have become public accountants had a new attractive field open to them, inside the railroads.

The role of the independent public accountant as auditor, which became the predominant factor in building the profession in Britain, prevailed in Britain because it was backed up by legislation creating a market for this role. Britain got the equivalent of the United States SEC Acts in the 1860's with provision for adequate accounting disclosure and certification by independent auditors.. No such legislation was forthcoming in America for another 70 years.

However, a new consulting role for the public accountant in America began to open up in the 1870's. The Corporate form required some concepts beyond the ordinary bookkeeper, and the growth of manufacturing corporations with complex inventories also required a high degree of expertise. So we find the advertisements of public accountants from this period stressing this semi-consulting role. A legitimate question might be to ask by what process the public accountant acquired this additional expertise. Few advanced textbooks were available and advanced college teaching was still twenty years off. The most probable answer is a blend of experience and natural selection. The individual had to do his own thinking on accounting matters without the crutch of AICPA Committees, SEC regulations, and Cost Accounting Standard Boards, a condition conducive of natural selection, and a few vibrant and hardy bubbles made it to the surface out of the body of an otherwise flat champagne.

Ethel Kingman commenting on these pioneers composed a fitting benediction. She wrote -

> "Those early accounting practices had for the most part been built up by men, each of whom singly wrested a living from society by his own active brain and stubborn courage. Each one was typical of the current phrase of those times - "A self made man."

CHAPTER NINE

PUBLIC ACCOUNTING IN WESTERN MASSACHUSETTS

Ernest Berg

Seventy-Five Years of Growth and Progress

The territory referred to as western Massachusetts embraces all of the Commonwealth lying approximately twenty-five miles west of Worcester running to the New York state line, comprising the principal industrial areas of Springfield, Westfield, Holyoke, Northampton, Greenfield, Pittsfield and North Adams.

The Earlier Years

Western Massachusetts at the turn of the century was well established as a busy and prosperous industrial area with particular emphasis on paper manufacturing and textiles. The City of Holyoke, with its unique system of canals providing efficient and inexpensive water power, was known as the "paper City" and, together with the production of the ingenious U. S. Government "money" paper by Crane Company in Dalton (Pittsfield section), western Massachusetts was the quality paper manufacturing center of the nation. Its textile manufacturing operations, extending all the way to North Adams in the northwest corner of the state, boasted such nationally known names as Skinner Satins, Fair Alpaca, Arnold Print and a host of others.

Into this busy, diversified atmosphere, the profession of public accounting took root, primarily through services provided by the newly established firms

A turn-of-the-century accounting office.

(mainly of Scottish origin) quartered in New York City. However, local and intimate accounting service was lacking and a golden opportunity prevailed for those who could establish a practice and step into the gap. Two such pioneers emerged in the persons of Frederick J. Hillman and Edwin S. Doubleday.

"Major" Hillman was a teacher of "commercial" subjects in the Northampton school system and Mr. Doubleday, a New Yorker, had gained experience and knowledge of western Massachusetts clientele through his contacts as a member of the staff of the venerable and prestigous accounting firm of Barrow, Wade & Guthrie. The ebullient Major Hillman (he is reputed to have worn spats and have carried a cane) founded the New England Audit Company, a firm that prospered from the start and eventually encompassed a clientele with home offices spreading as far afield as Birmingham, Alabama. He was years ahead of his time in the promotion of what is now loosely referred to as "management services" and his consultation services were widely sought by business executives while, at the same time, his firm's audit coverage expanded.

Mr. Doubleday, who established the firm that still bears his name, has the distinction of having been granted Massachusetts CPA certificate #1 which hangs on the wall of the present firm of Doubleday, Allen & Grimaldi of West Springfield where his son, Edwin C. Doubleday, who joined the firm in 1907, presides as senior partner after 68 years of service.

Messrs. Hillman and Doubleday dominated the profession in western Massachusetts until 1914 when an office was opened in Springfield by Clinton H. Scovell and C. Oliver Wellington, two able accountants who had established a partnership in Boston several years before. Scovell, Wellington & Company very quickly assumed a position of leadership, and, as the firm spread throughout the east, its Springfield office, with its rapidly growing volume and staff, became the firm's proverbial tail wagging the dog

That the western Massachusetts area was being properly and adequately supplied with competent accounting and management service by these three principal firms plus the usual complement of individual practitioners and small firms that had come into being, is best exemplified by the reluctance of any national accounting firm to establish a base in western Massachusetts during this period although there were such firms with sizable area clients. Obviously, in those earlier days, generally accepted accounting principles were those so considered by each particular accounting firm to be suitable in relation to its service to a particular client. It was not until 1913 that income taxation became a factor and, undoubtedly, such institutions as the Securities and Exchange Commission, the Accounting Principles Board or the Financial Accounting Standards Board would have been too bold to contemplate.

Depression

This, then, was the rather blissful state of the profession in western Massachusetts when the great depression descended, marking the end, or at least an interruption, of an era. The less hardy members of the industrial community were forced to curtail activities drastically and, in some instances, cease operations entirely, as a result of which accounting services were cut back, especially in the management services areas (cost systems, budgetary controls, etc.) where the western Massachusetts practitioners had been so proficient.

The post depression years brought gradual business recovery to western Massachusetts and the accounting profession grew in expertise and performance with the same three firms dominating the area but with additional small local firms and independent practitioners sharing the recovery. Scovell, Wellington & Company was still under the management of the original partners; Major Hillman had retired to less demanding fields but the firm of New England Audit Company was continued and expanded under the name of Hitchcock & Company, and the Doubleday firm carried on under son Edwin C's able direction, his father having passed away. Among the affluent clientele were such familiar names as Massachusetts Mutual Life Insurance Company, Moore Drop Forging Co. and Package Machinery Company (Scovell Wellington) National Blank Book Co., United States Envelope Co., and Chapman Valve Co. (Doubleday), and American Abrasive Co., A. C. Dutton Lumber Co. and W. F. Young, Inc. - Absorbine Jr. (Hitchcock), all purely local companies, locally serviced. Also, as a source of pride and accomplishment for the area accountants were enterprises, started from scratch, that were assisted and nurtured to fruition in some measure by close association and cooperation between accountant and client; such corporations as Acme Chain Corp., Lestoil, Inc., Stanley Home Products, Inc., Friendly Ice Cream Corp., John H. Breck Corp., and others which attained national prominence. Personal satisfaction and reward evolved from the rather intimate relationships that practice in the smaller community afforded. Then, in addition to these larger business enterprises, there was always the myriad of other types - banks, retailers, hospitals, colleges and sundry others - enough to maintain the staffs of the western Massachusetts practitioners - large and small.

War

The slow, steady growth of the post depression years was suddenly plunged into confusion and chaos with Pearl Harbor. The Springfield Ordnance District was established to monitor war production. Demands from older expanding clients and an ever increasing list of new clients swamped the practitioners. Manpower was disrupted by the call to the armed services of many experienced staff members, and new recruits, at least those with accounting experience, were hard to come by. The complications of excess profits taxes, contract renegotiations and similar war created problems made life quite difficult, albeit profitable, for the area practitioners who were resigned to 10 hour days and 60 hour weeks.

Post War to Present

Many practicing accountants were of the opinion that, after the war, their practices would return to the relative complacency of the late thirties but this was not to be, at least in western Massachusetts. Area industry, greatly enlarged by the wartime bulge, continued to grow and prosper and the accounting profession expanded along with it.

Then, as the post war years rolled on, the impact of corporate mergers and consolidations was felt, causing temporary disturbance to accounting practices in western Massachusetts. Some of the larger area clients were lost to national accounting firms serving the acquiring companies. Also, by this time, most of the original partners of the larger local accounting firms were approaching retirement age and the partnerships faced management problems. Possibly because of this and the growing multi-national aspect of business operations, Scovell Wellington & Company, in 1962, merged with Lybrand Ross Bros. & Montgomery (now Coopers & Lybrand) and, in 1972, Hitchcock & Company was absorbed by Main Lafrentz & Co. In the interim, however, a number of smaller firms had been established and the accounting clientele of western Massachusetts continues to this day to have ample, competent and intimate personal service available from many small accounting firms and individual practitioners.

Among firms currently in practice in western Massachusetts, in addition to the aforementioned original three, are (Springfield) Aaron Smith Bergman & Co., Downey Sweeney & Fitzgerald, Meyers Bros., Handelsman Menzel & Adeletti, Sullivan Piechota & Co. and Fred A. Wright & Co; (Holyoke) Casden & Casden, Greenspan & Greenspan, Joseph D. Kalicka & Co. and Petlock Judelson & Co.; (Westfield) Chapin & Harmon; (Greenfield) Roy B. Chapin & Co., and (Pittsfield) Apple & Albano, plus others too numerous to mention specifically.

Personalities

Departed practitioners who played a prominent part in the history of public accountancy in western Massachusetts and left their indelible imprint upon the profession were, among others: Theodore Woodward, Harold Treworgy, Nelson Foley and Alfred Read (Scovell Wellington), George Hitchcock, Irving Kaplinsky, George Snow and Roland Morse (Hitchcock & Company), Harry Burnett and Donald Snow (Doubleday) and Joseph Cushing, Morton Miner, Harry King, Fred Wright, Jonas Heit, Abraham Greenspan and Henry Downey. Veterans still in the picture (either retired or semi-retired) include Edwin Doubleday (with his 75 year old firm), William Johnston (Scovell Wellington - now Coopers & Lybrand) and Ernest Berg (Hitchcock & Company - now Main Lafrentz) along with others who have ceased to play an active roll in professional affairs.

Educational Support

Western Massachusetts has been fortunate in the regional educational facilities provided for the training of prospective candidates for careers in accountancy. American International College, Western New England College (successor to the Springfield Division of Northeastern University) and the University of Massachusetts at Amherst have been a training ground for junior staff accountants over the years and, in fact, have provided the area firms with recruits when the supply in other areas was totally inadequate. These institutions, with an emphasis on an accounting curriculum not found in many colleges today, have played an important part in the growth and development of public accountancy in western Massachusetts, something for which the practitioners are appreciative and grateful.

On the other hand, the practicing accountants have made their contribution by serving on the faculties of the colleges, particularly in the evening programs. An outstanding example of the extent of this contribution is the case of a practicing certified public accountant and teacher in Springfield who has attained the pinnacle of success as president of American International College, a prime source of well educated accounting graduates. Dr. Harry J. Courniotes, CPA, bears a unique distinction as one of the very few CPA college presidents in the nation, if indeed there are any others, a position he administers with prestige and aplomb. Other area CPAs in practice have entered the teaching profession and have served with distinction, some on a full time basis, but none with the lofty attainment of Dr. Courniotes.

Western Massachusetts Practice and its Relationship with the Massachusetts Society of CPAs

Springfield, the business and industrial center of western Massachusetts is located approximately 90 miles west of Boston. Fifty years ago, this meant about four hours of commuting time. Today, with the Massachusetts Turnpike, the travel time is closer to two hours (from portal to portal). In spite of this reduced time span, active participation of the western Massachusetts group in the Society's meetings in Boston has been understandably lacking, with few exceptions. Round trip travel of four hours to attend a three or four hour meeting may be considered unrewarding unless the subject matter of the meeting is imperative. To supply the local aspect of the Society's activities, a western Massachusetts Regional Committee conducts a program of its own, availing itself of some of the programs produced in Boston in addition to locally oriented seminars and speakers. The matter of Chapters, similar to some of the larger states, geographically, has been proposed from time to time but the membership in the western area is hardly large enough to support or warrant a Chapter, hence the continuation of the Regional Committee plan.

Participation of western area members in the management of the Society also has been rather sparse, again because of the remoteness to central headquarters. However, it has been the established custom of the Society to have at least one member from western Massachusetts on its executive committee and, during recent years, two western members (Ernest Berg - 1962-1963 and Donald Dupre - 1972-1973) were presidents of the Society. At least three members have served on the Massachusetts Board of Public Accountancy: Edwin S. Doubleday many years ago, Ernest Berg 1953-1957 and 1967-1971 (2 terms), and John Sweeney - 1964.

Future

As western Massachusetts continues to grow and develop, the future of public accountancy and the role of the CPA, according to forecast, should follow the progress of CPA's everywhere. The advent of the national firms in Springfield has undoubtedly broadened the base for inter-national service which could not be adequately provided by the strictly local practitioners of the earlier years. However, with new enterprises springing up, developing and prospering under the tutelage and personal contact of the smaller independent practitioners, there always will be a place for individual competency and judgment, regardless of the size of the firm providing the service.

With young men and women, better educated in accounting knowledgeable of business management, continually entering the field, whether in western Massachusetts or elsewhere, opportunities for successful practice in this western portion of the Commonwealth should abound in the future as they have in the past.

CHAPTER TEN

EARLY MASSACHUSETTS ACCOUNTANTS AND FIRMS

Anthony Krzystofik

Public accounting in Massachusetts has been practiced by a number of prominent accountants and firms. Most of these firms have passed from the scene, however, some of these early firms are still in existence today. In practically all of these cases the firms have had a number of name changes either through the addition of partners or mergers. In several cases the lineage of these firms can be traced to accountants who played important roles in the early history of the Society or the profession. In Western Massachusetts two of these early firms are still in existence today. In the case of Doubleday, Allen & Grimaldi, which has been in existence since 1896, the son of the founder Edwin S. Doubleday is still a practicing member of the firm. In the second case, the Springfield office of Main Lafrentz and Company can trace its lineage to the New England Audit Company which was founded by Major Frederick James Hillman in 1906. Both Edwin S. Doubleday and Frederick J. Hillman had important roles in the early history of accounting in Massachusetts. Today the firms they founded are still maintaining this important role in professional accounting in Massachusetts.

Edwin S. Doubleday

Edwin S. Doubleday had the distinct honor of having been presented Massachusetts CPA Certificate Number 1 on January 17, 1910. The first CPA

Registration Act provided that a Board of Certification be established for the registration of public accountants in Massachusetts and the Law designated the Bank Commissioner to administer the Act. In 1909 Mr. Doubleday was appointed by the Bank Commissioner as a member of this first Board of Examiners. The first registration certificates were issued by the Commonwealth through the Office of the Commissioner of Banks under the provision of the General Laws, Chapter 93, Section 37. The certificates were issued annually and required a five dollar renewal fee. A copy of the certificate issued on January 26, 1923 still hangs in the office of the founder's son Edwin C. Doubleday in West Springfield. One of the earlier certificates was returned on the Bank Commission and reportedly was framed and exhibited in the Commissioner's office.

On September 5, 1923, Edwin S. Doubleday was issued Certificate Number 1 by the new Board of Registration authorized under the Acts of 1923, Chapter 470. This certificate also hangs in the office of Edwin C. Doubleday.

Mr. Edwin S. Doubleday was born in Columbus, California on February 3, 1861 and although a native of California his ancestry for generations back was of New England stock. The progenitors of the American Doubledays came to America from England in 1676 and Edwin S. was the eighth generation of that name in the country. He was educated in the public schools of California and New York, graduating with distinction in the class of 1880 from the College of the City of New York. Immediately after graduation he became associated with his father's mercantile establishment in New York. For five years, from 1888 to 1893, he managed a branch of that concern in Australia. In 1896 he withdrew from commercial pursuits to take up the profession of public accounting, first in New York City and then moving to Massachusetts around 1900. He practiced accounting

EDWIN S. DOUBLEDAY
1861 - 1926

EDWIN S. DOUBLEDAY

Certified Public Accountant

Certificate No. 1, Massachusetts

274 Main Street

Telephone 2098

SPRINGFIELD, MASSACHUSETTS.

NEW YORK

41-43 Wall Street	**Telephone**
43-49 Exchange Place	**7517 Hanover**

EDWIN DOUBLEDAY'S ADVERTISEMENT AS SHOWN IN SPRINGFIELD CITY DIRECTORY --- 1911

The Commonwealth of Massachusetts

Department of Civil Service and Registration

Board of Registration of Certified Public Accountants

— BE IT KNOWN THAT —

Edwin S. Doubleday

having passed all examinations and complied with all the requirements prescribed by statute and the Board of Registration of Certified Public Accountants is registered as a

Certified Public Accountant

and is entitled to practice as such and is empowered to assume such title under the authority of Chapter 470 of the Acts of 1923.

In Witness Whereof *this certificate No. 1 is granted this 5th day of September 1923*

Board of Registration of Certified Public Accountants

Edwin J. Pride, Chairman

Daniel B. Lewis, Secretary

EDWIN S. DOUBLEDAY'S CERTIFICATE ISSUED IN 1923
TO REPLACE ORIGINAL CERTIFICATE NO. 1 ISSUED IN 1910

until his death on September 18, 1926.

Edwin C. Doubleday, son of Edwin S. Doubleday, was born on September 25, 1888. He received his early education in Vermont, New York, Baltimore, Springfield and attended prep school in Virginia. He left the Virginia prep school in 1907 and entered the public accounting office of his father. Edwin C. prepared for the CPA examination by taking correspondence accounting courses from Alexander Hamilton Co. He received CPA Certificate Number 447 on February 14, 1925 which still hangs in the office next to his father's certificate.

Both Edwin S. and Edwin C. Doubleday were members of the American Society of Certified Public Accountants, a predecessor organization of the AICPA. Society membership certificate number 2257 issued to Edwin C. Doubleday and number 2258 issued to Edwin S. Doubleday on August 1, 1925 still hang in the West Springfield office of the firm.

Over the past seventy-five years the firm has had the following changes in name and partnerships:

Edwin S. Doubleday
Doubleday, Farquhar & Doubleday
Doubleday, Burnett & Snow
Doubleday, Burnett, Snow & Shea
Doubleday, Snow & Sargent
Doubleday, Snow & Allen
Doubleday, Allen & Grimaldi

George J. Allen and Francis V. Grimaldi are the present partners of Edwin C. Doulbeday.

Edwin C. Doubleday, while now in his 88th year, still is an active member of the partnership. He arrives at his office at nine each day and works until approximately one o'clock in the afternoon. And, if need be, he brings a bag of work home for the rest of the day and over the week-end. Besides his active work day, Mr. Doubleday finds time for fishing, photography, gardening and stamp collecting.

Major Frederick James Hillman

Frederick James Hillman founded and incorporated the New England Audit Company in 1906. The company, in addition to its main office in Springfield, had branches in Boston and Worcester. The company operated chiefly in the northeastern section of the United States but conducted business as far west as Denver, in several of the Southern states and in Canada.

Major Frederick J. Hillman, eighth American generation of this family, was born in Hawley, Massachusetts on March 23, 1879. He spent his early years there and in Northampton. He became a student at Child's Business College in Springfield, later taking courses at Zanerian Art College in Columbus, Ohio. After completing his studies he became a member of the faculty of Child's Business College in Springfield and held this post for several years. The name of the school was changed to the Springfield Business School and Mr. Hillman became the principal of the Commercial Department. During this period Mr. Hillman perfected his skill as a public accountant. In 1906 he founded the New England Audit Company which he was to operate for twenty-two years. He was a fellow of the Certified Public Accountants and one of the first certified public accountants in the Commonwealth.

During his professional career in Springfield he held a number of high offices in civic, political and social organizations. During World War I he served as an officer assigned to the general staff in Washington. In 1927 Major Hillman resigned from public accounting to become executive secretary of the Springfield Chamber of Commerce. In the late 1930's Major Hillman joined the management engineering firm of Stevenson, Jordan and Harrison, Inc. of New York City which he was associated with until his retirement in 1953. Major Hillman returned to Massachusetts to live in Worthington until his death on May 10, 1957.

Harold Peters and Walter Leary assumed control of the original New England Audit Company in 1927 and operated the firm under the name of Hillman, Peters and Leary until April 1, 1929. In 1929 Peters left the firm to become controller of the National Union Radio Tube Company in New York while Walter Leary went into the brokerage business in Boston.

George K. Hitchcock, John R. Quint and Ernest A. Berg assumed control of the firm in 1929 and practiced under the name of Hillman, Peters and Company until 1934. At that time John R. Quint, the manager of the Boston office of the firm, left to establish his own practice in Boston. George K. Hitchcock and Ernest A. Berg reorganized the firm under the name of Hitchcock & Company and operated until 1972 at which time the firm was merged with Main Lafrentz & Co.

It is interesting to note that the public accounting firm originally started by Major Hillman in 1906 is still practicing in Springfield after approximately seventy years of professional service.

CHAPTER ELEVEN

EARLY PUBLIC ACCOUNTANCY IN MASSACHUSETTS

Linda H. Kistler

In this paper, the evolution of public accountancy in Massachusetts will be traced from the 1890s to 1913, when passage of the Sixteenth Amendment to the Constitution revolutionized the American tax system and vastly broadened the profession's opportunities for service. Topics which will be discussed include founding of a professional public accounting society in Massachusetts, events leading to the passage of Massachusetts' first registration act for CPAs and early accounting ethics in Massachusetts.

A Society is Born[1]

The Boston Directory, source of many intriguing fragments of information on early Massachusetts accounting, listed accountants from the very early 1800s. The classification "Accounting and Auditors", however, did not appear until the 1881 Directory; and the heading "Public Accountant", was first used in 1897. By 1900, the names of accountants who were to become the Socoety's founders had appeared for several years in the Directory, and these men undoubtedly were familiar figures in the Boston business community.

Massachusetts was not a pioneer in the development of a public accounting professional organization. An accounting society in New York was formed as early as 1882. However, Massachusetts public accountants did participate in very early professional organizations at the national level before a formal organization was formed within the state. The first national public accounting organization, the American Association of Public Accountants (founded in 1887) lists three Bostonians as signatories to its original constitution and by-laws.

Numerous English public accountants arrived in New York during the 1880s. Their influence apparently was limited to the New York area until around 1895, when three English accountants were known to have opened practices in Boston. Reference to early Bookkeepers' Associations predate 1900. For example, the Massachusetts Institute of Accounts was formed in 1896, and was an outgrowth of the Boston Bookkeepers' Association. These very early organizations apparently were open to all accountants, and records indicate that some public accountants were active members although the focus of these groups was predominatly toward industrial bookkeeping and accounting.

While the formal birth of a professional society of public accountants in Massachusetts occurred on February 13, 1900, the first meeting of the founding group actually took place on October 23, 1899. George S. Chase and his nephew, Harvery S. Chase, who were in public practice on Congress Street, sent a brief invitation to fifteen of the "best known Auditors and Expert Accountants" in Boston. The purpose of the meeting was to discuss what action should be taken with respect to potential legislation on the "Certification of Accountants" by the state. Referring to passage of certification laws in New York, New Jersey, Pennsylvania, Illinois, and Wisconsin, the Chases urged local public accountants to organize themselves in preparation to amend and improve a good bill or to oppose any unsuitable bills that might be proposed in the Massachusetts Legislature.

The initial meeting was attended by only seven of the original invitees and the Chases. Those present decided to issue another invitation to a wider group of practitioners. Harvey S. Chase was appointed Acting Secretary, and the next meeting (called "the first regular meeting of the Massachusetts Society of Public Accountants") was set for February 13, 1900.

The meeting on February 13 and a subsequent meeting on March 6, 1900, were more successful and a Constitution and By-laws were adopted. Although formal incorpoartion took place nearly a year later on February 14, 1901, the Massachusetts Society marks its founding from the original meetings in February and March, 1900.

A review of early records implies that an important objective of the new organization was to lobby for CPA legislation favorable to the members of the new group. The established public objective of the new society was: "...the elevation of the profession of accountancy...and the promotion of the interests of its members." Clearly, a certification law in Massachusetts was a primary concern of the group which was formally chartered under the name, Incorporated Public Accountants of Massachsuetts (IPA).

The Organization

Charter officers of the fledgling Massachusetts Society were: Amos D. Albee, President; William Franklin Hall, Vice President; Harvey S. Chase, Secretary; Charles F. Kellogg, Treasurer; and Augustus Nickerson, Auditor. George S. Chase, Frederick C. Tufts, and William H. Herrick were included on the Executive Committee. Other charter members were Herbert F. French, Charles C. Kurtz, George W. Manson, William C. Newell, Thomas S. Spurr, and George T. Stoddard.

Incorporation of the new accounting group did not go unnoticed. A local press notice called attention to the name of the new organization:

> "The name of the corporation was selected with a view of establishing the title 'Incorporated Accountant' upon as high a plane in the profession in New England, as the title 'Chartered Accountant' has in Old England, or that of 'Certified Public Accountant' in New York and other states, which have adopted the certification of public accountants by the State.
>
> It is quite possible, of course, that Massachsuetts and other New England States may hereafter adopt similar laws for certified public accountants, in which case, very likely, the I.P.A. may be transformed into C.P.A., but until such a law is actually passed by the Legislature, the new corporation proposes to support, to the best of its ability, both the professional duties and the professional rights of its members, as well as those of the profession at large and of the public."

This press reference supports the earlier conclusion that a fundamental objective of the new organization was to assure that any legislation respecting public accounting would be favorable to practitioners.

The American Association of Public Accountants and several state societies also extended a welcome to the new Massachusetts group. The early demonstration of cooperation and assistance between Massachusetts and national and state associations continues today. The Massachusetts Society, other New England state societies, and the American Institute of CPA are closely bound together by common professional objectives and interests. One doubts that Massachusetts' public accounting leaders in 1900 envisioned the far reaching effects of their efforts to unite public accoutants in Boston. During the seventy-five years since the founding group of fourteen Boston Accountants first met, the Massachsuetts Society of CPAs has grown to a flourishing, dynamic organization of more than 3,600 Fellows and Associates.

CPA Legislation

Although the first Massachsuetts public accounting society originated in 1900, a bill for certifying public accountants had been introduced in the Massachusetts Legislature two years earlier, on February 1, 1898. This bill was referred to the Committee on Mercantile Affairs which did not recommend passage; and the bill was rejected on February 24, 1898. Note the efficiency and dispatch with which the proposed legislation was handled. Introduction, study, and rejection of the bill were completed in just 24 days! The expeditious treatment of this bill offers some insights into the simplicity of the legislative process three-quarters of a century ago.

Despite the early rejection of CPA registration, the movement toward licensing public accountants was accelerating across the country; and Massachsuetts was no exception. Addressing the issue directly, Harvey S. Chase (a charter member of IPA) and others signed a petition which accompanied House Bill No. 1031, introduced January 24, 1907, seven years after the Incorporated Public Accountants was founded. The proposed legislation would have established a bpard of registration for accountants in Massachusetts. Principal requirements for certification to practice as an expert public accountant were: to have practiced public accounting for a period of five years, to receive approval by the board, and to pay a $10 fee. On March 12, 1907, the Joint Committee on Ways and Means recommended withdrawal of the bill, and the proposal died.

The 1907 failure didn't deter Massachusetts public accountants. In 1908, William Dillon, then serving as Secretary of IPA, and others introduced a petition together with a similar registration bill (House No. 447). Principal change in the 1908 bill was an increase in the registration fee to $25. The 1908 effort failed, although the Ways and Means Committee recommended that the matter be referred to the next General Court.

In 1909, two bills for certification of public accountants were introduced. House Bill No. 244 was supported by a petition of G. Duthie Strachan (also an IPA member) and others, and Senate Bill No. 182 was supported by William Dillon's petition. The bills were modified by amendments and substitutions, and were finally consolidated during their legislative journeys through both Houses. By May 12, 1909, the amended bill had been passed by both Houses and became effective on October 1, 1909.

The CPA Registration Act provided that a Board of Certification be established for the registration of public accountants in Massachusetts, and the law designated the Bank Commissioner to administer the act. The first Board of Examiners consisting of Amos D. Albee, Edwin S. Doubleday, Herbert F. French, Frederick S. Fuller, and G. Duthie Strachan, was appointed. Merrrs. Albee, French and Strachan were active members of the IPA during this period.

The young organization of Massachsuetts public accountants obviously exercised considerable influence upon the development and successful passage of the first public accountancy registration act in Massachusetts. The historical facts provide clear evidence of the intense involvement of the IPA in support of the law. Unquestionably, these early dedicated accountants influenced enormously the development of the public accounting profession in this state. The professional reputation and collective influence of Massachsuetts CPAs in 1975 owes a large debt to those early colleagues whose efforts culminated with the 1909 passage of a registration law for public accountants.

Early Organization of the IPA

The present organization and by-laws of the Society are necessarily more complex than those of the original group. However, several aspects of the early organization merit discussion because they provide insights into the evolution of the Society and life in Boston 75 years ago.

The objectives of the Incorporated Public Accountants of Massachusetts as stated in the By-laws "shall be social, and for the elevation of the profession of Public Accountant and Auditor and the promotion of the interests of its members." The first objective implies that the group considered social interchange an important function of the organization, although no clear evidence exists to conclude that social aspects were of paramount importance. The second and third objectives probably reflect the fundamental purposes of the organization--to foster professional development and to promote the interests of the membership.

Current by-laws of the society reflect the evolutionary nature of professional development both within the organization and in public accountancy generally. Today, the society's stated objectives are "to unite for common purposes the members of the accounting profession; to promote and maintain high professional and moral standards; to safeguard the interests of Certified Public Accountants; to advance the art of accounting; to develop and improve accounting education; and to encourage cordial relations among accountants." Note the relative positions of the social objectives of the society--first in 1900 and last in 1975. Today, the Massachusetts Society of CPAs emphasizes professional development and maintenance of high professional and ethical standards. Moreover, safeguarding of members' interest is only one of six explicitly stated objectives. In contrast, the protection of members' interests apparently was a strong motivating factor in founding the organization in 1900.

Two classes of members were established in 1900. Fellows, defined as "any male (emphasis added) person who is a citizen of the United States or who has declared his intention of becoming such citizen," comprised the basic membership group. Honorary Membership status could be conferred by unanimous vote of the Fellows present at any regular meeting following submission of a person's name to the Executive Committee. The category of Associate Member was added to the original by-laws in 1905. Male exclusivity was assured by requiring that only "male persons" could apply for associate membership.

Distinctions between Fellow and Associate in the early years were established by the membership requirements. A Fellow was required to have continuously maintained an office and practiced for a period of at least five years during which at least one year immediately preceding application had been spent in Massachusetts. An alternative to the first condition was to have practiced as a public accountant for four years of which at least the last two years had been spent in Masssachusetts. Residency requirements were not necessary for Associate members, but they were required to be in practice and to have been recommended by at least two Fellows of the society.

Each applicant for membership was required to submit recommendations from at least two Fellows, and the Executive Committee was charged with investigating the applicant and reporting to the full membership, which then voted on the candidate. Election was by ballot and three negative votes were sufficient to reject an applicant.

Membership in the early days was not automatic. The minutes of the Executive Committee reveal a strong preoccupation with membership actions, and numerous instances of delays were reported while the worthiness of an individual for membership was investigated. For example, the minutes of the Executive Committee for November, 1910, report that the application of Mr. James D. Glunts was received and action delayed until the next meeting. Then, in January, 1911, the minutes record:

> "The application of Mr. James D. Glunts was read and letters from applicant's references. It was decided that the Committee request further evidence of the candidate's ability and that the Secretary be requested to procure same and present at the next meeting of the Committee."

Finally, in February, 1911, the Executive Committee approved Mr. Glunts' application; and on March 9, the full membership voted to admit him as a Fellow. After a delay of four months, Mr. Glunts' application was approved. Since the entire membership consisted of only 61 Fellows and 4 Associates in 1911, it is obvious that membership was far from automatic. This episode also may reflect the leisurely pace of life in 1910, and contrasts sharply with today's highly structured and complex society.

The Executive Committee occasionally rejected an application for reasons that might be viewed in 1975 as capricious. For example, the minutes of October 8, 1908 Executive Committee meeting reveal an interesting decision:

> A letter from Mr. Horace S. Bassett dated October 3rd was read by the Secretary with reference to his application having been rejected in that he thought that the Executive Committee had rejected the same under a misapprehension and it was voted that the Secretary advise Mr. Bassett that the reason for the rejection was that it had been decided for the present not to admit any more Associate members.

The arbitrary nature of this decision would be unacceptable in a professional

Accountants

2452 BOSTON [1911] DIRECTORY

Incorporated Public Accountants of Massachusetts

*Denotes Certified Public Accountant of Massachusetts

Denotes Honorary Member

FELLOWS

*
ALBEE, AMOS D., 53 State St. Boston
*ALBEE, HERBERT H., 53 State St. "
Pittsfield
BARDWELL, WALLACE E., 124 Summer St. "
Boston
*BASSET, HORACE S., 200 Devonshire St. "
*BISHOP, GEORGE L., 59 Temple pl. "
*BOYDEN, WALTER L., 6 Beacon St. "
*CHANDLER, ASA E., 905 Old South bldg. "
*CHASE, ARTHUR T., 84 State St. "
*CHASE, CHAS. DYER, 31 State St. "
CHASE, GEORGE S., 84 State St. "
*CHASE, HARVEY S., 84 State St. "
*COMINS, EDWARD P., 84 State St. "
*COOLEY, MORGAN L., 73 Tremont St. "
*DAVIS, HERBERT T., 8 Congress St. "
DILLON, WILLIAM, 50 Congress St. "
*DOUGLAS, ROBERT, 166 Essex St. "
DYSART, ROBERT J., 28 State St. "
EDWARDS, TRUMAN G., Old South Bldg. "
*FRENCH, HERBERT T., 166 Essex St. "
*GLUNTS, JAMES D., 35 Congress St. "
*GREELEY, HENRY N., 53 State St. "
*HALL, JAMES W., 53 State St. "
*HALL, WILLIAM FRANKLIN, 53 State St. "
HARPER, RICHARD L., 53 State St. "
HERRICK, WILLIAM H., 24 Milk St. "
*HILLMAN, FREDERICK J. Springfield
Boston
KELLOGG, CHARLES W., 35 Congress St. "
Brookline
†KURTZ, CHARLES C., 46 Pernow St. "
*LOVE, HENRY D., 84 State St. Boston
*LUTHER, J. SEYMOUR, Jr., Old South Bldg. "

*LYALL, GEORGE, 27 State St. Boston
*MANSFIELD GIDEON M., 53 State St. "
MANSON, GEO. W., 113 Devonshire St. "
*MARVIN, HAROLD A., 73 Tremont St. "
*MASTERS, J. EDWARD, 60 State St. "
*MOYER, ORLANDO C., 59 Temple Pl. "
NEWELL, WM. C., 141 Milk St. "
*NICKERSON AUGUSTUS, 53 State St. "
*OAKEY, FRANCIS, 84 State St. "
*PARKER, EDWARD L., 50 State St. "
PARSONS, JOSEPH S., 214 Columbus Av. "
*PARSONS, THOMAS P., 1107 Tremont Bldg. "
*PIPER, HENRY A., 953 Old South Bldg. "
*POPE, CHARLES H., 166 Essex St. "
*PRIDE, EDWIN L., 8 Congress St. "
*RAND, WALDRON H., 59 Temple Pl. "
*SANGER, GABRIEL, 166 Essex St. "
*SAWYER, HOLLIS H., 131 State St. "
*SETCHELL, MORTON E., Old South Bldg. "
*SPURR, THOMAS S., 294 Washington St. "
*STEELE, F. R. C., 131 State St. "
*STEWART, ANDREW, 28 State St. "
*STORER, NEWMAN W., 59 Temple Pl. "
*STRACHAN, G. DUTHIE, 59 Temple Pl. "
TUFTS, FREDERICK C., 24 Milk St. "
*TUTTLE, CHARLES H., 84 State St. "
*WELLINGTON, C. OLIVER, 714 Tremont Bldg. "
*WRIGHT, CHARLES H., 9 Emrose Ter. "
WRIGHT, RICHARD W., 953 Old South Bldg. "
WRIGHT, WALTER C., 45 Milk St. "
*WRYE, WALTER C., 84 State St. "
*WYMAN, GERALD, 131 State St. "

ASSOCIATES

ALBREE, EDWARD C. Swampscott
BYRNES, ARTHUR T., 53 State St. Boston

DYSART, HUGH, 28 State St. Boston
WOODBRIDGE, J. M., 257 Washington St. Newton

Advertisement of Incorporated Public Accountants of Massachusetts as it appeared in the 1911 Boston City Directory.

Accountants

Certified Public Accountants of Massachusetts, Inc.

CHARLES H. TUTTLE President.
AMOS D. ALBEE, Vice President.
HERBERT F. FRENCH, Treasurer.
WALDRON H. RAND, Secretary.

FELLOWS

ALBEE, AMOS D., 53 State St. Boston
ALBEE, HERBERT H., 53 State St. "
BASSETT, HORACE S., 200 Devonshire St. "
BISHOP, GEO. L., 59 Temple pl. "
BOYDEN, WALTER L., 6 Beacon St. "
CHANDLER, ASA E., 905 Old South bldg. "
CHASE, ARTHUR T., 84 State St. "
CHASE, CHARLES DYER, 31 State St. "
CHASE, GEO. S., 84 State St. "
CHASE, HARVEY S., 84 State St. "
COMINS, EDWARD P., 200 Devonshire St. "
COOLEY, MORGAN L., 73 Tremont St. "
DAVIS, HERBERT T., 40 Central St. "
DOUGLAS, ROBERT, 49 Federal St., "
DYSART, ROBERT J., 40 State St. "
EDWARDS, TRUMAN G., 1126 Old South Bldg. "
FRENCH, HERBERT F., 166 Essex St. "
GLUNTS, JAMES D., 35 Congress St. "
GREELEY, HENRY N., 53 State St. "
HALL, JAMES W., 53 State St. "
HALL, WILLIAM FRANKLIN, 53 State St "
HARPER, RICHARD L., 53 State St. "
HILLMAN, FRED'K. J., Court Sq. Bldg. " Springfield
KELLOGG, CHARLES F., 35 Congress St. Boston
LOVE, HENRY D., 84 State St. "
LUTHER, J. SEYMOUR, Jr., 932 Old South Bldg. "
LYALL, GEORGE, 79 Milk St. "
MANNIX, WILLIAM H., 134 State St. Boston
MANSFIELD, GIDEON M., 606 Exchange Bldg. "
MARVIN, HAROLD A., 73 Tremont St. "
MASTERS, J. EDWARD, 60 State St. "
MOYER, ORLANDO C., 1125 Old South Bldg. "
NICKERSON, AUGUSTUS, 53 State St. "
OAKEY, FRANCIS, 84 State St. "
PARKER, EDWARD L., 50 State St. "
PARSONS, THOMAS P., 812 Tremont Bldg. "
PIPER, HENRY A., 953 Old South Bldg. "
POPE, CHAS. H., 166 Essex St. "
PRIDE, EDWIN L., 40 Central St. "
RAND, WALDRON H., 59 Temple pl. "
RISLEY, ARTHUR L., 6 Beacon rm 721 "
SANGER, GABRIEL, 166 Essex St. "
SAWYER, HOLLIS H., 60 Congress St. "
SETCHELL, MORTON E., 932 Old South Bldg. "
SPURR, THOMAS S., 294 Washington St. "
STEELE, F. R. C., 131 State St. "
STEWART, ANDREW, 40 State St. "
STORER, NEWMAN W., 59 Temple Pl. "
TUTTLE, CHAS. H., 84 State St. "
WRIGHT, CHARLES H., 9 Emrose Ter. "
WRIGHT, RICHARD W., 953 Old South Bldg.
WRYE, WALTER C., 84 State St. "
WYMAN, GERALD, 131 State St. "
WELLINGTON, C. OLIVER, 40 Central St

ASSOCIATES

ALBREE, EDWARD C. Swampscott
BARDWELL, WALLACE E., 124 Summer St. Pittsfield
BYRNES, ARTHUR T., 53 State St. Boston
DYSART, HUGH, 40 State St. Boston
MANSON, GEO. W., 113 Devonshire St. "
WOODBRIDGE, J. M., 457 Washington St. Newton

HONORARY

KURTZ, CHAS. G., 46 Vernon St. Brookline
PARSONS, JOSEPH S., 214 Columbus Ave. Boston

The 1912 Boston City Directory contained an advertisement of the Certified Public Accountants of Massachusetts, Inc., successor organization of the IPA.

society today. A subtle form of discrimination is found in the provision that a "no" vote by three members automatically rejected a candidate. This "black-ball" system could effectively bar an otherwise qualified candidate from membership.

The blanket discrimination against females during the early years of the society is in marked contrast to society by-laws in 1975. Recognition of the generally low status of women in American society in those pre-suffrage days does not erase the sting of an all-male accounting organization deliberately excluding qualified females from membership. One cannot fail to speculate that the lack of women in public accounting today may be traced in part to those early practices which excluded females.

These early by-laws probably reflect rather accurately the customs of similar professional organizations around the turn of the century. Rather than dwell upon the discriminatory aspects of the early group, a more fruitful approach is to point to the society's current nondiscriminatory practices. Without exaggeration, the Massachusetts Society of CPAs has achieved fundamental social, as well as professional, progress during its 75 year history.

An initiation fee and annual dues were assessed by the Incorporated Public Accountants of Massachusetts. Fellows were charged an initiation fee of $15 and Associates were assessed a $10 fee. At the inception of the society, annual dues were $10 per year, and increased to $15 after 1906 (a precise date could not be verified).

An extraordinary portion of the recorded minutes of the Executive Committee deal with problems of assessment and collection of dues and initiation fees. Several accountants were dropped from membership for non-payment of dues; and the preoccupation with financial matters implies the organization may have experienced some period of fiscal austerity.

The organizational structure of the IPA was similar to the society's present structure. The by-laws provided for a President, a Vice-President, a Secretary, A Treasurer, an Auditor, and an Executive Committee which included the President, Secretary, and Treasurer, plus three Fellows. Today, the society's officers have been enlarged to include a first Vice-President and two Vice-Presidents. Also, the Executive Committee now consists of all officers, the immediate past president, and eight elected Fellows.

Early Professional Ethics

A discussion of the evolution of Massachsuetts public accounting would be incomplete without an analysis of early professional ethics. Keeping in mind similar developments in law and medicine, it is useful to seek documentation of a professional code of conduct during the infancy of public accounting. The most direct evidence of established ethical standards is found in the by-laws under Article X, Penalties:

> Section 1. If any member of the Corporation (1) violates any of the by-laws of the Corporation, or (2) is convicted of a felony, or misdemeanor, or (3) is held by the Executive Committee on the complaint of any member, to have been guilty of any act or default discreditable to a public accountant, his membership in the Corporation shall crease by a resolution of the Executive Committee presented before the Corporation and supported by a two-thirds vote of the Fellows present at any regular or special meeting; but before such resolution shall be presented by the Executive Committee, they shall give the member an opportunity of being heard in his own behalf.

These early rules are much less detailed than the society's present regulations under Article VII--Professional Conduct and Discipline. However, the founders of Massachusetts public accounting displayed remarkable foresight in recognizing the importance of appropriate professional conduct and they sought to enforce elementary ethical standards in public accounting practice.

Note under item (3) above, that a member could be expelled from the Society if he was found to have been guilty of any act or default discreditable to the profession. A search of early minutes of meetings from 1906 to 1911 indicates that the organization actively enforced the code of conduct established in its by-laws.

An incident during 1910 and 1911 illustrates the concern of the IPA in the conduct of its members. Mr. G. Duthie Strachan apparantly was involved in an act that some members considered discreditable to the profession. Mr. Strachan was one of the early leaders of IPA who had served on both the Executive Committee and Legislative Committee and had led the movement to register public accountants under the first CPA law in 1909. Moreover, he had served on the first Board of Examiners, a very powerful position in the profession. Clearly, he was one of the most influential public accounting practitioners of his time.

Initial record of charges against Mr. Strachan appeared in the Minutes of the May 1910 Annual Meeting:

> Mr. William Dillon referred to the serious charges recently made in the public press against one of our members, and moved the reference of the matter to the Executive Committee to examine into and report: the motion was seconded and voted.

Specific charges against Mr. Strachan were not noted in the minutes of either the Executive Committee or the general body.

Second reference to the matter occurred in the September 1, 1910 minutes of the Executive Committee:

> The President was requested to call upon Mr. Strachan, the member accused on the complaint of a member, to have been guilty of an act discreditable to public accounting; and suggest that he resign his membership in the Corporation.

A meeting of the Executive Committe only one week later rescinded the earlier decision and the minutes of the September 10 full meeting of IPA record this recommendation:

> The Executive Committee reported on the reference to it of the complaint of the published actions of another member discreditable to a public accountant, that the report of a subcommittee, having in charge duties connected with the investigation, had not been received in full; progress was reported and a request for further time.

Next reference to the Strachan case occurred in the October 5, 1910 minutes of the Executive Committee:

> The President (Charles Tuttle), as a committee to wait upon Mr. Strachan, the member accused of acts discreditable to a public accountant, reported having seen the member and having advised him to resign, and that Mr. Strachan had refused to resign.
>
> It was noted that the Secretary prepare a report to the Corporation expressing the intention of this Committee to arrange for a hearing at which the accused member may be heard in his own behalf.

This action of the Executive Committee was reported to the main body at the October meeting. A search of the minutes through November, 1911 revealed no further reference to the complaint against Mr. Strachan. Whether the matter was quietly settled is not certain. However, the official list of Fellows and Associates includes the name G. Duthie Strachan as of October 7, 1911 nearly a year and a half after initial charges were brought.

The importance of the Strachan case lies not in the nature of the charge against him, nor in the apparent failure of the organization to resolve the case expeditiously. Rather, the important points are that charges were brought, the matter was reviewed, a request for resignation was made and refused by the accused, and finally, the accused member was offered an opportunity to speak on his own behalf. These actions imply that this early group of public accountants were sensitive to the public image of accounting practitioners. Moreover, the organization monitored the public acts of its members, and a judicial procedure was in place to protect both the accused member and the organization.

Another aspect of professional conduct merits brief mention in this discussion. The early organization allowed and even encouraged, its members to solicit clients through the medium of advertising.

In the early 1900s the Boston Directory is replete with examples of public accountants and auditors advertising their services to the public. The accounting profession regarded advertising as a legitimate method for soliciting business, and the ethical implications of the procedure were ignored. Solicitation of clients through advertising was a practice that continued for a significant period after 1910.

A Name Change and Horizons Expand

The Incorporated Public Accountants of Massachusetts revised its by-laws, and applied for a new charter in 1911. On March 21, 1911, the Certified Public Accountants of Massachusetts, Incorporated, received a charter. Following a decade of growth and development from a small group of 14 public accountants, the organization had expanded to a dynamic and influential organization of 61 Fellows and 4 Associates in 1911. On November 9, 1911, the IPA voted to dissolve and the CPA of Mass., Inc. came into existence with the Executive Committee and members of the old organization forming the new group. An era had ended, and the public accounting profession in Massachsuetts was on the threshhold of new growth and service to the business community.

The income tax amendment in 1913 opened new horizons for public accounting services. These developments, together with an analysis of the Society's evolution during the 1920s and the Depression of the 1930s, will be discussed in another chapter.

FOOTNOTES

[1]The author is indebted to the early work of Ethel S. Kingman, whose monograph, "Accounting in Massachusetts" was used as both a basic source and final authority for developing certain events discussed in this paper.

CHAPTER TWELVE

HISTORY OF THE MASSACHUSETTS SOCIETY OF CPAs --- 1910 to 1930

Linda H. Kistler

Introduction

An earlier paper on the history of Massachusetts CPAs described the founding of the first professional society of public accountants in the state. This article traces the society's evolution from around 1910 to 1930. The period covers the peaceful years before World War I, the war years, the enormous prosperity and economic growth of the 1920s which culminated in the collapse of 1929, and the beginning of the most severe economic depression this country has ever endured. Extraordinary industrial growth presented opportunities for the fledgling accounting profession; and the history of the Massachusetts Society of CPA's mirrors to some extent the larger developments taking place in the state and throughout the country.

This paper presents a broad overview of major activities within the society and then examines the ongoing controversy surrounding adoption of a code of professional development activities of the organization.

From 1910 to 1930 --- An overview

The predecessor organization of the present society, the Incorporated Public

SOCIETY MEDAL AWARDED EACH YEAR FOR HIGHEST HONORS ON CPA EXAMINATION

Accountants of Massachusetts, in 1911 voted to form a new organization called the Certified Public Accountants of Massachusetts, Inc. (the name was changed to the Massachusetts Society of Certified Public Accountants, Inc. in 1922). Membership consisted of fifty-four Fellows, six Associates, and two Honorary Members in 1912.

Not surprisingly, society members were not required to be certified. The first Massachusetts CPA registration act became effective in 1909, and the presence of non-CPAs in an organization formed in 1900 was inevitable. However, the early advertisements of the society failed to distinguish CPAs and non-CPAs, a fact that may have impeded full professional recognition by the public. Membership policies led to a serious identity crisis some years later when the professional goals and attitudes of CPAs and non-CPAs began to diverge.

The early years of the society were marked by an extraordinary preoccupation with amendments to by-laws, and membership applications, investigations, and approvals. A careful reading of the minutes for this period leads to a conclusion that the problem of low attendance at many meetings may have been attributable to the time consumed by routine procedural matters.

Continuing attention to recruitment of members implies that some Massachusetts CPAs simply would not support the new organization. A comparison of society membership and total numbers of registered CPAs tends to sustain this conclusion.

By 1923, the society had grown to 143 members, while the total number of CPAs in the state exceeded 300. Attendance during the preceding decade was very low, averaging from five to twenty members per meeting; and the attendance problem may have hindered efforts to attract important speakers to meetings. In 1924, only 152 of the 411 Massachusetts CPAs were members of the society, and in

1925, the totals were 178 and 477 respectively. By 1930, however, membership exceeded 250 and average attendance at monthly meetings had risen to eighty members and guests. Society minutes imply that mandatory membership in the American Institute of Accountants may actually have had a negative impact on the organization's efforts to enroll CPAs.

The Massachusetts CPA Law. Almost from the beginning, the registration act for Massachusetts CPAs was controversial. Unlike the law of many other states, a government official (the Bank Commissioner) controlled the registration of CPAs. Professional accountants recognized the desirability of an independent board of examiners, and in 1912 an amendment to the law was prepared for submission to the legislature. The Bank Commissioner opposed the bill and the proposal was dropped, but not forgotten.

In 1914, the society's Legislative Committee supported an act to establish a Board of Examiners appointed by the Governor, whose members would consist of a majority of CPAs. Further, the bill provided for a waiver of examination and issuance of certificates to all accountants certified under the original 1909 registration act. Significantly, the act included a reciprocity clause for CPAs from other states provided that standards of the applicant's state were equal to those of Massachusetts, and that applicants met certain basic requirements of Massachusetts law. The bill did not pass, despite concerted effort by the Legislative Committee.

In 1922, attempts to change the Massachusetts law were more successful. Two sections were revised. One section authorized the Bank Commissioner to issue a certificate to any applicant deemed to fulfill the necessary qualifications and professional experience. More importantly, a second section stated that a person who was not registered could not hold himself out as a CPA. The penalty for violating this provision was a $500 fine and/or imprisonment for not more than six months.

Finally, in 1923, Massachusetts CPAs succeeded in effecting a complete revision of the 1909 law. The legislation was introduced by the Bank Commissioner, and as originally written, it would have transferred administration of all CPA-related matters to the Director of Registration, which would have placed CPAs under civil service! Needless to say, the initial legislation was vigorously opposed by the society.

A more appropriate bill finally evolved and was enacted by the legislature. Its principal features were: (1) Administration was vested in a five-member Board to be appointed by the Governor. Four members were to be CPAs, and the fifth member would be a Massachusetts attorney. (2) The law conferred broad powers on the Board: "...It shall make such rules and regulations as are necessary for the proper conduct of its duties." Members of the society voiced apprehension at the lack of specificity in that section, but the legislature insisted upon delegating very broad discretionary power to the Board. (3) The provision allowing a registered public accountant to refer to himself as a CPA was retained; and the section prohibiting nonregistered accountants from claiming CPA status also remained.

Abolition of the annual license fee was enthusiastically received. Mr. J. Edward Masters, of the society's Legislative Committee, remarked: "...A very objectionable feature which existed in our old law was having to renew your certificate every year and pay $5, which of course, was the least objectionable, but it was the thought, I think, that we had to be licensed like an <u>ordinary dog license</u> (emphases added) or anything of that sort every year in order to be a certified public accountant, and I am glad to say that that has been abolished." (Minutes of Annual Meeting, May 28, 1923). One can only speculate on those early members' reaction to the present biannual $30 licensing fee.

Society members were justifiably pleased with their success in obtaining a CPA law that placed administrative responsibility in the hands of an independent Board.

The CPA Examination. Society records do not specifically refer to a formal, written CPA examination until 1912; and the 1909 law clearly did not require a written examination prior to issuance of a certificate. In 1912, however, the September meeting was devoted to discussion of the "practical questions" in the last examination. The test consisted of eight questions, of which five were required for passing within a four-hour period. Two examiners (Messrs. Albee and French) contributed to the discussion, and their comments imply that a rather liberal grading policy was employed.

In 1914, several changes in examination procedures were implemented. The examination consisted of a combined theory and auditing section; practical accounting (two full days); and commerical law. Experience requirements were: (1) High school education or equivalent; and (2) two years' practical accounting experience. The Board of Examiners was enlarged to seven members, from the five-member original Board, but was still under the control of the Bank Commissioner. The marking system was altered in an unspecified manner, and an examinee failing any subject was required to pass the entire examination again.

The fall of 1917 was marked by success on the CPA examination of two Massachusetts women, Alice M. Hill, and Gertrude Briggs, who became the first two female CPAs in the state. It should be noted that they were specifically barred from membership in the society at that time because the by-laws restricted membership to males until 1922. Ethel Kingman became the first female Fellow of the Massachusetts Society, when she was admitted in 1925. Gertrude Briggs and Alice Hill also were admitted later that year.

Before 1918, examination questions were prepared and graded in Massachusetts, despite the availability of examination questions from the American Institute of Accountants. The 1918 CPA examination questions were supplied by the AIA for the first time, and Massachusetts joined many other states already using uniform questions supplied by the national organization.

By 1920, more than 250 candidates sat for the CPA examination in the state, and some society leaders began to express concern over the maintenance of high professional standards. Moreover, the number of accounting students alarmed Waldron Rand who "...uttered a timely warning concerning the need of those in the profession to taking their profession seriously, and referred to the misleading advertisements in various magazines, in which, if one were to believe all that had been printed on the subject, accountants were making fabulous salaries. He said, moreover, that one correspondence school alone had some 14,000 members enrolled, and that accounting schools throughout the country were flooded with applicants." (Minutes of November 10, 1920).

Utilization of AIA examination questions was nearly rescinded in 1922. The society registered strong opposition to a Board proposal to discontinue AIA questions and substitute those of the Board. A resolution passed by the society noted that 38 states were using examinations provided by the AIA, and concluded that abandonment of AIA examinations "...would be unwise and would seriously retard the development of the profession of accountancy in Massachusetts."

(Minutes of March 27, 1922). Opposition to the change apparently was successful, and AIA questions continued to be used, with marking and grading carried out in Massachusetts. By 1927, candidates were required to be reexamined only on parts failed, and the Massachusetts Board continued to grade the examinations.

Until the 1930s the Massachsuetts Board of Registration of CPAs graded the examinations provided by the American Institute. In 1939, Mr. Charles Rittenhouse, a member of the Board of Registration, met with the society's Executive Committee to discuss the question of reciprocity between states and the fact that examinations were not graded by the American Institute of Accountants. He reported that the Board generally favored reciprocity but felt that Massachusetts law was in conflict with reciprocity because it required that certificate holders be residents of the state. The Executive Committee decided that a change in the CPA law was unlikely, and the matter was deferred.

With respect to the grading of examinations, the procedure used by the Board of Registration was to engage two qualified accountants to prepare answers to the questions, which were then reviewed by the Board and modified, if necessary. These two men graded all examinations; and marginal papers were reviewed by the Board to assure grading consistency. In some instances, papers were graded twice.

After some discussion, the Executive Committee voiced support for grading of the examinations by the American Institute. However, examination papers, while remaining in the custody of the AIA, should be readily available to the Board of Registration. Specific action on the issue was advisory in nature because a decision could only be made by the Board. However, possibly because of the society's recommendation, Massachusetts later joined other states in utilizing the grading facilities of the American Institute.

In another related development, the 1927 Education Committee recommended awarding a gold and silver medal to the two candidates achieving high scores on the CPA examination. No action was taken that year but the 1928 Committee continued its efforts to offer the awards. Initially, only the gold medal was awarded; and honorable mention was given to both the second and third highest candidates. The first Massachusettts gold medal recipient was Karl W. Baker, and he received the award in 1928.

An annual awards meeting was introduced in 1930. One meeting each year was devoted to honoring new CPAs and invited guests, and to recognizing medal winners for the prior year's examinations. The custom has continued 45 years, and it is one of the most popular events of the society.

Society Leaders and National Activities. From the beginning the state society maintained a close affiliation with national accounting organizations and with accounting groups in neighboring states. As a consequence of state society membership, Fellows also joined the American Association of Public Accountants, a national accounting group founded in 1887. Dual membership was required as early as 1912, and Massachusetts CPAs were hosts to the national convention of AAPA in Boston in 1913. The national meeting was preceded by nearly a year of planning and preparation; and apparently it was a great success.

Several Massachusetts men were active in national accounting affairs. Waldron H. Rand, a local practitioner and leader of the state society, was elected President of the American Institute of Accountants, the successor organization of the AAPA. He served two years (1918-1920) as President of the AIA, following membership on the Institute's Council, and service as Vice-President. Mr Rand also provided outstanding leadership during the state society's early years, serving as secretary, president, and member of the executive committee. His influence on public accounting in Massachusetts and his contributions to the Society were extraordinary; and he continued to serve both state and national groups until his death in 1929.

In 1921 a new national organization, the American Society of Certified Public Accountants, was formed by a dissident group of CPAs, displeased with some of the AIA's policies. The new CPA group restricted memberhsip to CPAs, published a monthly journal, The Certified Public Accountant, and actively supported legislation which would restrict the practice of public accounting solely to CPAs. The organization offered leadership in areas of activity in which the AIA was weakest, including strong advocacy of the CPA certificate as evidence of professional competence.[1]

A Massachusetts man, E.L. Pride, was elected president of the American Society of CPAs in 1924. Mr Pride addressed that state society following his election to national office. He spoke about the aims and purposes of the group and stated his intention to work toward a merger of the two competing national accounting organizations (AIA and ASCPA). A fundamental obstacle to union of the two groups was the AIA policy of admitting non-CPAs to membership. About 300 of the 1800 members of the American Institute were not certified public accountants at that time. The American Society of CPAs believed that non-CPAs detracted from the prestige, public image, and objectives of professional accountants.

The American Institute tried to counter some of the ASCPA's influence by establishing regional chapters across the country, including one in New England. The first regional meeting was held in Boston in 1920, and it was the first of many subsequent meetings during the 1920s.

Competition between the two national organizations precipitated an "identity crisis" in the Massachusetts society. Society members began to question the policy of admitting non-CPAs to full membership in the society. In 1922, E.L. Pride led a heated discussion opposing admission of any non-CPA to the state society. He stated that, in his opinion, a mistake had been made in the by-laws which allowed non-CPAs to be admitted as Fellows. Despite objections, members voted to admit seven non-CPAs to membership as Fellows at the October, 1922 meeting.

The issue continued to occupy the attention of the Executive Committee during the fall of 1922. After much discussion, the Committee recommended that a referendum vote be taken on the question of whether membership in Massachusetts Society of CPAs should be limited to CPAs. The Society's identity crisis was finally resolved in September, 1923, when the society voted to restrict membership of a Fellow to "...any citizen of the United States who is a certified public accountant under the laws of Massachusetts...". (Minutes of September, 1923). At the same meeting, the members directed the By-Laws Committee to review the by-laws and amendments submitted by members, and report back to the full membership at the annual meeting in May, 1924. It was obvious that extensive modifications of the by-laws were necessary.

A number of by-laws revisions were approved in 1925. Among the most important amendments were: (1) Non-CPAs were reclassified as Associates. (2) An

Associate member was automatically elevated to the status of Fellow upon issuance of a CPA certificate. (3) A majority vote of the Executive Committee was sufficient to approve an applicant for membership. A vote of the full membership was discontinued; and this change effectively abolished the "blackball" system of prior years. (4) Finally, in an obvious attempt to attract new CPAs to the society the initiation fee was reduced to $15 from $25.

The influence of the rival American Society of CPAs was obvious during the 1920s. The Membership Committee complained of difficulty in attracting new members due to the activities of the ASCPA and the fact that the Massachusetts Society of CPAs maintained close ties to the AIA. In 1924, the Membership Committee recommended that the society sever its affiliation, real or apparent, with <u>any</u> national organization. No action was taken by the society.

A careful reading of the minutes during this period leads to a conclusion that the organization's membership problems and general lack of support from Massachusetts CPAs may have been attributable to its close ties with the AIA, and to the presence of non-CPAs in an organizaiton which called itself a society of CPAs. The conflict of the ASCPA and the AIA did not subside until the two national organizations were united during the 1930s. Unquestionably, resolution of the CPA versus non-CPA identity crisis ultimately helped to strenthen the professional image of Massachusetts CPAs.

Attempts to project a professional image also had been complicated by the appearance of a fraudulent CPA diploma mill.[2] In 1920, an organization called the National Association of Certified Public Accountants was formed in Washington, D.C., which had no CPA law at the time. The primary function of the diploma mill was to sell CPA certificates to anyone able to pay a fee. The flood of bogus certificates frightened professional CPAs who justifiably feared a diminution of public confidence and professional stature. After some difficulty, a court injunction against the organization was finally obtained; and when the group could no longer issue its fradulent "CPA degrees", it went out of business. The episode had important implications for the Massachusetts group, which then began to re-evaluate its own practice of admitting non-certified accountants.

The Society As A Social Organization. During its early years, the society fulfilled an important social function for Boston accountants. Indeed, social activities were a much more important part of society affairs in 1920 than in 1975. The first annual field day was held in July, 1914, at the Villa Napoli, Nantasket. The outing included members' wives and friends, and it was the forerunner of many highly successful outings which have continued for more than sixty years. The popularity of the annual frolics is evidenced by enthusiastic membership support. During the period, the annual outing was the most widely attended meeting, and far exceeded average attendance at regular meetings.

The annual outings were not the only occasions to which women guests were invited. In April, 1911, the society held its first Ladies' Night, which was attended by more than 60 people at the Hotel Vendome. Activities of the evening included a speech by Edward L. Suffern, President of the American Association of Public Accountants, professional entertainment by a monologuist, a soprano soloist, and a five-piece orchestra which provided music for dancing until midnight.

The first Ladies' Night was followed by highly successful similar events during the 1920s. The Copley Plaza was a popular location for the annual evening; and the Pemberton Inn was the scene of the annual field day outing for six years during the 1929s. World War I caused cancellation of the field day in 1918, although Ladies' Nights continued to be held.

One of the organization's most important social events took place in April 1925, when the society celebrated its 25th anniversary. A formal dinner was held at the Hotel Somerset, and nearly 150 members and guests attended. Many important state and national accounting dignitaries joined the celebration. Highlight of the evening was a 25-year history of the Massachusetts Society by Harvey S. Chase, a charter member of the original group. Apparently, no expense was spared in making the evening a success. Records reveal that the celebration cost the society's treasury more than $1,100, a significant sum in 1925 dollars!

An Important Court Case. In 1926, a court action involving a dispute over the ownership of accountants' workpapers became a matter of concern to the society and its members. The case was Ipswich Mills vs. William Dillon, et al. The lower court judge held that the worksheets were the property of Ipswich Mills, even though they had been prepared by Mr. Dillon, a CPA, in the normal course of an independent audit.

The adverse decision was appealed to the Massachusetts Supreme Court; and legal counsel of the American Institute of Accountants actively participated in the appeal, in cooperation with the Massachusetts society. Litigation costs were paid by the AIA. In 1927, the lower court decision was overturned. The Supreme Court held that workpapers are the property of the accountants who prepare them, in the absence of an agreement to the contrary. This landmark decision established an important precedent on workpapers that continues today.

The News Bulletin. In 1922, the society attemped to establish a bulletin of the organization's activities. Only four issues were published, each comprising a one or two page summary of information for public accountants. Apparently, there was insufficient support within the society to warrant continuance of the Bulletin in 1922, because it died after only a few months. However, a pamphlet was revived in 1928. The News Bulletin, predecessor of the Massachusetts CPA Review, was first published on October, 1928 in mimeographed form. It has been an important communication and educational device for nearly half a century, and its contribution to the professional development of Massachusetts CPAs is immeaurable.

Evolution of Professional Ethics

Evidence of commitment to a code of professional conduct for society members can be traced to the initial meetings of the Incorporated Public Accountants of Massachusetts. During the period from 1910 to 1930, the organization addressed the task of adopting a code of ethics, and its efforts were not altogether successful.

The exercise of a blackball technique to exclude otherwise qualified applicants was not uncommon during the early years. One of the most obvious examples of personal bias was the repeated application of Clinton H. Scovell for membership. Mr. Scovell's first unsuccessful application had been placed before the society in 1910. During this period, three negative votes (for any reason) were sufficient to reject an applicant. For example, Mr. Scovell's application for membership was defeated in 1912 by a vote of eleven in favor of Mr. Scovell and six against.

Immediately, an attempt to amend the by-laws was made. The proposed revision would require an applicant whose election failed to wait at least one year before re-submitting his application. The close proximity of Mr. Scovell's rejection and the proposed revision apparently was not a coincidence. The following month, the amendment was voted upon, and passed. Mr. C. Oliver Wellington questioned the reasons for the amendment, and voiced an impassioned plea to change the by-laws and eliminate personal bias from the society. He proposed a new amendment that would require only a two-thirds vote of the Executive committee for election to the society. In addition, two letters from Fellows in support of the candidate were necessary.

In May, 1912, Mr. Wellington's amendment failed. It should be remembered that Mr. Scovell had first applied for membership in September, 1910. Two years later he had been rejected again (after several interim attempts). The available evidence implies that personal bias, rather than a lack of professional qualifications was the principal reason for his continued rejection.

Mr. Wellington continued to support changes in the election process during the next five years, with a notable lack of success. Mr. Scovell again applied for membership in 1913 and was rejected once more.

It was not until 1925 that the by-laws on membership were revised to eliminate the blackball technique. Professional qualifications became the principal criterion for admission of an applicant. Equally important, membership applications were reviewed by the Executive Committee, instead of the full membership. Approval by a simple majority of the Executive Committee was sufficient for entry into the society. Twenty-five years after its founding, the Massachusetts Society of CPAs achieved an important step toward establishing a truly professional organization.

Controversy surrounding Mr. Scovell reappeared in society records in 1915, when his firm was accused of unethical conduct in placing an advertisement for accounting services in a New York magazine. Mr. Oliver Wellington, a Fellow of the society and also a member of the firm C. H. Scovell and Co., received an admonishment in the form of a resolution from the Executive Committee which stated: "...In the opinion of the Executive Committee this advertisement was undignified and of a character detrimental to the best interests of our profession..." (Minutes of Executive Committee, November 10, 1915).

In December, Mr. Wellington asked to address the Executive Committee to explain his position regarding the advertisement. He expressed embarasement, disclaimed responsibility, and stated that he believed the head of his firm (Mr. Scovell) had been unaware of its publication. The Committee voted to accept Mr. Wellington's regrets, and the matter was dropped.

This incident is not an isolated example of ethics problems during the period. The issues of price-cutting, advertising, and unprofessional conduct were frequently discussed during the period 1915 to 1925, and an ethics committee had been established as early as 1912 to review a problem relating to fees. Advertising was common during the early years, and in 1912, the Boston Directory contained an advertisement paid by the society. By 1925, however, the practice had been discontinued.

In February, 1914 the society voted to include the Precepts of Professional Conduct as proposed by the AAPA. The Precepts were to be inserted as a supplement to the by-laws of the Massachusetts society. However, at the April, 1914 meeting, the inclusion of precepts was reconsidered, and copies were simply mailed to members. The effect of this action was to avoid explicit endorsement of a formal code of conduct. Apparently, members were unwilling to make a public commitment to a professional code of ethics.

An explicit, enforceable professional code of conduct is one hallmark of a professional organization and from time to time, the society returned to the subject. During the period 1910-1920, the AIA led national efforts to develop a code of conduct. At its May 1917 annual meeting, the Massachusetts society resumed discussion of a code of ethics which had been proposed by the American Institute. After much discussion, the society voted to postpone action.

Nevertheless, the activities of the American Institute were followed closely. In 1918, the annual meeting of the AIA approved the recommendation that a standing committee on ethics be established to censor advertising materials, and in 1919 the national organization approved a rule of conduct that prohibited the distribution of circulars and other publicity devices without the consent and approval of the Committee.[3]

In 1921, the state society endorsed the AIA position by sending copies of the national organization's resolution opposing advertising and soliciting for business to each Massachusetts CPA. Nevertheless, a formal code of ethics was not adopted by the society at that time.

In 1926, the Society's president, Stanley G. H. Fitch, reported that the Executive Committee had given preliminary consideration to adoptions of rules of professional conduct. He said that progress had been made, and noted that other state societies had already adopted a code. He urged the Massachusetts group to join the movement.

Favorable action on adoption of a code of ethics was delayed until the 1930s. Nevertheless, individual members, and the society as a body, began to adhere to the established code of the American Institute of Accountants. Customs change slowly, and the formal adoption of a code of professional conduct was not an easy process. Massachusetts accountants can point to many noteworthy achievements during the period from 1910 to 1930. Not the least among these was recognition that a professional organization has an obligation to welcome all qualified applicants regardless of race, creed or sex.

Professional Development

The importance of professional development in the life of CPAs was recognized by the Massachusetts Society of CPAs from its founding in 1900.

Prior to 1910, despite the preoccupation with membership details and by-laws revisions, numerous meetings concentrated on discussion of current accounting topics. Problems of inventory valuation, depreciation, accounting terminology, and cost systems were a few of the topics analyzed at monthly meetings. A number of important people addressed the group during the early years, and among the most note worthy was Justice Louis D. Brandeis, who spoke to the society in 1909.

Not surprisingly, Massachusetts corporation tax laws and federal income tax statutes received much attention. In 1913, the Tax Commissioner spoke to the society, and many state tax authorities and representatives of the Internal Revenue Service addressed members at later meetings.

In 1918, the War Income Tax Law was reviewed. The speaker traced the history of income tax legislation in the United States from the Civil War, when an income tax law was in operation, through passage of the 16th amendment of the U.S. Constitution in 1913. He noted that revenue collections in the Boston office in 1918 had increased to $100 million from $1 million a few years earlier! The contrast between taxes collected almost sixty years ago, and those from the New England Region today is worth a moment's reflection.

Newly revised Massachusetts Corporation tax laws were scrutinized in 1920 and 1921. In January, 1920, the history of the corporate tax law in Massachusetts was traced from 1864, when a local tax on machinery and real estate was levied on domestic corporations, to the most recent legislation. The 1920 law was complex, and society members devoted a number of meetings to analysis of the law.

The calibre of speakers and the topics discussed at regular meetings of the society was high. In 1922, a speech by attorney James Mudge on Stock Dividends was exceptionally comprehensive, and J. Chester Crandell of Scovell, Wellington gave a talk on the subject of managing a CPA office in 1923. The fact that both topics continue to be discussed more than fifty years later is a tribute to the durability of some accounting problems! The speakers and the professional level at which subjects were evaluated also indicates the dedication of early CPAs to continuing professional development.

In 1926, the society prepared and published a report of the Special Committee on the Massachusetts Certificate of Condition. The report was considered so valuable that it was mailed to all Massachusetts Corporations which were required to appoint an auditor to certify the certificate of condition. The society supported efforts to amend the Massachusetts Excise tax to simplify preparation of the return in 1927. Its March meeting was devoted to review of the revised law, and it provides evidence of the importance members placed on the taxation segment of their practices.

Beginning in 1925, the society sent a delegate to the New England Conference; and through its participation in the activities of the New England

Council during the next 50 years, the society has played an important role in the economic development of the New England Region.

One of the most noteworthy meetings of the society took place in September, 1929. Mr. Robert H. Montgomery, of Lybrand, Ross Bros. and Montgomery, spoke to 175 people on the subject, "The Future of the Accounting Profession." Mr. Montgomery was a giant of the profession during this period, and his address to Massachusetts accountants is evidence of the group's stature after nearly three decades of existence. The society had begun to exercise the type of influence in Massachusetts that its leaders had always sought.

Conclusion

This paper has reviewed and evaluated the progress and problems of the Massachusetts Society of CPAs from 1910 to 1930. The two decades were marked by many changes in the accounting profession, both at the state and national levels. An increasing commitment to professional development, broadened influence within the state, acceptance of a uniform CPA examination, and a growing sense of the need for a code of professional ethics are a few of the accomplishments of the period.

FOOTNOTES

[1]John L. Carey, The Rise of the Accounting Profession, 1896-1936, American Institute of Certified Public Accountants, (1969), pp330-32.

[2]Ibid., pp.281-82.

[3]Ibid., pp. 231-32.

CHAPTER THIRTEEN

HISTORY OF THE MASSACHUSETTS SOCIETY OF CPAs --- 1930 to 1940

Louis S. Corsini

The decade of the 1930's was an important era in the history of the accounting profession in the United States and in Massachusetts. The country was experiencing serious financial difficulties as a result of the Crash. Capital markets had dried up, the banks had failed and had upset the entire credit structure, and a majority of Americans were without purchasing power and were angry about it. It was clear that the *laissez faire* attitude of the 1920's could no longer serve the American people. The public demanded and obtained greater governmental regulation.

Previously there were no generally accepted accounting principles. Auditing standards, based on the 1917 and 1929 Federal Reserve pamphlets, "Verification of Financial Statements," were still evolving. Financial accounting and reporting practices were grossly inadequate and indeed must be considered among the reasons for the Crash.

To resolve the problems concomitant to the financial reporting system of American industry, Congress passed hundreds of reform laws in the early 1930's, including The Securities Act of 1933, and the Securities Exchange Act of 1934, which among other things created the watchdog Securities and Exchange Commission to administer the securities laws. The result of this legislation and of the Federal Revenue Acts, also passed during the 1930's, was the precipitation of the development of both a sound body of accounting principles and auditing standards and an enlargement of the scope of the auditor's work and responsibility. Henceforth, the independent accountant would be viewed as a professional.

The Society

By April 1931, the society's membership totalled 296, of whom 262 were Fellows, 32 were Associates, and two were honorary members. Ten years later, the society's membership had increased to 454, of whom 339 were Fellows, 112 were Associates and three were honorary members. These were years of building, of dedicated service, and above all of learning.

During the 1930's the society had no permanent address. The Executive Committee simply convened at the president's office. At its frequent meetings, the committee charted the society's business, a task which was considerably time consuming. The general membership gathered monthly, from September through April, usually at the Chamber of Commerce Building, at 80 Federal Street, to listen to guest speakers knowledgeable in accounting matters. Attendance was excellent, running from 80 to 150. The cost per member, including dinner, averaged $1.00 to $1.50. In addition, numerous technical sessions were held to keep the membership abreast of changes in the federal taxation laws. The 1932 Revenue Act alone contained 750 changes, and it was followed by the Acts of 1934, 1936, 1938, and 1939. The 1932 Act, the result of the federal government's "horrifying" $3 billion deficit for fiscal 1932, raised the corporate tax rate to 13 3/4% and made the salaries of presidents and federal judges subject to taxation.

Committees

In 1931 the society had four standing committees -- Legislation, Publicity, Meeting, and Education -- and three special committees -- Bylaws, Membership, and Natural Business Year.

The Legislation Committee was particularly active in the early years. In 1930 Massachusetts Governor Allen created a permanent Board of Tax Appeals, largely on the recommendations of the Legislation Committee. The tax rate in Boston at that time was $30.80 per thousand, and many people believed that it was too high. The committee was successful in amending legislation filed by the legal profession to restrict the preparation of legal documents to attorneys. This legislation, if it had been enacted, would have seriously curtailed the accountant's work, as it would have prevented a public accountant from proffering advice and preparing reports necessary to his practice, and from appearing before public officers or bodies. In 1935 members of the committee assisted in the administration of the Massachusetts Unemployment Compensation Acts. It was also about this time that the Legislation Committee seriously considered adopting the same position as lawyers with regard to privileged communications. However, the society never acted on this issue.

The Meetings Committee performed admirably. There was a well-beaten path between the Harvard Business School and downtown Boston, where the monthly meetings were held. Harvard professors Ebersole, Lewis, McNair, Cabot, Dewing, Walker, Sanders, and Cole addressed the society on various topics during this time. Other noted speakers were Professor Kester of Columbia University; Colonel Arthur H. Carter, managing partner of Haskins and Sells; J.M.B. Hoxsey of the New York Stock Exchange; John L. Carey, Secretary of the American Institute; Walter A. Staub of Lybrand's; Henry G. Long, Massachusetts Commissioner of Corporations and Taxation; Norman E. Webster, Chairman of the New York Stock Board; Carman G. Blough, Chief Accountant of the SEC; Morris E. Peloubet of the

American Institute; R.W.R. Glover of the American Institute; and William W. Werntz, Chief Accountant of the SEC.

Their subjects were timely and eternal. They confronted accounting issues which still pose problems today, such as the valuation of investment securites for balance-sheet purposes and related reserves, the basis for foreign currency conversions in consolidation, the question of capitalizing equipment held on a rental-purchase basis, and various disclosure problems. Speakers also addressed more general issues such as auditing machine (fore-runner of computerized) accounting systems, ethics and honesty in business affairs, and the accountant's relationship to corporate management. Most of these presentations were well received and were generally followed by a question-answer period in which lively discussion ensued.

The Education Committee was very active in trying to find new ways to serve the membership. In 1931 it proposed the establishment of an accounting library for the members. This was never acted on, since arrangements had been made to give members access to the Harvard Business School library. And, of course, there was the Kirstein branch of the Boston Public Library.

At various times the Education Committee sponsored tax conferences, accounting forums, and educational meetings. In 1934 the Education Committee recommended an annual scholarship for the best essay submitted on selected accounting topics. Those that were considered exceptional were to be published in the News Bulletin. The essay contest was first held in 1937; the subject was "The Future of Professional Accountancy." L. I. Swindell won first prize. The Education Committee also suggested holding luncheon discussions to increase interest in the profession and the society among younger members. At the first such meeting, held in December 1936, attendance was high, comprised primarily of staff accountants. The Education committee also sponsored the annual awards dinner, which feted successful CPA examination candidates.

The Publication Committee was charged with the responsibility of releasing information of an educational nature. Preparation of the News Bulletin consumed most it its time and effort. At one point there was serious discussion about discontinuing the Bulletin because of the poor response from the membership; fortunately the Bulletin survived. In 1940 the Publication Committee was able to report that the society was mentioned in 71 news items in and around Boston.

The Natural Business Year Committee had the thankless task of petitioning attorneys to set up fiscal closings for clients on dates other than calendar year end. The purpose was to spread the accountant's work more evenly throughout the year.

Although the Accounting Principles and Auditing Procedures Committee was not formally established until the 1940's, the area of its concern originated in the 1930's. First, there were the accounting principles emanating from SEC legislation; second, there was the need to extend audit procedures as a result of several cases of collusive fraud that had been uncovered in the late 1930's. These caused the American Institute to recommend some very important audit procedures, including the physical test of inventory quantities, the confirmation of accounts receivable by direct communication, and important revisions in the short-form report.

Other committees came and went as the need arose. If one wanted to serve on a committee but did not wish to work too hard, he might consider the Arbitration Committee, which assisted in settling disputes between merchants. This committee went years without a single call for its services. Ad hoc committees were set up to handle technical sessions and matters of current interest. A banking committee was created to work with the Robert Morris Associates on disclosure standards. The year could not pass without some unfortunate committee having to consider the perennial problem of the Massachusetts Certificate of Condition format.

In 1934 the Massachusetts Board of Registration of Public Accountants formally adopted a code of professional ethics. In the next year the Bylaws Committee of the society began to consider a written code to guide the members in the practice of their profession. It was not until 1937 that a code of ethics was adopted and became part of the bylaws. Much thought went into the preparation of the code, and the final verison leaned heavily on the codes adopted by the Massachusetts Board of Registration, the American Institute of Accountants, and the New York Society of CPA's. The Ethics Committee was immediately established to see that the new code was obeyed. Apparently there was a problem with competitive bidding, particularly for engagements involving municipalities, quasi-municipal agencies, and banks. The society believed that such practices were demeaning to the accounting profession and not in the public's best interest. Althought the committee did little in the way of censure, its existence tended to inhibit undesirable practices.

Advertising, too, was a bit of a problem. It was not uncommon for CPA s to incorporate "tax consultants" on their letterhead, a practice generally overloooked. Instances of advertising by non-society members were referred to the Massachusetts Board of Registration, as were cases involving unregistered accountants who nonetheless did the work of the public accountant. Occasionally, the Executive Committee chastised a firm for soliciting clients of fellow members. It was rare for a member to be dismissed from the society, although it did occur for serious transgressions.

Certification in Massachusetts

At the beginning of the decade, in order to qualify as a CPA, one had to have earned a high school diploma, have two years of public accounting experience, and pass an examination prepared and graded by the American Institute of Accountants, but administered by the Massachusetts Board of Registration. Within a few years the experience requirement was changed to three years. In 1932, the examination, which had been given only in the spring of each year, was moved to the fall. In that same year, New York passed a law, effective January 1, 1938, requring an individual to hold a bachelor's degree. Massachusetts would not do this until the 1960's.

Massachusetts did not recognize certificates of other states until the society pressed the matter. In 1929 Mr. Peloubet of the American Institute wrote to the society, urging it to consider the notion of reciprocity. The ideas expressed in Mr. Peloubet's letter were endorsed, and the society took the issue to the Massachusetts Board of Registration, which in 1930 agreed to recognize out-of-state certificates held by people who had received them while residents of those states.

Admittance as a Fellow to the Massachusetts Society presumed that the appplicant had met the requirements of the Massachsuetts Board and the sponsorship of two Fellows (later changed to one) was required. The Executive Committee passed on each applicant's qualifications and if they were found to be in order, the individual's name was published in the next monthly notice following the application. If no objections were raised, the candidate was elected to membership.

In May 1931, 210 candidates were seated for the examination, and 16 passed all parts. In November 1939, 188 were seated and 32 passed all parts; the average age of the candidates was 30, and 86 held college degrees.

Administrative Matters

The 1930's were lean years. Dues were $10 for Fellows and $5 for Associates. However, as members experienced difficult times, dues deliquencies became a serious problem and consumed a good deal of the Executive Committee's time. The society was not disposed to drop members for nonpayment of dues, in view of economic conditions, so in 1931 the treasurer was authorized to loan the current year's dues to members experiencing difficulty. In 1932 the society again endeavored to help its own by requesting all unemployed members to register with the society's secretary, and a list of these members was furnished to society members with the request that they be given preference in filling vacancies.

Day-to-day matters were attended to by society officers, with the assistance of their respective firms. In 1936, Mr. French suggested appointing a part-time secretary to the president, and on June 2, Mrs. Ruth M. Welton was selected for the position. Mrs. Welton, who was employed by Lybrand's at the time, had been doing work for the society since 1929, thanks to the munificence of that firm. Mrs. Welton subsequently was named executive secretary and until her retirement in 1954 proved to be a most valuable asset to the society.

Travel in those days was not what it is today, and many society members urged that the society establish chapters outside of Boston. This was never done, but over the years the society has made a concerted effort to hold technical sessions, conferences, and meetings in different parts of Massachusetts.

Political Involvement

Normally, society members were rather low-keyed in airing their political views. But in 1932 the membership apparently felt a sense of urgency about the state of the nation and the society sent telegrams to each Massachusetts Senator and Representative in Washington exhorting immediate balancing of the federal budget through the reduction of government costs and a broadening of taxation. It was unlikely that anyone heeded the message, but an article in the New York Times of March 25, 1933, quoted the White House as saying:

> President Roosevelt expects to end the fiscal year with a balanced budget on ordinary government expenses and perhaps with a slight surplus.
> The balanced budget is to be effected, the President reasons, by employing his so-called capital budget.
> Under this system only the ordinary expenses of the government would be charged against annual income. Extraordinary expenditures, such as are being incurred in pending and prospective legislation, could be charged against the future as a debt redeemable in thirty or forty years, and only the interest on bonds would be taken from current revenues.

Some of the society members could not support such a policy, and Mr. Crandell remarked at a meeting, "Expenditures for capital items should be eliminated unless they could be met from current income -- income of future generations should not be mortgaged." More than one society speaker reminisced about the era of President Taft (1909-1913) as "the good old days."

The National Economy League, founded in 1932 with more than 75,000 members in Massachusetts, probably expressed the thinking of many society members at the time. The League believed that the fundamental cause of the

Depresison was the intolerable burdens imposed upon industry, property, and individuals by the increased cost of government. Unfortunately, the press labelled members of the League as tax dodgers and argued that the organization was stimulated by big business interests for selfish motives.

The society was not one to shirk its public responsibility when the need arose. During the first administration of Boston Mayor Maurice J. Tobin (1939 - 1940) society members volunteered to review, without compensation, the office practices, accounting systems, and administrative procedures and controls of several city agencies for the purpose of making the government function more efficiently. Many of the recommendations resulting from that effort subsequently were adopted by the city.

The Certificate of Condition

At the beginning of the decade the court handed down a controversial decision which caused a great deal of agitation among businessmen and accountants. The case was United Oil Co, v. Eager Transportation Co., et al. The court stated that the directors of Eager were to be held liable for the debts of the company as a result of the misleading manner in which balance sheet items appeared in the Massachusetts Certificate of Condition.

The Eager balance sheet showed assets, at cost, on the debit side and related reserves on the credit side. The court contended that the reader was entitled to rely on figures on the asset side as representing gross values in the absnece of any notes that reserves were applicable in reducing these values.

At this time about 28,000 certificates were being filed each year, and the ramifications of the Eager decision were staggering. Therefore, a bill was filed and subsequently passed which stated that no report of condition shall be deemed false if prepared in accordance with the usual method of keeping accounts. The new law also gave the Commissioner of Corporations and Taxation authority to prescribe the format of the Massachsuetts Certifcate of Condition. The society was instrumental in designing the new form.

The National Organization

Until 1936 there were two national organizations -- the American Institute of Accountants and the American Society of Certified Public Accountants. Many believed that the existence of two organizations was not in the best interest of the profession. Therefore, in February 1933, the society passed a resolution stating that the profession should be represented by a single national organization and conveyed this to the two national organizations. In 1935 the society endorsed a similar resolution, passed at a meeting in Atlantic City, in which representatives of all state societies participated. The two organizations finally merged in October of 1936, becoming the "American Institute of Accountants, the National Organization of Certified Public Accountants." To everyone else, it was simply called the "Institute."

Society members were very active in the national organization. Attendance at the annual meetings was always a treat for society members. In June the schedule for the necessary number of Pullmans would be furnished to the railroad so that when October finally came, all would be ready. The Massachusetts Society delegation usually required two cars.

In 1935 the annual meeting was held in Boston and was an astounding success. It also cost the society $1,890.

People

The objectives of a professional organization are to serve the needs of the membership so that they can better serve society and increase the stature of the profession in a deliberate manner. It can be fairly stated that the Massachsuetts Society went a long way toward meeting these objectives.

The men and women who served the society during this period were first-rate. Extremely capable, intellectually and administratively, they sought to raise the standards of their profession for the greater good. Many of them worked tirelessly for the society, taking on unnecessary headaches, giving countless hours of their time, and donating the services of their respective firms. Hundreds of changes in tax laws and developments in accounting principles and auditing procedures were discussed and interpreted in technical sessions and meetings so that members could better serve their clients.

One proof of competence is achievement and the national organization recognized this. Two society presidents -- Percival F. Brundage and J. Harold Stuart -- were to become presidents of the American Institute. Mr. Brundage also held the position of Budget Deputy Director under President Eisenhower. Donald P. Perry and Homer N. Sweet served as vice-presidents in the American Insitute. Several others also participated actively in the affairs of the American Institute, including service on the Executive Committee and the Council.

All officers of this period were active in civic projects and community affairs. Many members served on the Massachusetts Board of Registration. Teaching and writing were fairly common among society members. Charles F. Rittenhouse, who achieved national recognition in 1922 when he was appointed accountant for the receivers in the bankruptcy of Charles Ponzi, served as head of the accounting department at Boston University, taught at Simmons College, and authored several textbooks and articles on accounting. Miss Ethel Kingman, Phi

Beta Kappa at Boston University and the first woman to be admitted to membership, would later write a history of the profession *Accountancy in Massachusetts*. James Willing served as lecturer on auditing at the Harvard Business School and at Northeastern University prior to becoming president of the society for the 1929-1930 term. Donald P. Perry was appointed Dickinson Lecturer at the Harvard Business School.

There were others who served the society in less public ways. Men such as J. Chester Crandell, Homer N. Sweet, and Earle M. French worked hard to increase membership, to involve everyone, and to make the society what it is today.

Herbert French, one of the founders of the society, died in May 1930. J. Chester Crandell, Hollis H. Sawyer, and Francis H. E. Walter, three of the society's most valued members died at the end of the decade.

Conclusion

The decade of the 1930's holds some very unpleasant memories for many people. There was radical change in political and economic thinking. For some, it meant a departure from the work ethic; for others, a new political ideology. For the society, it meant the beginning of a new era in which the practice of public accountancy emerged as a recognized profession. It is fortunate for us that the leaders of the society understood this and planned accordingly. In decorum, technical matters and individual concern, they established a style which we can look back on with pride.

FOOTNOTES

Edwards, James D. History of Public Accounting in the United States. East Lansing: Bureau of Business and Economic Research, Michigan State University, 1960.

Kingman, Ethel S. Accountancy in Massachusetts, A Brief Study. Boston: Massachusetts Society of Certified Public Accountants, Inc., 1952

CHAPTER FOURTEEN

HISTORY OF THE MASSACHUSETTS SOCIETY OF CPAs --- 1940 to 1960

Louis S. Corsini

The War Effort

As the nation began to mobilize, accounting matters and professional development were perforce set aside. Manpower and material were being diverted to the war effort, and practically no one would remain untouched. Accountants, like everyone else, served their country in governmental administrative jobs and as fighting men in the armed forces. By July 1945 approximately 80 Massachusetts CPA s were serving in the armed services.

At the beginning of the war there was a relative scarcity of accountants, yet the Massachusetts State Director of Selective Services publicly stated that there was no shortage of accountants in the commonwealth. The society disagreed, not for the purpose of exempting accountants from service, but rather to persuade selective service authorities that accountants should be utilized in their professional capacity. The society urged the American Institute to use its influence in New York and Washington for the same end. State societies throughout the country were making similar requests. The first, rather foreboding approach by the American Institute to the selective service system was humorously related by John L. Carey. Representatives of the American Institute met with an individual who had been a practicing lawyer prior to the war and who believed, as many lawyers did, that accountants who did tax work were in fact practicing law. His response to the American Institute was a simple declarative: "I am allergic to accountants."

It was not until August 1943 that the Bureau of Selective Service issued Local Memorandum No. 115, which included accountants in the list of critical occupations. Deferments were difficult to obtain, but by 1944 registrants between the ages of 30 and 37 benefited from a substantial relaxation of the requirements for occupational deferment. At about the same time, the War Manpower Commission issued a directive requiring essential industries located in the metropolitan Boston area to adopt a 48 hour work week. Among the few exceptions was the accounting profession.

As part of its contribution to the war effort, the society, in the summer of 1941, passed a motion whereby any member serving with the armed forces would have his dues abated during the period of service, upon application to the society. In addition, the society, which had been requested to assist in reducing gasoline consumption by one-third, urged its members to eliminate unnecessary driving.

The society also formed a Special Committee on Wartime Problems to coordinate activities of members and all accountants in Massachusetts. Some of the committee's specific objectives were to provide accountants to meet the government's needs; to eliminate nonessential work; and to cover clients for members serving in the armed forces. At the time there was little question that a significant number of principals in practice were overworked because of the shortage of trained personnel. In order to ease the burden, the executive committee proposed a training course for new staff men. The course, comprised of 11 weekly sessions on elementary auditing practice, had an average attendance of 38.

Civic efforts were also made by the society during the war years. Elbridge A. Bollong served as Chairman of the Professional Division in the 1942 campaign of the Greater Boston United War Fund. In 1943 the society donated $100 to the American Red Cross, "not to establish a precedent but to recognize an emergency." The society helped subsidize the war effort by purchasing $2,000 of U.S. Bonds at 2 1/2%. In addition, several members contributed time on a special assignment for the U.S. Navy Department.

When the war ended, there was some concern that there would be high unemployment. As veterans began to return home, the society formed a committee, which functioned effectively until mid-1947, to provide assistance to these men and women. Committee members and other society members furnished information regarding the opportunities and responsibilities of public accountancy, a field that expanded along with the rest of the economy in the boom years following the war. A number of public accounting firms inaugurated on-the-job training programs for veterans under the GI bill of Rights, with the approval of the State Board of Collegiate Authority, the agency which assisted the government in this undertaking. Under these programs veterans received part of their compensation from the government during the training period. "Contemporary Accounting," a refresher course for public accountants, was offered in the fall of 1945 by the American Institute and was used by several colleges for veterans and others.

The society also feared the war had taken its toll on standards of performance in accounting and auditing. Donald P. Perry recognized this. In an address to the society entitled "Rehabilitating the Internal Controls," delivered in October 1945, he stated:

> "Laxity in following prescribed routines may have been a frequent result of the strains and stresses accompanying the wartime volume of work and the difficulties of providing adequate supervision and review. Laxity has by no means been confined to accounting. Poorly laundered linen, uncooperative sales service in our retail stores etc. are all evidence of the deterioration of standards of service."

Perry was not the only one to lament the decline in standards. In 1945, in order to ensure the maintenance of integrity and quality of the CPA's work, it was suggested that the society become active in policing the work of its members by reviewing financial statements covered by auditor opinions. The suggestion was not generally accepted.

Society Activities

In light of the expansion of society activities, it was obvious that the society needed a home of its own. Lybrand's for many years had graciously extended to the society the use of their office, facilities, and personnel. Therefore, on April 14, 1949, it was recommended to the Executive Committee that the society establish a permanent office staffed by a full-time executive secretary and a secretarial assistant. The new office would be financed by regular dues.

After three years of planning, a permanent office was leased on the sixth floor at 44 School Street. Ruth Welton, then assistant secretary, declined to accept a permanent appointment, but served as full-time interim executive secretary in the organization and administrator of the new office. Her successor, Agnes Bixby, was appointed on January 1, 1954, and proved to be an able administrator. She served the society for 20 years, until April 30, 1974.

When Miss Bixby joined the society, she was its only employee and worked

November 1953: (left to right) Ruth M. Welton, Executive Secretary; Mark C. Walker; George W. Pierce (standing); John L. Carey, Executive Director A.I.C.P.A.; Haorld Wald, President M.S.C.P.A.; Arthur Foy, President A.I.C.P.A.

Our new office, Reception Room showing Conference Room and Library through doorway at left.

1950 Annual Meeting in Boston

with only a few committees. In those halcyon days, the office had to close down for two weeks at a time when she was away on military duty. At the time of her retirement, Miss Bixby had five assistants and worked with more than 40 committees.

In February 1950 the society passed its fiftieth year. At the preceding year's meeting of the American Institute at Los Angeles, blue ball-point pens were distributed on behalf of the Massachusetts Society, which bore a gold seal with the head of an Indian and the words:

Boston Tea Party - 1950

Massachusetts Society of C. P. A. ' s

Golden Anniversary

Dues and Membership

During the war the annual dues were $10.00. On May 1, 1945 they were increased to $15.00 for Fellows residing or having their place of business within 25 miles of Boston as measured from the State House. The dues remained at $10.00 for other Fellows and at $5.00 for Associates. In 1957 the dues were increased to $25.00 for members within 25 miles of Boston who possessed a certificate for more than three years.

Total membership ran as follows:

	Total	Fellows	Associates	Honoraries
1940	454	339	112	3
1950	1,036	705	327	4
1960	1,626	1,299	323	4
1970	2,539	1,886	650	3

Not until 1950 did the membership reach the 1,000 mark. Between 1954 and 1974, the membership increased from 1,228 to 3,350. Massachusetts membership in the American Institute reached 1,000 in 1958 and this entitled the Massachusetts Society to another seat on the Institute Council.

In 1953 Harry C. Bentley, founder of Bentley College, was elected to honorary membership. In 1954 Ruth Welton was accorded the same honor. J. Harold Stewart was appointed to head the Second Hoover Commissions's Budget and Accounting Task Force in 1953.

During the 1940's and 1950's the society lost some of its finest members. Donald P. Perry, past president, teacher, and active member of the American Institute died in 1957. Other past presidents deceased were Edwin L. Pride, founding member (1941); Harvey S. Chase, founding member (1946); Homer N. Sweet (1948); George T. Finnigan (1950); F.R. Carnegie Steele (1955); William Boynton (1955); James Willing (1958); Richard Seamens (1959); and Charles P. Rittenhouse (1960). Other members decreased were Arthur T. Chase, honorary member (1955); Gardner Ward Chase, active member and strong supporter (1952); and Alice M. Hill, one of the first women to pass the state CPA exam (1956).

Committees

The Ethics Committee undertook relatively few activities during the war years. In 1942 the committee heard a case of client solicitation and employee hiring without informing the former employer. The evidence was circumstantial and inconclusive and the charges were dismissed.

Beginning in 1945, paid listings in the New England Telephone and Telegraph Directory were reviewed to determine if there were any violations of the society's Code of Ethics. In later years listings would show only the practitioner's name and

UNIVERSITY CLUB, BOSTON - MARCH 1959

Left to Right: Agnes L. Bixby, Executive Director, MSCPA; John F. Clarke, President, MSCPA; William Bixby, Budget Commissioner, Commonwealth of Massachusetts; Arthur Koelbel, Vice President, MSCPA.

the initials CPA, but in 1945 listings appeared under such headings as "Tax Return Preparation" and "Accountants - Bank Auditing." These advertising practices, though not specifically prohibited by the code violated its spirit and the committee believed that such practices should be discontinued. As late as 1959, the listings in the classified telephone directories of Boston and outlying districts revealed that a large number of CPAs (non-society members) were being listed in boldface type under the heading "Certified Public Accountants" and a similarly large number under "Tax Return Preparation." Both practices constituted violations of the Code of Professional Conduct.

It was also in 1959 that the American Institute asked the society for its opinion on the proposed revision of the Code of Ethics regarding the matter of independence of financial interests in any audit client. After reviewing the proposal, the Ethics Committee endorsed the concept, and further, proposed similar revision in the society's Code. The American Institute's proposed revision was accepted at its 1961 annual meeting.

In 1941 the society established a committee for the collection of historical information. Some of the fruits of the committe's labors were seen in Miss Kingman's excellent monograph Accountancy In Massachusetts - A Brief History, published in lieu of the April 1952 issue of the News Bulletin. In 1957 the committee began a scrapebook for preserving newspaper clippings on matters of interest to the society which is available in the society's library.

Public relations efforts were generally rather meager during the 1940's; in 1942, for example, there were only 12 newspaper items and a few radio spots. However, during the 1950's the society made a concerted effort to improve the image of the accounting profession. A large segment of the population did not know what a CPA was or did. The society sought to clear the haze in a number of ways. A booklet entitled The CPA Exam; Gateway to a Profession was mailed to legislators. Considerable amounts of educational and informational material were distributed to small business owners, banks and legislators. By 1953 there were a few TV shows, primarily on individual federal income tax matters. Many high-powered members of the society appeared on WHDH-TV, "Dateline Boston" and WBZ-TV and also did radio spots on WNAC, WHDH and WEEI. The shows continued throughout the decade.

The Public Relations Committee was also active in furnishing speakers for various service organizations, including the Lions, Kiwanis and Rotary groups. In 1959-60, society members spoke at 31 high school "vocational days" around the state.

Membership in the society furnishes, among other things, the privilege of hearing authoritative speakers on matters of professional interest, the give and take of tax, accounting, and auditing forums and most important the opportunity to meet people. The Meetings Committee has had overall responsibility in this area.

During the war the committee sponsored programs of timely concern. In 1942 Gerhart H. Seger, editor of a New York German language weekly, delivered an address to a worried society membership on "The War and the Fifth Column in America." Other sessions addressed the problems of public accounting and national defense; special accounting problems, such as cost-plus-fixed-fee overhead distribution, the amortization of war plant facilities and the termination of war contracts.

The steady stream of prominent speakers continued with Carman G. Blough, Maurice E. Peloubet, Victor M. Stempf, Walter E. Staub, John L. Carey, Paul

Grady, Percival F. Brundage, all of the American Institute, Professor Thomas H. Sanders of Harvard University and Professor Olsen from Dartmouth College.

The number of guest speakers began to taper off in the 1950's. Most meetings were still being held at the Parker House, but some were held at the University Club at Trinity Place. Sessions were becoming more and more technical and were being put on by the society's own members. In addition, costs were rising. Dinner meetings during the war had cost $2.50; by 1960 the cost had risen to $4.50. A round-trip railroad ticket to the American Institute's annual meeting at Detriot in 1941 cost $42.75; by 1960 the cost had risen to approximately $55.

On April 23, 1945, approximately two weeks before V-E Day, the Massachusetts society gave a dinner at the Copley Plaza Hotel for Ira Mosher, recently elected president of the National Assocation of Manufacturers. Tickets were $5.50 per person. It must have been an important meeting because more than 300 members attended and even Massachusetts Governor Maurice L. Tobin spoke briefly. Homer N. Sweet served ably as toastmaster.

Joint meetings were held annually with the Robert Morris Associates and the National Assocation of Accountants, and at various times meetings were held with other accounting-oriented groups.

From time to time the society hosted the annual meeting of the American Institute. In both 1943 and 1950 members of the American Institute from all over the country assembled at the Copley Plaza Hotel in Copley Square for the three-day annual event. Each year society members also celebrated the annual party held in the Louis XIV Ballroom at the Somerset Hotel.

For many years the society has awarded gold and silver medals to the two candidates who score the highest on the CPA examination. The weighting formula for the determination has changed from time to time, as shown below.

	Weight		
	Early 1940s	Late 1940s	Early 1950s
Accounting Problems	3	5	5
Accounting Theory	3	2	3
Auditing	3	3	4
Law	1	2	2

	Weight		
	Late 1950s and Early 1960s	Late 1960s and Early 1970s	As of 1974
Accounting Problems	5	5	2
Accounting Theory	4	5	1
Auditing	5	5	1
Law	2	1	1

Not only the weighting, but also the examination itself has changed, in terms of length and degree of difficulty. Originally the CPA exam took only two days. Accounting practice and theory took one day and auditing and commercial law one-half day each. In 1943 the exam time was increased to two and one-half days, the same as it is today.

In 1945 most states were using the uniform CPA exam prepared by the American Institute. Two Massachusetts men - Donald P. Perry and Ernest A. Berg - later served as chairmen of the AICPA Board of Examiners, which was responsible for achieving uniformity of examination throughout the nation. However, in the early 1940's the success ratio of candidates taking the exam was quite low, and the American Institute had been criticized for making the exam too difficult. Interestingly enough the results of the November 1945 exam were substantially higher than they had been in previous years. Of the 165 candidates who sat, 11 passed all four parts, and about one-third passed accounting problems. Even today neophytes to the profession invariably hear from their seniors how difficult the exam used to be.

A very fine practice which continues to this day is the annual awards dinner sponsored by the Education Committee. Here, successful exam candidates are feted and awards are given. In the mid-1950's the award was a copy of The CPA and His Profession. The practice of giving an award continues.

In addition to the annual awards dinner, the Education Committee also sponsored a number of other educational meetings. In 1946 a series of weekly meetings was held for the benefit of junior accountants. In 1948 the committee inaugurated a program to benefit students of accounting at local colleges and schools offering accounting at the college level. This program was designed to acquaint students with the activities and aims of the profession. Students from Harvard, Babson, Boston College, Boston University, MIT, Bentley and Northeastern were invited to attend the society's technical meetings. The society also formed a student accounting group.

The first annual Vocational Day for accounting students was held at Northeastern University on February 7, 1949. Eleven hundred students attended. The program included addresses entitled "Public Accounting as a Career," "The Viewpoint of the National Firm," "The Viewpoint of the Local Firm," and other topics of interest to potential entrants to the profession.

Subsequently, the committee was active in disseminating information regarding public accounting to students through educational forums held at universities and secondary schools throughout the state by showing the American Institute career film, Accounting - The Language of Business. This film, produced in 1953, was based on an hypothetical conversation between a CPA and a friend's son who was considering career opportunities. It depicted various types of problems encountered by the practicing CPA. Among the other American Institute-produced films were The CPA (1959) showing a day in the life of a partner in a local accounting firm and Men of Account (1968) made by the Canadian Institute of Chartered Accountants and modified by the American Institute for U.S. audiences.

In 1948 the Massachsuetts Society and the American Institute sponsored a three-day study conference for CPA's at the Harvard Business School to deliberate contemporary problems of theory and practice confronting the profession. A similar conference was held in 1951 at Dartmouth College. These two conferences evolved into what is now the New England Graduate Accounting Study Conference. Held on college campuses, the meetings were originally scheduled shortly after Labor Day, but now convene in the spring. At the first conference, speakers at the technical sessions included Maurice E. Peloubet and Alvin R. Jennings, both of New York. Society member Howard Greene served admirably as the program chairman.

The Committee on the News Bulletin was relatively quiet during the early 1940's. For instance, during the year ended April 30, 1944 only two issues of the New Bulletin came out; by 1946 that number had doubled. The time and manpower simply had not been available during the war years.

In 1946 the Bulletin added a department entitled "Your Round Table," a forum for the discussion of accounting problems; answers were provided to questions sent in by members. In 1947 another feature was added, "The President's Corner."

In 1948 the News Bulletin took on new format and content. Issues varying in length from 20 to 28 pages were published on the first of each month, beginning on September 1, 1948. Each pocket-size issue had one feature article, shorter contributions by society officers and committees, brief news items and several departments. In honor of the society's fiftieth anniversary, the 1949 issues had white and gold covers.

In 1951 the Bulletin accepted advertising for the first time to help defray costs. But it was not until the mid-1950's that the society voted to accept only high-quality advertising relevant to the accounting profession.

Commencing in September 1958, an annual literary award was presented to the author of the most outstanding article published in the Bulletin during the preceding publication year, as judged by three past presidents of the society. The first such award, sponsored by Robert Boyer & Co., was presented to Dorothy G. Willard, author of the article "Tax Accounting Methods." The award has encouraged society members to research and write on critical accounting problems which require clarification and resolution, and in doing so, respective authors have facilitated the work of their colleagues and their profession. The practice of giving the award has continued to the present day.

By the late 1950's the committee had been renamed the Publications Committee. In September 1959 the News Bulletin also assumed a new name and another new format. The name change was the first since the Bulletin had made its initial appearance in 1928. The new name, of course, was the Massachsuetts CPA Review. Ever since 1949 the publication had a cover and beginning in 1959 and continuing for a year, the cover of the new Review featured pictures of the Freedom Trail. The content, however, remained basically the same.

In order to write by-laws, a layman must have a strong sense of duty. That sense was always present in the meticulous work of the By-Laws Committee. In the mid-1940's by By-Laws Committee worked on an amendment to facilitate the election of officers and to improve the method of electing the nominating committee. The committee's 1947 exhaustive study of the by-laws resulted in several important improvements. In 1956 the by-laws were changed again to provide for two vice-presidents. These changes led to a more smoothly functioning society.

The Committee on Accounting and Auditing Procedures was established in 1945 to review the 25 Accounting Research Bulletins and 22 Statements in Auditing Procedure issued by the American Institute, and to advise the Massachusetts Society membership on the contents of the above at meetings and technical sessions, and to answer questions on accounting and auditing procedure submitted by members of the society. One of the Committee's first activities was to make suggestions to the Office of the Commissioner of Banks about prescribed audit procedures in connection with statutory examinations of banks. Although the committee occasionally studied the problems of the Massachusetts Certificate of Condition, most of its time was devoted to American Institute pronouncements.

In 1947 special local committees began operating outside the greater Boston area, specifically in Worcester and Springfield, to serve central and western Massachusetts. In 1951 committee appointments were also made in the New Bedford and Fall River areas to serve the southeastern part of the state. These committees helped to increase membership, expand services, and can be credited

NEW ENGLAND ACCOUNTING STUDY CONFERENCE
DARTMOUTH - 1963

with making the society a truly statewide organization.

Other committees were formed during this period to handle the needs of the growing profession. In 1950 two advisory committees were formed - one aided industrial accountants; the other, individual practitioners. In the mid-1950's as the accounting profession was on the brink of moving into management advisory services, a Management Services Committee and an Estate Planning Committee were formed.

Taxation committees have been and always will be important in society matters. To keep the members abreast of current developments in tax law during these years, taxation committees sponsored technical sessions, annual all-day conferences, a variety of tax assistance programs and frequent notes in the News Bulletin. The major tax revision of 1954 provided an abundance of work for the Taxation Committee.

In 1960 there were four standing committees - Education, Legislation, Program, and Public Relations. There were also four area committees - Central Massachusetts, Southeastern Massachusetts, Western Massachusetts, and Berkshire County. Nineteen special committees, three of which were charged with cooperating with other professional groups and another three devoted solely to taxation also existed.

Legal Matters

In 1943 the case of the Lowell Bar Association v. Birdie T. Loeb, et al tested the issue of whether the preparation of tax returns constitutes the practice of law. The defendant employed about 100 workers, one lawyer, and one accountant and advertised that the company would prepare an individual's federal income tax return for $2, state return for $2, or both for $3.75. Judge Morton of the Massachusetts Superior Court found in favor of the plaintiff. He reasoned that since a tax return is a legal document, it involves the work of an attorney.

The Massachusetts Society was concerned enough about the ramifications of such a decision to file an amicus curiae brief with the Massachusetts Supreme Court, which heard the case on appeal. Fortunately, the high court modified the decision of the lower court by holding that the preparation of tax returns by the defendant did not constitute the practice of law. The court held that:

> The proposition cannot be maintained, that whenever, for compensation, one person gives to another advice that involves some element of law or performs for another service that requires some knowledge of law, or drafts for another some document that has a legal effect, he is practicing law. All these things are done in the usual course of work of occupations that are universally recognized as distinct from the practice of law.

However, the Loeb case did not resolve the question of whether the preparation of complicated tax returns constitutes the practice of law.

In 1946 the Legislation Committee successfully defeated proposed legislation which would have discriminated unnecessarily against CPA's i.e., the old argument that CPA's practice law.

In 1949, Tax Court Bill HR 3113 was proposed to eliminate the future admission of CPA's from practice in that court. The American Bar Association fought vigorously to make the Tax Court a court of record and stongly supported the Administrative Practitioner's Bill. Both maneuvers were aimed at ensuring that only lawyers would practice before the Tax Court. Fortunately, the status of the Tax Court, i.e., as an agency in the Executive Branch remained unchanged, and the

Administrative Practitioner's Bill was completely redrafted. Congress never did act on the bill.

At about this time Representative Wilbur D. Mills of Arkansas sponsored a bill to establish a Tax Settlement Board to simplify and facilitate the settlement of tax matters informally, particularly for small businesses and individuals. The society endorsed the bill, but it did not pass because it was unacceptable to lawyers.

In Massachusetts, the Appellate Tax Board denied to CPAs the privilege of appearing before that board on behalf of others. The society's protests were to no avail. In a letter dated April 18, 1951 the board stated that it was not inclined to change its position.

PAs and CPAs

After the war the society considered placing restrictions on noncertified accountants practicing public accounting. Reaction to this effort by noncertified accountants led to the establishment of the Massachsuetts Association of Public Accountants. This organization's objective was to obtain legislation for the continuing licensing of non-CPAs. The society was unalterably opposed to any legislation of this type.

By the fall of 1950 the Massachusetts Society and representatives of the Massachusetts Association of Public Accountants had met to discuss the possibility of the two organizations reaching an agreement on a regulatory accountancy bill for introduction in the 1951 legislative session. The two organizations were able to agree, but on March 19, 1951, the Committee on State Administration submitted an unfavorable report to the legislature, recommending that any action be delayed until the next annual session. The proposed legislation would create a State Board of Accountancy comprised of five CPAs and two PAs to replace the Massachsuetts Board of Registration of CPAs. In December 1951 the Massachsuetts Association of Public Accountants took the offensive and filed Bill No 1392. The bill provided for the registration of public accountants as a continuing class. No one would be able to practice public accountancy unless registered as a public accountant. The Board of Accountancy would consist of seven public accountants who would have charge of registering all those who would practice public accounting.

For the third straight year the society had to deal with legislation on the regulation of accountancy. On January 28, 1952 the bill was debated before the House and the question put to a vote. The vote sustained the recommendation of the State Committee on Administration which had submitted an unfavorable report on the bill. The society had won after a hard fight.

The American Institute

When the American Institute began to issue pronouncements on accounting and auditing matters, Thomas H. Sanders, a professor at Harvard University and a member of the Massachusetts Society was appointed Director of Research for the Committee on Accounting Procedure. Unfortunately, when the war began Dr. Sanders had to resign to undertake duties related to the war effort. During the committee's life, which lasted until 1959, when it was superseded by the Accounting Principles Board, 51 Accounting Research Bulletins were issued. Only seven Accounting Research Bulletins were issued during the war. Since the bulletins were not binding on members of the American Institute, their adoption was based on general acceptability on the part of the business community.

In 1945 the American Institute approved a plan of coordination with the state societies to bring about closer friendships and relationships, assist societies in serving their members better, and coordinate efforts to resolve accounting problems and disseminate information. The result has been the creation of an organized public accounting profession.

But the American Institute also had to mend fences with some of its members because, as John L. Carey pointed out, there were many who suspected that the organization was unduly influenced by the larger accounting firms. From the earliest days of the organized profession, tension had existed between the large and small accounting firms. The post-World War II mergers of smaller firms with larger ones alarmed small practitioners, who may have feared that all accounting work would ultimately be done by the large firms. Louis H. Penney, a past president of the American Institute conducted a study to allay the small practitioners' fears. The study showed that it was frequently the small firms that initiated merger activities and that in the years 1946 through 1961 only 163 mergers took place. Another study, by Marvin Stone, showed that from 1946 to 1966 the number of CPAs associated with the ten largest firms had increased from 2,950 to 11,850 a 401 percent increase, whereas the total number of CPA's increased from 20,778 to 94,284, a 453 percent increase.

In 1951, in another move to interest local practitioners in the Institute, the Advisory Committee of Local Practitioners was created. This committee developed programs to meet the needs of small practitioners and also publicized the services available to them through the American Institute. These efforts were reasonable successful in improving relations between the national organization and small practitioners.

The American Institute also expended considerable effort to improve public relations with those outside the profession. The chief approach was the occasional distribution of booklets to special-interest groups. Recognizing the expanding services that accountants could offer banks, nonprofit organizations, and the like, committees were established to deal with such matters.

The American Institute was doing other things as well. It joined in the fray to fight proposed legislation which would adversely affect the practice of CPAs. It was prepared to go to the U.S. Supreme Court for a review of the Agran case or some simialr case if the Treasury Department intended to make it impossible for CPAs to practice before that department. Fortunately, that was not necessary, for in January 1956, the Secretary of the Treasury issued a statement to the effect that CPA's could continue to practice as they had in the past. But it took until 1965 for Public Law 890332 to pass both houses of Congress with the following provision:

> Any person who is duly qualified to practice as a CPA in any state may represent others before the Internal Revenue Service of the Treasury Department upon filing with that agency a written declaration that he is currently qualified and is authorized to represent the particular party in whose behalf he acts.

The statute ended 30 years of controversy.

In the 1954 revision of the Internal Revenue Code, the Institute's Tax Committee made 213 recommendations for changes in the proposed code, 105 were adopted.

In 1956 the American Institute initiated its continuing education program. This had long been the wish of Donald P. Perry, who had for much of his career fought for the upgrading of educational standards. The Institute Council also adopted the recommendation that a bachelor's degree be required for a CPA certificate and that as soon as possbile, postgraduate study devoted to accounting and business subjects also be required.

Massachusetts Society members were always active in the American Institute and its councils. The following members served as officers:

1936	Charles F. Rittenhouse	Vice President
1940	C. Oliver Wellington	President
1945	Homer N. Sweet	Vice President
1946	Percival F. Brundage*	Vice President
1948	Percival F. Brundage	President
1948	J. Harold Stewart*	Vice President
1949	J. Harold Stewart	President
1956	Donald P. Perry*	Vice President
1959	Edward J. McDevitt	Vice President
1961-63	Roger Wellington	Treasurer

*Gold medal award winner's citation from the AICPA for distinguished service to the profession.

On June 1, 1957 the American Institute of Accountants was officially renamed the American Institute of Certified Public Accountants.

FOOTNOTES

Carey, John L. *The Rise of the Accounting Profession to Responsibility and Authority 1937-1969*, New York: American Institute of Certified Public Accountants, Inc. 1970.

Edward, James D. *History of Public Accounting in the United States*. East Lansing: Bureau of Business and Economic Research, Michigan State Universiry, 1960.

Kingman, Ethel S. *Accountancy in Massachsuetts, A Brief Study*, Boston: Massachusetts Society of Certified Public Accountants, Inc. 1952.

CHAPTER FIFTEEN

HISTORY OF THE MASSACHUSETTS SOCIETY OF CPAs --- 1960 to 1970

Louis S. Corsini

The 1960's were exciting years for the accounting profession. Mergers, acquisitions, legislation and legal battles, and complex financial arrangements caused a flurry of activity at the AICPA. Accounting Principles Broad opinions and research studies were released more frequently than ever before and CPAs throughout the country were hard pressed to stay abreast of new developments.

In addition, public accounting as a profession began to emerge. The image of the CPA was beginning to assume definition in the eyes of the public. Investors, too, were awakening to the importance of the auditor's role and the significance of the attest function. The SEC and the financial press were largely responsible for thrusting the profession into the public view. The SEC was an always felt presence in the background, and the press, seemingly startled by the discovery of such an important yet unrecognized individual in the reporting process, were in turn harsh and merciful - but rarely neutral - in their treatment of the accounting profession. The Accounting Principles Board was alternately criticized and pitied, but rarely lauded. Generally accepted principles were continually questioned, and the few lawsuits of the period were highly publicized.

Occasionally the society came under fire, as did the American Institute for allegedly being under the control of the large national firms. When such a charge was leveled in 1967, the following statistics were gathered from the society's records. Of the 1797 Fellows and Associates, 20 percent and 34 percent, respectively, were affiliated with national firms; and in the past 15 years, 51 of the 178 elective offices, or 29 percent, were with the large firms. So although there was some truth to the charge, the situation was not as bad as many small practitioners believed.

Within the profession and the society, it was the era of professional development, education, and adaptation to continual change. The society worked hard to meet the challenge. New committees were formed to deal with emerging problems, old committees were revived, and professional development courses became a part of life for every practicing CPA.

As the complexities and volume of economic activities increased, it was apparent to the profession that candidates seeking admission to the accounting profession had to meet high educational standards. During the 1940's and 1950's, Donald P. Perry had fought long and hard to raise these standards. However, it was not until the 1960's that new standards were imposed.

On January 1, 1960, the Massachusetts Board of Registration set forth the new rules for applicants sitting for the CPA examination. Applicants had to meet one of the following three requirements:

1. (a) Education - high school graduate with two years' full-time study or equivalent in business subjects
   (b) Experience - four years
2. (a) Education - college graduate
   (b) Experience - three years
3. (a) Education - master's degree in business administration

(b) Experience - two years.

On December 1, 1966, a further requirement was added. Applicants would now be required to meet the education and experience requirements under (2) or (3) above.

Social Activities

In 1961 the time for election of officers was changed from May to January in order to give the incoming slate a little more time to acclimate to the rigors of executive office. The practice of appointing committee coordinators to report to the executive committee on the progress made by various committees was instituted early in the 1960-61 year. It looked as though it was going to be a big year, as 250 member had volunteered to serve on the various committees. In 1962 an operating guidebook was prepared for the executive committee, officers, and committees of the Massachusetts Society, since an effort had been made to formally inform officers and committees of their duties and objectives.

By the beginning of 1968 the society had outgrown its facilities at 44 School Street and was considering moving to One Center Plaza, which offered a five-year lease at $12,481 per annum. The move took place that summer to the new quarters which offered 50 percent more space. The move also led to the installation of an updated accounting system for the society, an improvement which had been needed for some time, and the addition of a full-time bookkeeper. Appropriations for new furniture were $5,000.

Financial condition, too, changed during the decade. Total fund assets more than doubled, although operations generally resulted in an excess of expenses over revenues.

	1961	1970
General Fund Assets	$ 14,679	$ 65,465
Admission Fund Assets	34,686	33,771
Furniture and Equipment Fund Assets	-	7,072
Total	$ 49,365	$ 106,308

By 1960 the society began to make serious efforts to enhance the image of the CPA. Tax articles and public releases were furnished regularly to local newspapers, speakers were supplied on request to various service organizations, and tax programs were prepared for radio and television by Howard Greene and Sam Shapiro. All combined to provide a real service to the public. But the society felt that these activities were still not enough, so in 1962 a publicity counsel, Gordon Sanders of the Boston Herald was engaged to prepare newspaper releases. In 1964 the society considered having the CPA's story carried in a supplement to the Sunday newspaper, at a cost of about $8,500, but nothing was done. When the idea was brought up again in 1969, costs had risen to about $12,000 and the idea was rejected once and for all.

As part of the concerted effort to improve the CPA's image, the Public Relations Committee sponsored the Dial-A-Tax-Expert program in March 1968. The first program was held in the conference room of the society offices. Twelve phones were installed, and 75 volunteers helped taxpayers on their federal and state tax returns. The 1968 program, which ran for two weeks, was advertised on television, radio, billboards, and in a feature article in the Boston Globe. Four thousand taxpayers called in for assistance. This program was so successful that it became a continuing service offered by the society.

Accounting education was a lively topic for discussion among society members in the early 1960's. There was little question that the accounting profession was expanding and that there would be a need for capable young men and women trained in accounting. The problem was, of course, that very few students had even the faintest notion of what public accounting entailed. Therefore, the society decided to make a concerted effort to reach out to students. Speakers appeared at Massachusetts' high schools on career day. The American Accounting Association publication, Young Eyes on Accounting, was mailed to high school vocational guidance departments. The society purchased from the American Institute the film, The CPA, to show to high school and college students; later in the decade the society acquired another film, Men of Account, from the American Institute and made it available to colleges and universities. In 1968 the Education Committee held a joint meeting with high school counselors from western Massachusetts. In the following year, the committee placed copies of the booklet, These CPAs Want You in local colleges and universities. The booklet listed firms offering employment.

The establishment of an educational foundation had been discussed for a number of years, but nothing had been done. By 1964, however, the society began to prepare the necessary legal documents to set up such a fund and to solicit financial gifts. The purposes and objectives of the fund were threefold:

1. To advance education and research relating to the discipline of accountancy;
2. To provide financial assistance to qualified students preparing for a career in public accounting or the teaching of accounting;
3. To assist business colleges and universities by providing student scholarship and loan funds.

Professional development grew so rapidly in the mid-1960's, that a part-time director was hired by the society. Three part-time directors, Dr. Robert G. Taylor of Northeastern University and Gordon Nelson and Andrew Petersen from Bentley College, held that post at various times until 1970, when it had become obvious that continuing education would not lessen and that a full-time director would be required. In 1970 Ted Flynn was appointed the first full-time director. Typical of the early courses were the six seminars entitled "Accounting Fees" and "Budgeting for Profit in Small Business." The professional development courses were generally a financial success. Attendance, on the other hand, was not encouraging. During the late 1960's only about 25 percent of the membership attended professional development courses.

In 1960 the State Tax Commission was directed by the General Court to study the advisability of a more simplified and equitable corporate income tax. This resulted in the passage of Chapter 756 of the Acts of 1962. The bill made some drastic changes in the Massachusetts Corporate Excise Tax applicable to both foreign and domestic corporations, changes which would simplify the computation and administration of the excise.

The society had considered actively advocating a policy regarding the formulation of these laws, but decided to remain neutral. However, the society did work very closely with the Department of Corporations and Taxation on amendments to the law pertaining to the Massachusetts Certificate of Condition. The purpose of the legislation was to simplify the filing requirements of the Certificate of Condition and to clarify the auditor's responsibilty relating to the financial statement contained therein. Three years of work went into the amendments, which became law on May 18, 1962.

In the summer of 1960 Boston's deputy mayor invited J. S. Seidman, president of the American Institue, to discuss municipal procedures in accounting at the city and state levels. Mr. Seidman recommended that Boston's municipal accounting procedures be modernized through the utilization of electronic data processing and a centralized system of accounting. The recommendations were well received, but it would be a few years before they were acted on. In that same year Mayor Collins of Boston requested various accounting firms in the city to donate their service to study operations of separate departments in city government and to make recommendations for streamlining government. The society responded by forming a subcommittee to take whatever action seemed fit and by performing some management advisory service.

In 1968 the society undertook a program to make available professional counseling and advising services, free of charge, to disadvantaged people of the black community who were attempting to establish their own businesses in the Roxbury area. The services offered included advice on tax matters, design and maintenance of business records, capital requirements, and other business problems. The society enlisted volunteer services from large CPA firms and from individual practitioners. The whole program was kept on a very low key basis, and there were no affiliations with other public service programs or with Mayor White's office. By December 1968, 55 black businessmen had received help through 75 participating firms.

In the fall of 1960 a big membership drive to attract more CPAs was launched. Since few new memberships resulted, the effort had to be described as unsuccessful. The membership drive did, however, assist the society in tightening its records. Information supplied by members revealed that many "practicing" CPA s had in fact been deceased for many years.

A second membership drive was more successful, producing 168 new members. The society also sought to increase the number of Associate members. Total membership during the decade increased by 913, to 2,539; the number of Fellows increased by 587, to 1,886, and the number of Associates by 327, to 650. The death of William Morse Cole reduced the number of honorary members to three.

In 1960 the Executive Committee voted to reduce dues for non-practicing CPA's and CPA's in government, but no action was taken by the membership. In 1963 dues were still $25 for Fellows; however, by 1966 they had risen to $30 for Fellows residing within 25 miles of Boston, $20 for other Fellows, and $10 for Associates. By the end of 1967 it was recommended that dues differentials for geographical location be eliminated, and the following dues structure was adopted:

Fellows -	
Certified for three years	$ 40
Less than three years	35
Associates -	
CPA s of another state	25
Other associates	20
Nonresidents	10
Retired members over 65	5

By 1962, with the completion of the Massachusetts Turnpike, the society president urged members from western Massachusetts to come to the city more often to attend society functions. It was felt that a centralized society was preferable to the formation of regional chapters.

During the 1960's Dorothy Willard was elected president of the National

Association of the State Boards of Accountancy. Miss Willard, who retired from the Massachusetts Board of Accountancy in 1969, had been vice-president of the society, editor of the News Bulletin, and recipient of the Massachusetts legislature citation. Ethel Kingman, the first woman member of the society, became the first woman to be elected to the Executive Committee.

John L. Carey of the American Institute and Kenneth W. Bergen of the law firm Bingham, Dana and Gould were elected to honorary membership in 1963 and 1967, respectively. Both William Morse Cole, Professor Emeritus at Harvard University, who was awarded honorary membership in 1960, and Harry C. Bentley, awarded honorary membership in 1967, died during the decade. Among the active and dedicated society members who died during this period were George F. Shannon (1962); James D. Glunts (1965); Arthur W. Koelbel (1966); Harry W. Wallis (1967); and Mark C. Walker (1970).

Committees

The society could very well be viewed as a collection of committees operating out of a common interest and from a common address. From the technical sessions of the Accounting and Auditing Procedures Committee to the awards dinner sponsored by the Education Committee, someone was always working on some assignment. A series of lectures on hospital accounting was offered in 1961, and the Hospital Accounting Committee was quite active in the later 1960's. Taxation committees - federal, state, and estate planning - were always very active, especially after the passage of the Revenue Act of 1962 and the Tax Reform Act of 1969.

Whether it is typical of the profession or just the members of the Massachusetts Society, reported violations of professional ethics have been relatively few and for the most part venial. During the 1960's the Executive Committee did not hear many cases. When, in 1964, the question of dual listings in classified directories came up, the committee ruled that in the case of CPA-Lawyers, only one listing in a classified directory would be permitted. Many society members carried these dual credentials, and protested vigorously to the American Institute, but their efforts did not change the society's position.

On the lighter side, the Executive Committee was notified that someone was using vanity plates with the initials "CPA". Since the Massachusetts Bar Association had taken a definitive position forbidding vanity registration and the practice appeared to be in violation of Sec. 3.01 of the society's code of ethics, a notice was sent out to the membership asking them not to use vanity plates; everyone complied.

The annual spring party, held at the Blue Hills Country Club in 1961, had moved to the Chatham Bars Inn by 1970. Dinner meetings, which were at the Parker House in 1960 for $5.00, were being held at Pier 4 in 1970 at a slightly higher cost. Dinner meetings featured many nationally known speakers including Leonard Spacek, Perry Mason, Andrew Barr, Edward Kennedy, Professors Don Smith and Bertrand Fox of Harvard, Mortimer M. Caplin, John L. Carey, Leonard M. Savoie, Robert Sprouse, David Linowes, John H. Knowles, M.D., John Lawler, Cleo F. Jaillet, and Owen L. Clarke. Gino Cappeletti of the Boston Patriots scheduled to speak at one of the October 1969 meetings drew one of the largest crowds ever, but at the eleventh hour something must have come up because Mr. Cappeletti never appeared.

On January 27, 1970, the society hosted the members of the Massachusetts General Court at the Grand Ballroom of the Sheraton-Boston. This gathering was initiated by Herman Steutzer and Ernest Berg, who had attended a conference on state legislature committees in Chicago. The purpose of the social get-together was for legislators and CPA s to get to know one another. The gala event was a huge success.

In the early 1960's the Education Committee sponsored the professional development program and, of course, the annual awards dinner, which always featured first-rate speakers. Successful candidates were usually given one of John L. Carey's books on the profession. At the 1966 awards dinner, Certificates of Recognition were given to three members - Ernest N. Griswold, Arthur P. Batchelder, and Stanley G. H. Fitch for 50 years in the society. Hugh Dysart, Sr., and Arthur F. Risley were honored in absentia.

The committee worked hard presenting workshops and seminars, particularly seminars in auditing standards, field work, and reporting. Other seminars included an IBM three-day course on data processing and a tax lecture series prepared by AICPA.

New Committees were always being set up as the need arose. In 1963 the By-laws Committee undertook a complete revision and codification of the by-laws. The study resulted in 40 substantive changes and other modifications, which were subsequently ratified by the membership. The changes became effective on May 1, 1967.

Also in 1963 two other projects were readied. One was a consultation service to assist small practitioners with their professional problem. The other project was the creation of a Practice Review Committee whose function was to uncover substandard reporting and to promote higher standards of professional performance. The latter committee, encouraged by the American Institute, was not to be disciplinary, but would rely on diplomacy, education, and persuasion. Other new committees were a Small Business Committee, which was very active for a short time working closely with the Small Business Administration, and the Massachusetts Certificate of Condition Committee.

In 1964 the Management Services Committee ran two successful programs which utilized cases in operations research, financial planning, and systems. During this period, the Practitioners' Advisory Committee set up the Emergency Professional Assistance Plan to provide services and assistance to the estate and clients of any deceased practitioners who had not made other arrangements, as well as to disabled practitioners who would be otherwise unable to provide quality services.

As legal liability problems began to emerge, the society appointed a Professional Liability Committee to deal with them, particularly in making arrangements for obtaining underwriters for professional liability insurance.

The Small Business Committee and the Committee on Relations with Bankers and Lawyers had programs designed to make these segments of the economy more aware of the services offered by CPAs. The Committee for Members in Commerce, Government and Education, originally known as the Industrial Accountants' Committee, held a number of successful luncheons at Purcells in an attempt to get these members more involved with society activities, but unfortunately the committee was allowed to die.

Other active committees were the Central Massachusetts Area Committee, the Management Services Committee, the Program Committee, and the Savings Bank Committee. By 1970 there were four area committees - Central, Southeastern, Western, and Berkshire County.

Each year the society co-sponsored the Northeastern University Tax Forum, as well as the annual fall New England Graduate Accounting Study Conference, held at some academic setting. In December of each year joint sessions were held with the American Society of Women Accountants, NAA, the Controllers Institute of America, the Federal Government Accountants' Association of Boston, the Tax Executives Institute, and the Institute of Internal Auditors.

The First Annual Spring Conference was held in May 1966 at the Chatham Bars Inn, Chatham, Massachusetts. The three-day technical sessions were a huge success. The conferences continued to be held there until 1970, when they were moved to Bermuda. The society also hosted the annual meeting of the American Institute in the fall of 1966, and the first and only meeting with the Financial Executives Institute was held on November 2, 1969.

The Massachusetts CPA Review

During the 1960's, and continuing to the present day, the *Massachusetts CPA Review* has been published every other month. Because some people felt that another vehicle was needed to keep the membership apprised of current newsworthy notes, the *CPA Newsletter* was created in 1962 to be sent out in alternate months from the *Review*. It was also about this time that Ethel Kingman's excellent column "We Remember" began to appear in the *Review*. Her column featured short historical notes and a brief obituary for deceased society members.

Beginning in 1964, entire issues of the *Review* were occasionally devoted to specific subject areas. The Internal Revenue Service under District Director Alvin M. Kelley was given an entire issue, as were bankers, SEC problems, accounting and auditing problems of defense contractors, and others.

In the mid-1960's Myron Greenside's bi-monthly piece on Massachusetts taxes was introduced, and this column soon became standard reading for society members. So, too, were the articles on taxation by George Brody and his successor in the mid-1960's, Joseph Flynn, whose column "Federal Tax Notes" still appears and is widely read by the membership.

Toward the end of the decade, new columns appeared, authored by new members. "Estate Planning," "What Others are Saying," "The CPA in Industry, Education and Government," and the "Editor's Corner" were just some of the departments that helped make the *Review* a truly useful magazine for the entire membership. Feature articles, most of which were written by society members, have continued to be timely and interesting and have certainly been largely responsible for making the *Review* a nationally recognized journal.

Legal Matters

Until 1959 the Massachusetts Society and the Massachusetts Association of Public Accountants had ignored each other. Then on December 19, 1959, the society voted to establish a committee to cooperate with the Massachusetts Association of Public Accountants. But the decade had barely begun when the society learned that the Massachusetts Association of Public Accouantancy under the guidance of its president, Rocco Antonelli, was planning to file new legislation with would strengthen the status of public accountants. The PA's bill, filed on December 4, 1961, provided for:

1. the licensing of public accountants;
2. equal representation with CPA s on the Board of Registration;
3. perpetual registration of public accountants, i.e., no phasing out via a grandfather clause.

AUGUST 19, 1963

Left to Right: Senator McKenna, Ernest A. Berg, Chairman MSCPA, Legislation Committee; Representative Stephen A. Davenport; Herman Stuetzer, Jr., President, MSCPA; Rocco J. Antonelli, President, MAPA; Max Hyman, Chairman, MAPA Legislation Committee; Senator George Keannelly.

The society took strong opposition to the bill which would allow persons to practice public accounting who had never taken an examination to establish their qualifications and who would be granted approval merely by reason of their own statement of qualifications. Fortunately, the bill was defeated on the floor of the House of Representatives on April 24, 1962.

But the battle was not over. On February 25, 1963, the Committee on State Administration conducted simultaneous hearings at the State House on two bills filed in that session which would regulate the practice of public accounting - the society's bill - House No. 2124 - and the Massachusetts Association of Public Accountant's bill - Senate No. 559. Both bills called for some type of regulation for the profession. The two major points of disagreement continued to be equal representation of PA's on the board and continuing registration for PA's as opposed to their being phased out.

The upshot of this was the passage of Chapter 663 of the Acts of 1963 by the Massachusetts General Court. The new law, entitled "An Act Abolishing the Board of Registration of Certified Public Accountants and Establishing a Board of Public Accountancy, and Further Regulating the Practice of Public Accountancy," was signed by Governor Peabody on August 19, 1963, and became effective 90 days later. Massachusetts thus became the 36th state to adopt regulatory legislation.

The new Board of Public Accountancy in Massachusetts, created through the enactment of Chapter 663, was comprised of five members - four CPAs and one PA. Only CPA members could act on matters concerning CPAs. The bill also established a Public Accountants Administrative Committee of five public accountants, one of whom would be the PA member of the Board. The committee was empowered to deal with matters involving public accountants, including registration. The era of the public accountant was drawing to a close, for registration would be only for those who had been in public practice prior to November 18, 1963. Legal fees incurred by the society in connection with the enactment of Chapter 663 approximated $13,500 less $1,500 contributed by the Massachusetts Association of Public Accountants to cover its share of the legal expenses.

Tensions between the two groups began to ease, and in January 1964, public accountants were invited to attend professional development courses sponsored by the society. There was even some discussion about admitting PAs into the society as associate members.

Massachusetts was not the only state that had to fight for regulatory accountancy legislation. The battle took place in nearly every state. In some states the issue went to the highest court, and as often as not restrictive legislation was not upheld. Actually, Massachusetts was considered as having permissive accounting laws; that is, anyone could practice accounting, but only those holding the CPA certificate could use the title CPA.

The American Institute changed its position on the issue several times. In the early 1930's it concluded that regulatory legislation would not serve the best interests of either the profession or the public. However, within a few years the American Institute adopted a more neutral posture, which it held until the early 1950's. However, in 1955 the national organization was forced to take a position in response to attacks by organized public accountants in many states. The neutrality position, characterized by passivity and defensiveness which in the long run could only lead to a watering down of CPA standards, was reexamined and set aside. Very shortly thereafter, the American Institute endorsed regulatory accountancy legislation to prohibit the continuing registration of public accountants, and in 1956 it published a "Form of Regulatory Accountancy Bill" as a guide to state societies planning legislation.

Throughout the decade the Massachusetts Society continually fought proposed legislation which would have the effect of downgrading the profession of public accounting. On December 9, 1964, the society's Executive Committee voted to oppose two new bills pending in the legislature. One proposal sought to allow all "municipal examinees," of the Commonwealth of Massachusetts or any of its subdivisions who were engaged in field audit work to register as public accountants, even though they continued in field audit work with the commonwealth. The second proposal sought to include corporations or their officers engaged in the practice of public accounting to be eligible for licensing as public accountants. Through the able assistance of Kenneth W. Bergen, legislative counsel, both bills were defeated.

Another piece of harmful legislation was proposed late in 1964. According to this legislation, whenever any law of a state agency required that a document of any agency of the commonwealth be prepared by a CPA, such requirements would be construed to mean a PA or a CPA. This proposal eventually became known as the "perennial Bartley bill", because from 1965 through 1969, this bill was introduced in the General Court, by Mr. Bartley and each year it was rejected. All of this legal activity forced the society to engage legislative counsel, William F. Malloy.

Other less important legislation dealt with compensation for board members and permission for state audit employees to register as public accountants after two years of audit experience. Late in the decade, legislation was introduced -

unsuccessfully - to impose liability on accountants who failed to disclose in their audit report any flagrant violations of law.

The American Institute of Certified Public Accountants

In 1959, after 18 months of deliberation, the Council of the American Institute approved the establishment of a Special Committee on Research Programs; its first objective was to determine the basic postulates and principles of accounting. Maurice Moonitz was appointed Director of Accounting Research and in 1961 _Accounting Research Study No. 1 - "The Basic Postulates of Accounting"_ - was released, followed within a year by _Accounting Research Study No. 3 - "A Tentative Set of Broad Accounting Principles for Business Enterprise."_ These studies were to be followed by many others and in theory were to provide a basis for many of the _Opinions_ of the Accounting Principles Board. Although this objective was not met, accounting research, so sorely needed, was nonetheless given some impetus.

In 1963 the AICPA prepared to make its bid for its opinions to have greater authoritative standing. This developed as a result of the Revenue Act of 1962, which enacted an investment credit to stimulate the economy. It was the accounting treatment of the investment credit that caused all the trouble. The Accounting Principles Board was divided on the issue, but finally was able to gather a majority in favor of spreading the credit over the life of the asset. Mr. Witschery, president of the American Institute, urged the Securities and Exchange Commission to support the board's conclusion, but it was not to be. The SEC published _Accounting Series Release No. 96_, which permitted alternative accounting treatments for the credit, an action that badly damaged the prestige of the board. As a result of the investment credit experience, the American Institute approved a proposal that Accounting Principles Board Opinions should be regarded as generally accepted accounting principles until they were subsequently disapproved or modified by the council. Furthermore, the burden of justifying departures from an APB opinion would be borne by the member departing from the opinion.

Up until 1966 the American Institute considered rescinding the ban on competitive bidding, but the issue died when the two-thirds vote necessary for repeal was not achieved. At the end of the decade the institute was contemplating the notion of incorporation of public accounting firms. At that time Massachusetts law forbade incorporation but within two years the law was changed and incorporation became a reality.

In October 1966 the American Institute held its seventy-ninth annual meeting in Boston. Approximately 300 members attended. It was also about this time that John L. Carey, who had served the American Institute for so many years and who had always maintained a close relationship with the Massachusetts Society, began to look forward to his retirement in 1969.

The CPA Wives' Club of Massachusetts, created at the annual meeting of the American Institute in Miami, October 4-7, 1964, was given the task of planning the social functions for the 1966 AICPA convention, which would be held in Boston. The CPA Wives' Club turned out to be more than ad hoc, for it has continued to operate and sponsor many worthwhile activities. One of the group's top priorities has been to raise funds for the Educational Foundation. The group has also been a socially integrating factor, as acquaintanceship among wives has led to acquaintanceship among husbands.

Accounting in Academia

A history of accountancy in Massachusetts would certainly be incomplete without some mention of the schools which prepare Massachusetts men and women for their careers in public accounting.

Harvard University began teaching accounting at about the same time the society was founded, in 1900. The first course was taught by William Morse Cole under the auspices of the Economics Department. The course was given as a vocational aid for students, and at first no academic credit was given. However, in 1908, when Harvard Business School was founded, accounting became a required subject for all first-year students. Boston University followed in 1913 by offering an evening program to business students. Accounting was a required course for every student. Classes were held at 525 Boylston street near Copley Square until 1938 when the university moved to the Commonwealth Avenue Campus. Bentley College of Accounting and Finance, the next to offer accounting courses, opened its doors to 30 students in Back Bay in 1917. Bentley was a two-year school until 1964, when it became a four year, degree-granting college. Northeastern University's College of Business Administration was founded in 1922 and in that same year organized its accounting program.

Outside the greater-Boston area, Holy Cross College first offered an introductory accounting course as an elective for upperclassmen in 1926. Later the accounting program increased its offerings substantially. A Holy Cross faculty member, Edward Peragallo, wrote on the history of accountancy before such writing became fashionable. His book _Origin and Evolution of Double Entry Bookkeeping; A Study of Italian Practice from the 14th Century_, published in 1938, was well received in academic circles.

Students in the Worcester area could also find instruction in accounting at the New England School of Accounting, a two-year school founded in 1926. Nichols College offered accounting courses shortly thereafter, and Worcester Junior College began offering instruction in accounting after World War II.

Western Massachusetts has had the good fortune to have three good schools offering accounting - American International College, the University of Massachusetts at Amherst, and Western New England College. Western New England and American International were both early entrants in the field of accounting instruction beginning in 1919 and 1926 respectively. In 1951, Western New England succeeded the Springfield division of Northeastern University which was primarily an evening school. The University of Massachusetts at Amherst opened the doors of its business school in 1947.

In addition to the greater-Boston schools already mentioned, Boston College's College of Business Administration opened in 1938 on Newbury Street, Back Bay. Babson College and Suffolk University followed shortly thereafter.

At the present time Massachusetts schools granting B.S. degrees with a major in accounting are American International College, Babson College, Bentley College, Boston College, Boston University, College of the Holy Cross, University of Lowell, University of Massachusetts, Merrimack College, Nichols College, Northeastern University, Salem State College, Southeastern Massachusetts University, Stonehill College, Suffolk University, and Western New England College.

Epilogue

At the present time the Massachusetts Society of CPAs has over 4,200 members (a far cry from the original 14), a staff of seven ably administrated by Theodore J. Flynn and his assistant Marianne Brush, and an operating budget of nearly a quarter of a million dollars. Further, the society has succumbed to the technological age by computerizing the records of all of its members. The expanded staff and increased member services have required moving to larger quarters at Three Center Plaza.

From 1970 to 1975, continuing education was probably the most talked about issue. In 1971, the American Institute of Certified Public Accountants presented a resolution urging states to adopt a continuing education requirement for CPAs eligible to practice public accounting. The concept was adopted by the council of the American Institute but implementation was left to the individual states. Massachusetts CPAs considered the proposal but in 1971 mandatory continuing education was not held in high regard. Even as recently as 1974 a survey of Massachusetts Society members indicated that the majority favored voluntary continuing education. Popular sentiment prevailed, and the society adopted a policy whereby each member was expected to voluntarily participate in 24 hours of continuing education. The society encouraged continuing education by expanding course offerings. Between the fall of 1970 and the fall of 1976, courses available to members increased from 13 to 55. In addition, the society joined with other New England states in a cooperative professional education program, increasing the total number of courses available in the New England region to over 115.

During the 1970's the society became seriously involved in the legislative process. A legislative analyst was employed part-time to identify issues affecting the profession; to develop an "early warning system" on pending legislation; and to assist the society in developing policy positions. A "Breakfast Meetings with Legislators" program was also instituted. This interaction was deemed essential for mutual understanding of the dynamics of the public decision-making process.

SOCIETY'S 75th ANNIVERSARY
ACCOUNTANTS DAY IN MASSACHUSETTS

(Left to right) J. Paul Finnegan, President-Elect, MSCPA; Governor Michael Dukakis; Victor Cohen, President, MSCPA; Theodore J. Flynn, Executive Director, MSCPA

Through such meetings both CPAs and legislators gained insight into each others' concerns, and the society began to play a more meaningful role in serving government and the profession.

On May 31, 1975, the Massachusetts Society of Certified Public Accountants celebrated its diamond anniversary at the Sheraton-Boston. The event commemorated 75 years of unremitting effort and dedication to society objectives on behalf of the members of the public accounting profession and the general public. Perhaps the words of past President Victor Cohen provide a fitting conclusion:

> We are accepted as a profession and our advice and counsel is sought after in the highest levels of government and industry. We have accomplished much of which we can be justly proud. But we must not rest on our laurels. To do so is only to regress. We must continually strive to even greater achievements and professional stature.

Footnotes

Carey, John L. *The Rise of the Accounting Profession to Responsibility and Authority 1937-1969*. New York: American Institute of Certified Public Accountants, Inc. 1970

CONCLUSION

This volume on accounting history has attempted to introduce readers to the extraordinary contributions of Massachusetts accountants during the last three centuries. In retrospect, the most surprising aspect of the authors' research was the discovery of the voluminous number of early accounting records and documents available in Massachusetts.

Three Centuries of Accounting in Massachusetts has touched upon mercantile, provincial and municipal accounting in the 17th century. It also has traced the development of public accounting in Massachusetts from the mid-19th century to 1970. Unfortunately, little information on accounting developments in the early 18th century are included - not because there is a paucity of data, but because many records are presently inaccessible. The state archives for much of this period have not been duplicated on microfilm and the material is simply not available to researchers. Steps are now being taken to establish proper storage for this material and the authors believe it may become available for examination within a few years.

The same lack of access is also true of the Treasurers' and Selectmen's accounts for the Town of Boston during the 18th century. Boston's accounts are now in the custody of the Boston Public Library but they have not been indexed. Despite these problems, Bill Holmes managed to inspect some of the town records and discovered a complete double-entry system in use by the Treasurer of Boston from 1780 to 1795. A more extensive analysis of these early documents is necessary to determine precisely when the double-entry system was introduced into Boston's municipal accounts.

Many sources of information on old accounting records are available in New England and particularly in Massachusetts. Baker Library at the Harvard University Graduate School of Business Administration has extensive files of the accounts and related business documents of many New England textile firms dating from the early 1800s. While some records have been examined by economists, social scientists and industrial historians, little accounting research has been conducted on this potentially fruitful source of accounting history. One can speculate that these early industrial records may contain the seeds of American cost accounting systems, and potentially valuable research awaits historians willing to invest the necessary time analyzing and evaluating these documents.

Another area for extensive accounting research may be found in the records of early Massachusetts and New England railroad companies. Preliminary investigation of fragments of these files has led the authors to conclude that the birth of the modern internal audit function and the application of statistical analysis to accounting data may be revealed by an analysis of early railroad accounts.

Finally, municipal accounting history in New England may be examined within the framework of the Town Meeting form of government, a tradition that dates from the 1600s. The essence of Town Meeting government has always been accountability. The earliest town records include rudimentary budgeting and auditing as normal functions by the late 1600s (see the Plymouth Colony records in Chapter Three); and appropriation accounting was well-established by the early 1800s. Unquestionably, Massachusetts and New England remain a virtually untapped lode of accounting history; and the several avenues for research mentioned there by no means exhaust the list for potential research.

How does one get into the business of uncovering and writing about accounting history in the early colonial years? It might encourage others to reflect on the fact that the authors are primarily accountants, each busy filling a niche in the modern accounting market, and with no specialized training in history research. The first job is to "get the feel" of the period in terms of the business climate, and in addition to the standard history texts, three books stand out in this respect:

"Builders of the Bay Colony" by Samuel Eliot Morison
(Houghton Mifflin Company, 1930)

"The Maritime History of Massachusetts, 1738 - 1860" by Samuel Eliot Morison (Houghton Mifflin Company, 1941)

"The New England Merchants in the Seventeenth Century" by Bernard Bailyn
(Harvard University Press, 1955)

The town records of Boston, printed and published by the City Record Commissioner in 1877, are an excellent source for on-the-spot lore from 1634 to the 1820's. These are very well indexed and easy to consult as to persons names, treasurers' reports, special committees, etc. Particularly interesting for the period 1644 to 1651 is Volume 32, the Aspinwall Notarial Records, which paint an extremely interesting day-to-day picture of business life during these years as seen through documents notarized by the town's early businessmen.

For the early accounts of the Provinces of Plymouth and Massachusetts the best sources are:

"Records of the Colony of New Plymouth in New England" and

"Records of the Governor and Company of the Massachusetts Bay in New

England" both edited by Nathaniel B. Shurtleff, M.D., the first in 1857 second in 1853, and printed by order of the Commonwealth.

For the rest there is the vast collection of State and City Archives, of smaller town archives, and the collections of a goodly number of local historical societies, all largely untouched by accountants. Nor should we forget the more prestigious files of the Massachusetts Historical Society, the Baker Library and the Aetheneum, for the most part beautifully indexed and easily consulted. The early merchants had a predilection towards litigation with one another and the judicial files of the various courts are an excellent source of materials since in almost all instances evidence in the form of accounts had to be filed in writing with the Court. The problem is not where to look but rather where first to look.

While the first part of the book relates to early accounting history in Massachusetts, Part II presents a comprehensive history of the first seventy years of the Massachusetts Society of Certified Public Accountants. Few professional accounting organizations have a more illustrious record of service and achievement; and the authors believe this history adds to the literature in accounting by tracing the evolution of one of the country's first accounting organizations dedicated to the professional development of public accountants.

Writing the history of the Massachusetts Society was a pleasant change of pace from the authors' regimen of teaching contemporary accounting. Most of the research and writing was performed at the Society's office, for it is in the library that the minutes of general meetings, executive committee meetings, other committee meetings and the annual meeting are premanently retained. In addition, at the end of each year, every committee submits a report summarizing the work accomplished during the year, and these also were available. For purposes of writing history one cannot ask for much more. The writing style and command of the English language, particularly of early members, is truly impressive; and it is a distinct pleasure to read through them.

Because minutes are documents of record, at best they only hint at the human interaction, the political battles and the petty squabbles within an organization. This is also true for the great personalities, the "characters" and the unsung heroes who are always relied upon to get the job done. For information of this type the historian must seek another source. One such source is correspondence, when available, but a better source of modern history is the people who were there, i.e., the observers and the actors, for they can provide the writer with a perspective on the times that is often difficult to glean from the printed page. In this instance the authors were extremely fortunate to be able to speak with the executive secretaries from 1936 to the present, Ruth Welton, Agnes Bixby and Ted Flynn about society issues and personalities. They were most cooperative, professional and an invaluable source of information. The authors had to guard against allowing their personal interpretations and biases to creep into the writing. This is a particularly sensitive problem when writing about living people.

Other sources of data utilized were: the Massachusetts CPA Review, the News Bulletin, society correspondence, local newspapers, and books on the profession, particularly those of John L. Carey.

Enough has been written here to show that the work presented in this volume is merely a beginning. The authors hope that readers will find this book both interesting and entertaining, as any history ought to be. They also hope their work will spur other accountants to join the small cadre of accounting historians in Massachusetts and other sections of the country where accounting history has heretofore been sadly neglected.

APPENDIX A

PAST OFFICERS SINCE ORGANIZATION OF THE ORIGINAL SOCIETY

Year	President	Vice President	Secretary	Treasurer
1900-1901	Amos D. Albee	William Franklin Hall	Harvey S. Chase	Charles F. Kellogg
1901-1902	Amos D. Albee	William Franklin Hall	Harvey S. Chase	Charles F. Kellogg
1902-1903	William Franklin Hall	Herbert F. French	Harvey S. Chase	Thomas S. Spurr
1903-1904	Herbert F. French	George S. Chase	Harvey S. Chase	Thomas P. Parsons
1904-1905	George S. Chase	Frederick C. Tufts	Harvey S. Chase	George W. Manson
1905-1906	Frederick C. Tufts	Harvey S. Chase	William C. Newell	William H. Herrick
1906-1907	Harvey S. Chase	Thomas S. Spurr	William Dillon	Charles H. Tuttle
1907-1908	Thomas S. Spurr	Augustus Nickerson	William Dillon	Herbert F. French
1908-1909	Augustus Nickerson* William C. Newell†	William C. Newell* Charles H. Tuttle†	William Dillon	Herbert F. French
1909-1910	William C. Newell	Charles H. Tuttle	Waldron H. Rand	Herbert F. French
1910-1911	Charles H. Tuttle	William Dillon	Waldron H. Rand	Herbert F. French
1911-1912	Charles H. Tuttle	Amos D. Albee	Waldron H. Rand	Herbert F. French
1912-1913	Waldron H. Rand	Newman W. Storer	Walter C. Wrye	Gerald Wyman
1913-1914	Waldron H. Rand	George L. Bishop	Walter C. Wrye	Gerald Wyman
1914-1915	J. Edward Masters	William Franklin Hall	George Lyall	Gerald Wyman
1915-1916	J. Edward Masters	William Franklin Hall	George Lyall	Gerald Wyman
1916-1917	F.R. Carnegie Steele	Edwin L. Pride	George Lyall	Gerald Wyman
1917-1918	F.R. Carnegie Steele	Edwin L. Pride	George Lyall	Gerald Wyman
1918-1919	Edwin L. Pride	Hollis H. Sawyer	George Lyall	Gerald Wyman
1919-1920	Edwin L. Pride	Hollis H. Sawyer	George Lyall	Gerald Wyman
1920-1921	George Lyall	Hollis H. Sawyer	Frederick B. Cherrington	Gerald Wyman
1921-1922	George Lyall	Hollis H. Sawyer	Frederick B. Cherrington	Gerald Wyman+ Robert Douglas†
1922-1923	Hollis H. Sawyer	Stanley G.H. Fitch	Frederick B. Cherrington	Robert Douglas
1923-1924	Hollis H. Sawyer	Stanley G.H. Fitch	Frederick B. Cherrington	Arthur T. Chase
1924-1925	Stanley G.H. Fitch	Frederick B. Cherrington	Charles F. Rittenhouse	Arthur T. Chase
1925-1926	Stanley G.H. Fitch	Frederick B. Cherrington	Charles F. Rittenhouse	Arthur T. Chase
1926-1927	Frederick B. Cherrington	Charles F. Rittenhouse	Percival F. Brundage	Arthur T. Chase
1927-1928	Frederick B. Cherrington	Charles F. Rittenhouse	Percival F. Brundage	Arthur T. Chase
1928-1929	Charles F. Rittenhouse	James Willing	Clifton W. Gregg	Arthur T. Chase
1929-1930	James Willing	J. Chester Crandell	Clifton W. Gregg* Albert E. Hunter†	Arthur T. Chase
1930-1931	J. Chester Crandell	Percival F. Brundage	Albert E. Hunter	Arthur T. Chase
1931-1932	Percival F. Brundage	Donald P. Perry	Albert E. Hunter	Arthur T. Chase
1932-1933	Donald P. Perry	Raymond D. Willard	Arthur W. Yardley	John F. Clarke
1933-1934	George S. Clarkson	Richard D. Seamans	Arthur W. Yardley	John F. Clarke
1934-1935	Richard D. Seamans	Homer N. Sweet	Arthur W. Yardley	John F. Clarke
1935-1936	Homer N. Sweet	Earle M. French	Arthur W. Yardley	John F. Clarke
1936-1937	Earle M. French	Arthur W. Yardley	J. Harold Stewart	John F. Clarke
1937-1938	Arthur W. Yardley	Anthony Jaureguy	J. Harold Stewart	Edward J. McDevitt
1938-1939	Anthony Jaureguy	J. Harold Stewart	Albert E. Hunter	Edward J. McDevitt
1939-1940	J. Harold Stewart	Albert E. Hunter	Edward J. McDevitt	Philip Saunders
1940-1941	Albert E. Hunter	Edward J. McDevitt	E. Ober Pride	Philip Saunders
1941-1942	Edward J. McDevitt	Philip Saunders	E. Ober Pride	Christopher Haworth
1942-1943	Philip Saunders	E. Ober Pride	Joel D. Harvey	Christopher Haworth
1943-1944	E. Ober Pride	Harvard L. Mann	Joel D. Harvey	Christopher Haworth
1944-1945	Harvard L. Mann	Joel D. Harvey	Clinton W. Bennett	John J. McIsaac

Year	President	Vice President	Secretary	Treasurer
1945-1946	Joel D. Harvey	Clinton W. Bennett	Harold A. Mock	John J. McIsaac
1946-1947	Clinton W. Bennett	John J. McIssac	Harold A. Mock	Norman H.S. Vincent
1947-1948	John J. McIsaac	Norman H.S. Vincent	Harold A. Mock	Richard S. Chamberlain
1948-1949	Norman H.S. Vincent	Harold A. Mock	James B. Willing	Richard S. Chamberlain
1949-1950	Harold A. Mock	Richard S. Chamberlain	James B. Willing	William Boynton
1950-1951	Richard S. Chamberlain	James B. Willing	William Boynton	Harold Wald
1951-1952	James B. Willing	William Boynton	John J. Harrington	Harold Wald
1952-1953	William Boynton	Harold Wald	Anthony F. Kearney	Mark C. Walker
1953-1954	Harold Wald	George W. Pierce	Anthony F. Kearney	Mark C. Walker
1954-1955	George W. Pierce′	Anthony F. Kearney	Lewis M. Foster	Mark C. Walker
1955-1956	Anthony F. Kearney	Mark C. Walker	Lewis M. Foster	Andrew Petersen
1956-1957	Mark C. Walker	Ernest A. Berg John F. Clarke	Lewis M. Foster	Andrew Petersen
1957-1958	Lewis M. Foster	Andrew Petersen George F. Shannon	Norman E. Jones	Arthur G. Flaherty
1958-1959	John F. Clarke	Duncan Edmands Arthur W. Koelbel	Norman E. Jones	Arthur G. Flaherty
1959-1960	Andrew Petersen	Norman E. Jones William A. Schan	Morris Goodman	Hamilton Young
1960-1961	Arthur W. Koelbel	Morris Goodman Herman Stuetzer	Howard F. Greene	Hamilton Young
1961-1962	Norman E. Jones	Herman Stuetzer Hamilton Young	Roger Wellington	Howard E. Hansen
1962-1963	Ernest A. Berg	Howard E. Hansen Roger Wellington	Edward W. Higbee	Dorothy G. Willard
1963-1964	Herman Stuetzer	Howard E. Hansen Maxwell A.H. Wakely	Robert Boyer	Dorothy G. Willard
1964-1965	Morris Goodman	Joseph B. Fyffe William Wright	Edward W. Higbee	Robert O.F. Bixby
1965-1966	Howard E. Hansen	Robert Boyer Dorothy G. Willard	Joseph Perroncello	Robert O.F. Bixby
1966-1967	Roger Wellington	Robert O.F. Bixby Richard J. O'Connor	Joseph Perroncello	Hugh Dysart, Jr.
1967-1968	Joseph B. Fyffe	Edward W. Higbee Joseph Perroncello	Theodore F. Tucker	Hugh Dysart, Jr.
1968-1969	Robert Boyer	Robert O.F. Bixby++ Earl F. Brown Donald R. Dupre	Theodore F. Tucker	Robert M. Kitchin
1969-1970	Robert O.F. Bixby	Joseph Perroncello++ Henry T. Downey Hugh Dysart, Jr.	Victor Cohen	Robert M. Kitchin
1970-1971	Joseph Perroncello	William Wright++ Joseph Chechile Theodore F. Tucker	Victor Cohen	Jordan L. Golding
1971-1972	William Wright	Donald R. Dupre++ Victor Cohen Robert M. Kitchin	J. Paul Finnegan	Jordan L. Golding
1972-1973	Donald R. Dupre	Earl F. Brown++ Jordan L. Golding Jerome P. Solomon	J. Paul Finnegan	William J. Hajjar
1973-1974	Earl F. Brown* Victor Cohen†	Victor Cohen++ Edward H. Pendergast, Jr. J. Paul Finnegan	Donald C. Wiese* Anthony T. Krzystofik†	William J. Hajjar
1974-1975	Victor Cohen	J. Paul Finnegan++ Wayne W. Jones Donald V. White	Anthony T. Krzystofik	George E. Manning
1975-1976	J. Paul Finnegan	Jordan L. Golding†† Anthony T. Krzystofik William J. Hajjar	Joseph R. Gilhooly	George E. Manning
1976-1977	Jordan L. Golding	Edward H. Pendergast†† George E. Manning David O. Shapiro	Joseph R. Gilhooly	Howard J. Peterson* Fred Alexander†

*Resigned +Died †Successor ++First Vice President ††President Elect

APPENDIX B

LITERARY AWARDS - MASSACHUSETTS CPA REVIEW

Year	Article	Author
1958	Tax Accounting Methods	Dorothy Willard
1959	Whither Materiality	William Holmes
1960	Planning and Controlling Income in Small Business	Roger Wellington
1961	The Business Approach to Auditing	Zack White
1962	Estate Planning for the Young Professional	Richard Knight
1963	The Market Value of Inventories	William Holmes
1964	SBIC's and Auditors	Roderick K. Macleod
1965	Internal Budgetary Controls - An Independent Accountants' View	James M. Lynch
1966	Recent Developments in Sub Chapter S	David Wheeler
1967	The Computer Administration of a Professional Office	Benjamin Benson
1968	APB Opinion No. 9 Revisited	Allan E. Oram
1969	Recognizing Management Service Opportunities	Jordan L. Golding
1970	Special Award for Dedication	Anthony Krzystofk
1970	Does the IRS Want Two Sets of Books	Alfred F. Falk
1971	Tax Shelter Investment in Oil and Gas Explorations - The Fund Concept	Benjamin Benson
1972	Special Award for his Dedication to the Massachusetts *CPA Review*	Joseph Flynn
1972	An Epithaph for the Accounting Principles Board	Philip E. Meyer
1973	So, What Else is New	William Holmes
1974	CPA, A Man for All Seasons	Jordan L. Golding
1975	Massachusetts Practitioners Tax Forum	James B. Karter
1975	Special Award for "Three Centuries of Accounting in Massachusetts	Linda H. Kistler Louis S. Corsini William Holmes
1976	Massachusetts Municipal Accounting	Walter W. Merrill

APPENDIX C

Massachusetts Society of Certified Public Accountants

AWARDS WINNERS

Exam.	Gold Medal	Silver Medal
1928	Karl W. Baker	
1929	Edward A. Stevens	
1930	Robert W. Smith	
1931	Dorothy G. Willard	
1932	Wilson Norfleet	
1933	John C. Potter	
1934	Curtis Campbell	
1935	Jay S. Hoffman	Janice E. Tarlin
1936	Richard G. Williams	Louis F. Quinn
1937	Robert Cherry	Winthrop Newcomb
1938	Warren S. Anthony	William F. Seward
1939	Rae D. Anderson	Wayne B. Wagar
1940	Nathaniel Lipschitz*	Gordon A. Stillings
1941	Lawrence H. Cousineau	Alfred C. Harcourt
1942	Richard T. Gourlie	Harry Winokur
1943	E. Frances Sondergard	Louis Hirshfield
1944	Helen R. Emery(Nowers)	Theodore Fellner
1945	Edward L. Leary	Walter P. Davidson
1946	Merton L. Alperin	Louis A. Casinghino
1947	Philip F. Brier	Edward J. Greenspan
1948	Gideon Blaisdell	Myron W. Glichouse
1949	Roscoe E. Irving	James J. White
1950		
May	Victor Havian	John King
Nov.	William Fletcher	John Judge & Victor Cohen
1951		
May	Charles Noble	Irving Popkin
Nov.	Howard Casey	Walter Merrill
1952	Norman Grandberg	John F. Murphy
1953	Gerald Holtz	John E. Stanick
1954		
May	James M. Lynch	Francis Gills, Jr.
Nov.	John D. O'Connell	Jeanne M. Downey

* Name changed to Lipton

Exam.	Gold Medal	Silver Medal
1955		
May	Richard M. Dorr	John W. Newton
Nov.	Robert W. Lentilhon	Daniel I. Peck
1956		
May	Vincent Allocca	Frank W. Smale
Nov.	David O. Shapiro	Robert C. Richardson
1957		
May	Ronald F. E. Hayes	Victor J. Fontana
Nov.	Stanley L. Saperstein	William A. Mann
1958		
May	Leopold A. Bernstien	Warren K. Wentworth
Nov.	Constanzo D. Fustolo	David P. Johnson
1959		
May	Ronald C. Baldwin	Warren S. Cooper
Nov.	Charles A. Morrison	Ronald G. Segel
1960		
May	Paul C. Wilson, Jr.	Robert F. Gayton
Nov.	Joseph A. Soetens	Robert F. Bolton
1961		
May	Russell Sample	Robert R. Bradley
Nov.	Carol A. Cotino	Michael Feit
1962		
May	Thomas V. Breen	Robert Boynton
Nov.	Paul Rigazio	Allen J. Reilly
1963		
May	Robert L. Fish	Vincent M. O'Reilly
Nov.	William H. Smith III	John J. Dias
1964		
May	Davide M. Villani	Robert H. Temkin
Nov.	Robert W. Hunter	Elliot Honnan
1965		
May	James F. Lafond	Paul E. Roche
Nov.	C. Akiba Hermann	Robert L. Caggiano
1966		
May	Richard Dieter	John Cherin
Nov.	Cece M. Smith	John A. Epeneter
1967		
May	Sanford C. Gunn	Anthony J. Woodworth
Nov.	David W. Mette	Charles H. Roscoe
1968		
May	Joseph S. Mulkern	David F. Kleeman
Nov.	John J. Lifford	Michael K. Schaefer
1969		
May	William L. Siddall	Herbert S. Alexander
Nov.	John H. Gilbert	Richard L. Woodside

Exam.	Gold Medal	Silver Medal	Bronze Medal
1970			
May	Walter S. Los, Jr.	George A. Vera, Jr.	
Nov.	Richard C. Wakefield	Paul R. Yecies	
1971			
May	Steven Seeche	Kenton J. Sicchitano	
Nov.	Paul N. Spigel	John M. Merrill	
1972			
May	Charles D. Poutasse	Norman F. Boucher	William J. Grenker
Nov.	Lee S. Parker	William P. Gately	Arthur Golden
1973			
May	Harold F. Oberkotter	Eugene L. Fisher	S. Hayden Anderson
Nov.	Richard F. Waters	John F. Duff	Patricia J. Shiley
1974			
May	Mary E. Ferris	Michael H. Murray	Robert E. Belensz
Nov.	J. Richard Andersen	David T. Thompson	Robert R. Langer Richard L. Trueblood
1975			
May	Alan Lederman	David B. Kaplan	John G. Szuflad
Nov.	Robert G. Murray	Patricia B. Norris	George D. Kinder
1976			
May	William J. Connolly	Richard H. Grueter	Joni A. Mace
Nov.	Lee Adrean	Richard A. D'Amore	Lynn P. Eiseman

Massachusetts Society of Certified Public Assountants

AWARDS WINNERS - HONORABLE MENTION

Exam.	First	Second	Third
1929	Harry Stoleek	Louis Lederman	
1930	Abraham M. Doctoroff	Herbert E. Henshaw Edward M. Wales	
1931	Robert J. Frederici	Michael J. Reagan	
1934	George A. Nikola		
1935	S. Forrest Kelliher		
1947	William J. Pruyn		
1953	Arnold London	Armin J. Frankel	David J. Lessels
1954			
Nov.	Willard R. Gallagher	Lawrence A. Kiley	Edmund M. Kladky Alan E. Symonds
1955			
Nov.	Bernard Moller		
1956			
Nov.	Richard F. Shea	Donald M. Budge	John A. Foppiano
1957			
May	Robert W. Beecher	John A. Malloy, Jr.	
1958			
May	Alfred S. Buckley	John E. Engdahl	
Nov.	Gilbert G. Desrochers	Paul J. Gerry	
1959			
May	Robert A. Stillman	Carl Packer	Frederic T. Hersey
Nov.	Robert A. Randall		
1961			
May	Robert E. Wunder		
Nov.	Burton A. Sage		
1962			
May	Jay D. Trepp		
Nov.	Richard F. McArdle		
1963			
May	Robert L. Wolf		
Nov.	Lazarus S. Donabedian	Leigh M. Gelser	William L. Gibbons Allen Kurinsky
1964			
May	William F. Maye		
Nov.	Timothy Burns	Robert Fenton	Norman LeBlanc Edward H. Pendergast James F. Russell

Exam.	First	Second	Third
1965			
May	Jerold B. Shocker		
Nov.	Jay S. Kamen	Wallace A. King	David E.Shaw
1966			
May	Bruce F. Horton		
Nov.	Daniel C. Tracy	Walter W. Topham	Ronald E. Bates Lawrence Speidell
1967			
May	Harvey A. Creem Douglas A. Fahlbeck		
Nov.	David M. June	John Plakans Burton Sonenstein	
1968			
May	John R. Whittemore		
Nov.	Warren A. Stebbins	David A. Garceau	John F. Garvey
1969			
Nov.	Edward B. Kostin	Alan R. Korpi	Paul E. Gricus
1970			
May	Robert H. Charron		
Nov.	Edmund J. Giardina	Raymond W. Hadrick	
1971			
Nov.	May Jane Anderson	Thomas M. Feeley	John A. Murray George B. Olson

THE DEVELOPMENT OF CONTEMPORARY ACCOUNTING THOUGHT

An Arno Press Collection

Baldwin, H[arry] G[len]. **Accounting for Value As Well as Original Cost** *and* Castenholz, William B. **A Solution to the Appreciation Problem.** 2 Vols. in 1. 1927/1931

Baxter, William. **Collected Papers on Accounting.** 1978

Brief, Richard P., Ed. **Selections from Encyclopaedia of Accounting, 1903.** 1978

Broaker, Frank and Richard M. Chapman. **The American Accountants' Manual.** 1897

Canning, John B. **The Economics of Accountancy.** 1929

Chatfield, Michael, Ed. **The English View of Accountant's Duties and Responsibilities.** 1978

Cole, William Morse. **The Fundamentals of Accounting.** 1921

Congress of Accountants. **Official Record of the Proceedings of the Congress of Accountants.** 1904

Cronhelm, F[rederick] W[illiam]. **Double Entry by Single.** 1818

Davidson, Sidney. **The Plant Accounting Regulations of the Federal Power Commission.** 1952

De Paula, F[rederic] R[udolf] M[ackley]. **Developments in Accounting.** 1948

Epstein, Marc Jay. **The Effect of Scientific Management on the Development of the Standard Cost System** (Doctoral Dissertation, University of Oregon, 1973). 1978

Esquerré, Paul-Joseph. **The Applied Theory of Accounts.** 1914

Fitzgerald, A[dolf] A[lexander]. **Current Accounting Trends.** 1952

Garner, S. Paul and Marilynn Hughes, Eds. **Readings on Accounting Development.** 1978

Haskins, Charles Waldo. **Business Education and Accountancy.** 1904

Hein, Leonard William. **The British Companies Acts and the Practice of Accountancy 1844-1962** (Doctoral Dissertation, University of California, Los Angeles, 1962). 1978

Hendriksen, Eldon S. **Capital Expenditures in the Steel Industry, 1900 to 1953** (Doctoral Dissertation, University of California, Berkeley, 1956). 1978

Holmes, William, Linda H. Kistler and Louis S. Corsini. **Three Centuries of Accounting in Massachusetts.** 1978

Horngren, Charles T. **Implications for Accountants of the Uses of Financial Statements by Security Analysts** (Doctoral Dissertation, University of Chicago, 1955). 1978

Horrigan, James O., Ed. **Financial Ratio Analysis—An Historical Perspective.** 1978

Jones, [Edward Thomas]. **Jones's English System of Book-keeping.** 1796

Lamden, Charles William. **The Securities and Exchange Commission** (Doctoral Dissertation, University of California, Berkeley, 1949). 1978

Langer, Russell Davis. **Accounting As A Variable in Mergers** (Doctoral Dissertation, University of California, Berkeley, 1976). 1978

Lewis, J. Slater. **The Commercial Organisation of Factories.** 1896

Littleton, A[nanias] C[harles] and B[asil] S. Yamey, Eds. **Studies in the Historv of Accounting.** 1956

Mair, John. **Book-keeping Moderniz'd.** 1793

Mann, Helen Scott. **Charles Ezra Sprague.** 1931

Marsh, C[hristopher] C[olumbus]. **The Theory and Practice of Bank Book-keeping.** 1856

Mitchell, William. **A New and Complete System of Book-keeping by an Improved Method of Double Entry.** 1796

Montgomery, Robert H. **Fifty Years of Accountancy.** 1939

Moonitz, Maurice. **The Entity Theory of Consolidated Statements.** 1951

Moonitz, Maurice, Ed. **Three Contributions to the Development of Accounting Thought.** 1978

Murray, David. **Chapters in the History of Bookkeeping, Accountancy & Commercial Arithmetic.** 1930

Nicholson, J[erome] Lee. **Cost Accounting.** 1913

Paton, William Andrew and Russell Alger Stevenson. **Principles of Accounting.** 1918

Pixley, Francis W[illiam]. **The Profession of a Chartered Accountant and Other Lectures.** 1897

Preinreich, Gabriel A. D. **The Nature of Dividends.** 1935

Previts, Gary John, Ed. **Early 20th Century Developments in American Accounting Thought.** 1978

Ronen, Joshua and George H. Sorter. **Relevant Financial Statements.** 1978

Shenkir, William G., Ed. **Carman G. Blough: His Professional Career and Accounting Thought.** 1978

Simpson, Kemper. **Economics for the Accountant.** 1921

Sneed, Florence R. **Parallelism in Two Disciplines.** (M.A. Thesis, University of Texas, Arlington, 1974). 1978

Sorter, George H. **The Boundaries of the Accounting Universe** (Doctoral Dissertation, University of Chicago, 1963). 1978

Storey, Reed K[arl]. **Matching Revenues with Costs** (Doctoral Dissertation, University of California, Berkeley, 1958). 1978

Sweeney, Henry W[hitcomb]. **Stabilized Accounting.** 1936

Van de Linde, Gérard. **Reminiscences.** 1917

Vatter, William J[oseph]. **The Fund Theory of Accounting and Its Implications for Financial Reports.** 1947

Walker, R. G. **Consolidated Statements.** 1978

Webster, Norman E., Comp. **The American Association of Public Accountants.** 1954

Wells, M. C., Ed. **American Engineers' Contributions to Cost Accounting.** 1978

Worthington, Beresford. **Professional Accountants.** 1895

Yamey, Basil S. **Essays on the History of Accounting.** 1978

Yamey, Basil S., Ed. **The Historical Development of Accounting.** 1978

Yang, J[u] M[ei]. **Goodwill and Other Intangibles.** 1927

Zeff, Stephen Addam. **A Critical Examination of the Orientation Postulate in Accounting, with Particular Attention to its Historical Development** (Doctoral Dissertation, University of Michigan, 1961). 1978

Zeff, Stephen A., Ed. **Selected Dickinson Lectures in Accounting.** 1978